Telling Memories
Among
Southern Women

Telling Memories Among Southern Women

Domestic Workers and Their Employers

in the Segregated South

Susan Tucker

Louisiana State University Press
Baton Rouge and London

Designer: Sylvia M. Loftin
Typeface: ITC Garamond Light
Typesetter: The Composing Room of Michigan, Inc.

Library of Congress Cataloging-in-Publication Data

Telling memories among southern women: domestic workers and their
    employers in the segregated South / [edited by] Susan Tucker.
        p.   cm.
    ISBN 978-0-8071-2799-5 (pbk.)
    1. Women domestics—Southern States—Interviews. 2. Afro-American
women—Southern States—Interviews. 3. Women domestics—Southern
States—History—Sources. 4. Housewives—Southern States—
Interviews. I. Tucker, Susan, 1950–
HD6072.2.U52A137 1988
305.4'3—dc19
                                                                88-9437
                                                                CIP

The paper in this book meets the guidelines for permanence and durability of
the Committee on Production Guidelines for Book Longevity of the Council
on Library Resources. ∞

In memory of Linda Ruth Adams, 1950–1971

Contents

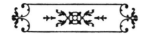

Acknowledgments

First and foremost, I extend my thanks to all of the women who agreed to be interviewed by Mary Yelling and me in the course of this project. Without their willingness to be interviewed, this book would not exist. Their generous sharing of their time and memories enriched not only my understanding but my appreciation of what Jacquelyn Dowd Hall has called "the front-porch culture of the South." The women who spoke with us treated us as neighbors, and I will always remember them—their kindness, their hospitality, and their lives. They set before me lasting gifts in their ways of speaking, and their often intimate accounts provided rich and diverse examples of courage, dignity, and tradition.

Mary Yelling, too, I thank for exposing me to such richness and diversity, as well as for her interviewing during 1981 and 1982. Her work stood as a keystone to the project, for without her, many of the stories concerning tensions between black and white women would not have been told. As a black woman talking with black women, she was able to establish a rapport more quickly than I was, and one of a somewhat different kind. Her own feelings about the interviews also gave me a much stronger, more personal, and more intimate view of the part of southern life I was trying to understand. Her belief in the project and her enthusiasm about the data were immensely important to me.

Especially in connection with the actual beginning of the project, I thank Richard Coram. Throughout, his attention to the progress of the work and his long-distance magic have been of a momentous nature. From Richard I learned to focus on one project, a lesson that often proved critical in the many years during which I transcribed and edited tapes.

Christin Loehr, Randy Bates, Nancy Anderson, Linda Hobson, Carter Smith, George Fuller, and Caroline Helwick read various drafts of the narratives and text. I thank them all. To Christin I am particularly grateful. On many days the thought of her encouragement was all that kept me going.

Numerous people helped me juggle part-time and intermittent full-time work, the work of mothering, and related daily stresses as I transcribed and edited the tapes. I thank Cynthia Kimmel for the refuge she gave me in her house, in her calm nature, and in her experience as a mother. Martha Leake gave me a few beautiful clothes during these years—gifts that cheered me. Stephen Hales provided complimentary pediatric care for my small child. Elizabeth Rayne listened to many of my problems, helping me to better sort through my past. She let me feel worthy of her gift of listening. She let me see a vision of myself long forgotten. Zonnie Breckinridge and Mary Campbell Hubbard gave me much-needed legal advice. I also thank Meg Cahill for her help with word processing during these years.

Dan Cullen, my editor for a time, gave me encouragement, long-distance friendship, and a sense that this book could actually be completed. John Easterly of LSU Press proved to be a most thoughtful reader, valued critic, and skillful editor. Now as I finish, his help seems a reward in itself to me, and a treasure of his own making to others who might be so lucky to work with him. I thank also all of the staff at LSU Press for their expertise and reassurances in readying the book for publication.

In 1985 I had the good fortune to become a fellow at the Newcomb College Center for Research on Women. The center was, and is, a continuing source of help, providing me with library privileges, a space to work away from home, and exposure to scholars. Among these, Beth Willinger has been a loyal friend and critic. Her countless readings of the manuscript, her many answers to questions, and her willingness to refer me to others have helped me to complete the book. On many days her laughter and good cheer provided the only opportunity for levity.

The Earl K. Long Library at the University of New Orleans kindly provided me with leave from my regular work as a librarian during January of 1986. I thank especially Sybil Boudreaux and Ethel Llama for their interest during 1985 and 1986.

Many other people helped me along by asking about my work. Their questions allowed me to see that the subject of domestic work is significant to others and made the hours spent working on the book feel not so solitary. Many people, for example, spoke with me on my journeys from home to my daughter's various baby-sitting, day-care, and school arrangements. Their casual questions and conversations validated my work. Greetings between mothers, these were often my only adult conversations for days. I wish to thank especially Annie Croffitt, Cida Lancaster, Hazel Brennan, Peggy Richardson, and Wanda Beverly. I also thank Luisa Lancaster, who allowed me another balance in life—the opportunity to live with her and to turn some of my attention away from myself, my work, and the care of a small child. And I thank Scott Olesen, who under the most difficult personal circumstances nevertheless always asked about my work.

This project also owes much of its existence to those people who had a part in my southern childhood. My father encouraged me to analyze the societal customs we practiced. My mother, the painter, provided me with an example of work centered upon many different renditions of one's immediate environment. Eula Mae Rudolph, the domestic who cared for me and my three sisters, taught me much—both by words and example—about the need to question the lives we led. These three persons were especially important to me as I went in and out of the memories of my childhood. For one thing, I learned from them the value of the process of work itself. No lesson has helped me more in beginning this work or in finding the perseverance and courage to complete it and, at the same time, care for my own child.

My parents also gave me much financial help during the periods in which I had to forgo full-time employment to work on this book. My sisters—Jane, Frances, and Julie—helped me by their steady friendship, happy dispositions, and optimism. In many moments of distress they made me like being a part of a southern family.

I also thank my daughter, Franny, whose birth in 1982 made me think differently about many aspects of domestic work. Her infancy and the infancy of the book coincided in such a way that the two brought peace that overrode fatigue and despair. I will always remember her beauty, her resourcefulness, her happy growth, her strong will, and her love during this period. I thank her for the wishes she spoke for me—for her coins thrown in fountains, for her birthday candles blown out for me.

I thank my stepdaughter Ginny for her funny stories, for her help with Franny, and for her irrepressible generosity. I thank my stepdaughters Maggie and Betsy for sidestepping masses of paper and for their other frequent side steps that attest to their flexibility and tolerance in the small and big issues of stepfamily life.

Finally, I thank my husband, Don Erwin, for miraculous acts of kindness during the last two years. His energy, his careful attention to the feelings of others, his notes on my desk, his juggling of parental and professional responsibilities, and his other stereotype-defying behaviors make every day truly easier than it would otherwise be. I count him as one of the great blessings upon my life and, surely, as the nicest person I have ever known.

Telling Memories
Among
Southern Women

Preface

In a sense this book is, above all, a personal one. It is a record of the stories as well as the silence I have heard all my life about two groups of southern women—black domestic workers and their white employers. It is my attempt to produce a collective memory of these women of the South, as well as my memory of hearing these women speak.

The greater part of the book is made up of oral history narratives. Within these narratives are the stories that individual domestics and their employers have chosen—consciously or unconsciously—to remember and tell about their lives.

Oral history is most simply defined as "the method of gathering and preserving historical information in spoken form." The oral history in this book is of a special kind, the kind that employs the recording of memories as the only means to ensure that "those who are involved in a particular facet of history be included if not in the writing of that history, at least as historical sources."[1]

Oral history, then, allows us to hear those memories of people who might not otherwise be heard and also to look more closely at the interplay of individual memory and historical forces. It appeared to me, particularly as I edited and transcribed the interviews with these southern women, that memory is actually the basis of history as it is understood by most people. Perhaps because I was talking with women who were the inheritors of a history involving silences as well as well-defined opinions and prejudices about race, class, and gender, their memories seemed to precede, accompany, and continuously influence their formal learning.

The southern women I spoke with, for example, typically remembered having gone to school knowing something of their parents', grandparents', and great-grandparents' memories of the past—the Civil War, the emancipation of the slaves, the Jim Crow laws, the Ku Klux Klan, the Great Depression. In the interviews they recalled these early memories as a sort of preconditioning to any formal education they may have

---

1. Oral History Association, *Oral History Evaluation Guidelines* (N.p., 1980), 3; Alphine W. Jefferson, "Echoes from the South: The History and Methodology of the Duke University Oral History Programs, 1972–1982," *Oral History Review,* XII (1984), 46–47.

subsequently had on race, class, and gender in the South. I do not mean to say that they spoke in such terms but that the way they spoke suggested to me that the previously acquired knowledge base, inherited, as it were, from their elders, strongly and continuously influenced, even shaped, their understanding of life. This inheritance, at its core, consisted of accounts of the self and the other—the other, more often than not, being defined by race. These early accounts remained vivid, much more vivid and influential than I had thought possible, in the memories of the women interviewed on this project.

The memories and facts seemed to coexist and inform each other in ways that I needed to keep continuously in mind in analyzing what was said. The interplay between them also reminded me of the interactive nature of learning, particularly the learning of one's own history, which, especially in the South, has undergone a process of continual revision. Within this interplay, southern myths, art, literature—as well as the southern belief system—have been created and re-created. And within this interplay, behaviors and actions have been shaped. The recording of these actions has been called history.

We have not, until quite recently, actively worked with this interplay of memory and history. In beginning to do so, we have discovered the means to find out the ways certain social and historical forces were perceived by those people who did not write of their experiences but were nevertheless "involved." Oral history, then, in both its methods and its theory, has enabled us to broaden our understanding of the past and our conception of history.

The recording of memories, the practice of oral history, seemed especially well suited to a study of domestic workers within the South. Oral history methods, particularly the use of the tape recorder, gave me access to the stories of people who had neither the time, the tradition, nor the inclination to write their history. The principals, the domestic workers, often worked long hours and had little schooling. Moreover, their work was done within the private home, without the benefit of co-workers and therefore without even a body of songs and chants such as often accompanied physical work done in groups.

In its theories, notably in its focus on the interplay of individual memory and historical forces, oral history also seemed quite suited to a study of domestic workers. They had vivid memories, and seemed to be quite vividly remembered by the whites, and yet they were not present in history books. Moreover, there seemed to exist significant silences within their own memories and the memories about them. The memories, for example, often showed me that in the past, white and black women did not speak to each other about race and class, and yet both of these were key factors involved within their lives and their interactions with each other and with other people.

I recalled such omissions from my own experiences. For example, I did not know much about the laws that governed segregation in my childhood, but I remember the separate waiting areas in my father's office. I remember going there with my mother and sitting in the white section. I remember, also, going with a baby-sitter, a young black woman whom I remember only as Alethea, and sitting in the colored section. I do not remember much about Alethea, but I remember the green leather chairs in the colored section. I remember asking about them. I remember that it felt good to still be a child and allowed to sit with Alethea, who seemed so much safer and closer to me than anyone else in the waiting area. As a child with a maid, I was exempt from the laws of segregation. I was exempt at least until I was a little older.

To me, then, southern racial custom was inextricably a part of any relationship I had with a black woman. Domestic workers and members of the families of domestic workers were the only black people I knew until I was twenty years old. Throughout my childhood and adolescence, there would be black women who cared for me and for whom I cared. And yet, the rules about race were always between us. These rules did not hang over me in a heavy way. But they were there—unspoken. We never even mentioned that we were of different colors. If I wanted to ask about black people, I asked about "your people." We thought it impolite to mention race. What was actually "impolite"—and far beyond that—was southern racial customs—the favoring of one race over another, the unequal schools and housing, unequal access to health facilities, bank loans, parks, buses, employment opportunities, and the myriad of other things.

On some level we white children sensed that something was wrong, but we could not see that we were at the center of it. The rules had been made long before for reasons no one would discuss. Children learned only that discussion of the rules was not permitted.

Our childish reticence was compounded by the reticence of the black women. The black domestics, of course, had been taught from earliest childhood the danger of speaking of racial inequality to whites. We were just children, but we would grow up. Thus, we had their silence to interpret along with their talk, a silence that grew larger as we grew older. This book is my effort to undo some of the silence.

In such undoing there is, of course, the process of selection, of choice. I was very aware, throughout the interviewing and editing, that, above all, the stories told were ones that these women were willing to share. They were stories selectively remembered, selectively repeated, and selectively recorded. Such a repeated selection process is one that has much bearing on the nature of this book, for it underscores the two effects of memory I noted throughout every interview: those of revision and reconciliation.

Revision occurs, of course, because the past that really was and the past that is remembered are always separate. Interpreting and reinterpreting the past are crucial for survival, strength, and carrying on. Such continuing interpretation allows one to move forward without condemning the self that was. In most of the interviews I found the general tendency to choose stories that show the "good" in one's life over the "bad," to choose, if you will, the revised version.

For white women, the choice to remember the "good" over the "bad" often led to the protest that "whites *did* give a lot to these black women," and other protests that the paternalistic system had worked well. But such protests were rarely without simultaneously voiced feelings of guilt and sorrow and some acknowledgment of the injustices of racial customs in the South. These white women had reinterpreted their memories in light of an awareness of social and political change that had sometimes been accompanied by education and self-analysis.

For black women, revision made possible the discussion of "bad times" —injustices and even cruelties—with a spirit of strength. Revision allowed the recollection of sadness and hurt feelings with dignity, so that they, too, might align themselves with life today and their present self-image.

In so doing, both black and white women seemed to achieve feelings of reconciliation with their past lives. The telling of their stories allowed them to re-create emotions and thoughts that previously had been unarticulated, to one degree or another. In speaking anew or for the first time of these memories, they reconstructed the past. The telling of their stories, then, seemed to become an act that changed the past. And hearing their stories caused me to continually revise and reconcile, to change my perceptions of the past as well.

*   *   *

I began this project with the goal of recording the memories of black domestic workers and their white employers in the part of the South where I grew up. I wanted to record these memories because I felt black domestics were important figures in the history of the South and especially in the history of the changing roles of women in the South. I suspected that the roles of black domestics went well beyond the stereotypical depictions, and I felt that they were a historical group little studied by scholars.

In literature and in the popular imagination, for example, the black domestic is cast as both mother to her own children and mother surrogate to white children. More important, she is often seen as a strong mother to both races of children. I recognized in such portrayals not only the stereotypical mammy figure but also other stereotypes of female behavior—the great attention to the needs of others, perseverance, manipulation, making do, forgiveness—that might tell us something about the environment in which southern children were raised.

Since black domestics were probably the only group of blacks who went daily into the private homes of whites, I also wanted to know more about the role of the black domestic as a go-between or interpreter for both races. From my own experiences, I felt that memories about domestic workers were central to almost any conversation of white southerners on race relations. The black domestic was almost universally cited as an example of a "good black," of one deserving of a better life. I wanted to hear more of such stories, to see if they showed any patterns, and to explore their meaning.

In addition, I wanted to find out if the memories of black domestics revealed any patterns that addressed this role of the domestic as go-between. I had overheard, and read of, black people similarly describing whites as "good whites" or "quality whites." Were such labels chosen by black domestics through a knowledge of white life gained by working in white homes?

Although my goals were specific, I had only a vague idea about how to collect such information. I am not a trained historian or sociologist. I began, moreover, alone, without the assistance of any teachers or colleagues, without a very clear idea of either what I was doing or where it would take me.

Nevertheless, in the winter of 1979 I launched my project. To establish certain standards, I relied mainly on two books well known in the field of oral history.[2] I had also worked on many large governmental survey research projects and drew upon the more rigid methods used in social science interviewing.

As it turned out, however, the formal questionnaire that I dutifully took to my first interviews often went unused. This questionnaire asked primarily technical and factual questions concerning wages, hours worked, Social Security, fringe benefits, housing, and so on. What I found was that, though these facts were important, they were not what people wanted to talk about. What was recalled and described in greatest detail was, instead, episodes from the speakers' lives, particularly those episodes dealing with the speakers in relation to other people.

Such memories, I came to see, involved many complicated, entangled feelings and thoughts on race and social customs, on mutual affection and simultaneous mutual distrust. Such thoughts and feelings proved more difficult to discuss than I had imagined. For some older black women, for example, the interview seemed to violate what I came to see was a taboo: the discussion of race relations with a white woman. For some white women, on the other hand, the interview addressed subjects that brought up much uncertainty, anger, and confusion about how many of their actions, thoughts, and feelings would be perceived by others. Indeed, in many interviews the women did not even wait to be asked questions, but began long monologues, leaving little space for questions. In other interviews the women would be almost reticent, necessitating many probes to draw out those subjects they were willing to discuss. Therefore, the questionnaire was, more often than not, set aside.

Although I tried to keep the speaker on a chronological track, I soon realized that the narrator must be allowed to depart from the questions if she wished to ramble. The information proved richer in detail and emotion than I had anticipated, but obtaining it required a willingness to let each interview take a different course. The interviews also required a willingness to enter into conversation, to discuss one's own feelings. Although I tried to delay such conversations until the end of interviews,

2. Willa K. Baum, *Transcribing and Editing Oral History* (Nashville, 1977); Cullom Davis, Kathryn Back, and Kay MacLean, *Oral History: From Tape to Type* (Chicago, 1977).

that was not always possible. My own feelings and ideas, and those of the other interviewer, therefore, may have influenced the stories told.

Interviewing in this more informal way was to continue from 1980 to 1985. I did all the interviews with white women and a little over half of the interviews with black women. Mary Yelling, a black social worker with whom I had worked on survey research projects, did the other interviews with black women. The narratives are marked with her name or my name accordingly. Her part was, of course, essential to the project. As a black woman interviewing black women, she was able to establish the necessary atmosphere of trust and harmony more quickly than I was. Her interviews, for example, generally took one or two visits. Mine with black women often took three or four. I believe the tone of the interviews she conducted and the types of details told to her convey a trust that comes from being of the same race as the interviewees. She also had contacts within the black community that I did not have.

We spoke with anyone willing to speak with us: referrals from social service agencies and churches, people waiting for buses, relatives, friends, and friends of friends. In all, ninety-two interviews were completed with women from Florida, Alabama, and Louisiana. All but five of the interviews were recorded on tape. The five not recorded on tape— because of mechanical failure or at the request of the speaker—were recorded in notes by hand.[3] The interviewing sessions generally ran from one and a half to three hours. Many short follow-up interviews were also conducted.

After each interview I transcribed the tapes in longhand, which took from fifteen to thirty hours for each interview. I transcribed all but three tapes myself. I chose to do so because I wanted to understand, as much as possible, the narrators' feelings and thoughts. I did not feel I could do so unless I actually heard those stories that their voices spoke with most emotion—heard and heard again, more analytically each time, each question and each response. In transcribing the tapes myself, I felt I had a much better chance of capturing the spoken voice in written words and of ultimately repeating those stories that seemed most important to the speakers or most representative of the collective past of domestic workers and their employers.

After the transcription I edited out questions, changed names, and presented the stories told as if they were spoken in one long monologue.

3. Recorded by hand was the interview with Mary Patricia Foley. Recorded in part by hand were the interviews with Corinne Cooke and Helen Reed.

The main purpose of this first stage of editing was to provide a life history of the narrator. Although we were asking the white women to speak primarily of someone else, some understanding of each woman's life seemed necessary to any record of her memories. Since we had attempted to maintain something of a chronology in all the interviews, editing for a life history was fairly easily accomplished. In some cases, however, the ordering of the interview changed in this first stage of editing.

I then reedited each narrative eight to ten times, trying to capture attitudes and feelings as shown in the words of the speakers. The main purpose of these additional rounds of editing was to present stories that revealed customs, characteristics, and feelings common among domestic workers and their employers. I also edited for clarity and simplicity, taking out portions of the narratives that seemed repetitious and working toward a compilation that could be easily read while still portraying the lives of the women speaking. In most cases one-fourth to one-fifth of the unedited transcriptions are included in the final edited narrative. In three cases, in which the interviews were extremely lengthy, however, only one-tenth or so of the unedited transcriptions appear.

I use the term *narrative* for these final versions because the form in which the accounts appear is clearly not the interview form. The narratives are, instead, the versions I heard and then, in many cases, rearranged. Therefore, one of my main cautions to the reader is to remember that each narrative is the product not only of the words of the interviewer and the interviewee but also of the evolving focus of the editor. That is, with each stage of editing, I removed portions of the interview, which altered the narrative. I did so to show the South as I heard it, to show the versions of women's lives I heard in the interviews. Someone else, at every turn, might have heard differently.

My intrusion as the editor was one that I was conscious of throughout the making of the book. My goals were to provide an accurate record of what was said and, at the same time, to make sure the reader is aware of my presence. In the former task, I tried to give careful attention to transcribing the words exactly as I heard them. Although I sometimes did change the order of the sentences from the tape to the narrative, my one strict rule was that I would not change the choice of words or the word order within sentences or within what became paragraphs. The women's use of language was my only means of showing their character on paper.

At the same time, however, I chose not to use dialect spelling, except in two cases. I chose to use standard English spelling for ease in transcribing, editing, and reading the narratives. I do not believe that I could have successfully transcribed and edited the tapes in dialect. This would have required some training that I lack.

However, I also hoped, in using standard English, to underscore that the narratives are the written rendition of the speakers' stories. The distinction between the written and the spoken seemed very important to me because so much of my subject centered around race. Being of the black race, in the Western world, has meant the assumption of the language of white people.[4] And though in the United States this assumption took place many years ago, in some ways it is still going on, because blacks do speak a sort of dialect, as do white southerners to a lesser extent. I felt that if I even tried to use dialect, I would belie the fact that my account is that of a researcher, something different from the actual dialect that either I, Mary Yelling, or the interviewees spoke—something different from what is on the tapes. I did not want to discount this difference.

I did retain the dialect spelling of the word *Nigra* for the pronunication of the word *Negro*. The pronunciation here seemed significant, for it was most often used by older white women who would never have used the word *nigger*, but who nevertheless seemed to find the use of *Negro* or *black* somehow difficult. There was something defiant and mocking in their retention of the word *Nigra* that I felt I should not change. I also retained the use of the word *Miz*, rather than substituting the words *Miss* or *Mrs.* Southern women, when they use a title for one another, do not generally say "Mrs." unless they have some important point to make about marital state. They sometimes say "Miss" for a title with a first name, but even this they most often pronounce as "Miz." I see this pronunciation as significant for the way southern women define themselves. I am not sure exactly how. I am not sure whether they define themselves less by their state of being married or not, for example. But I could not change the pronunciation. I did try, and the use of "Mrs.," particularly, seemed so false—to even the written rendition—that I returned to the pronunciation as I heard it.

Forty-two edited narratives from the interviews are included in the book. The narratives are arranged by subject in five parts and an epilogue, and within each part they are grouped by race (blacks first) in chronological order according to the year of each speaker's birth. The recording of memories, of course, does not lend itself easily to subject categorization, and the reader may find recurring themes that are dominant in one part and yet run throughout the book.

4. Franz Fanon, *Black Skin, White Masks,* trans. Charles Lam Markmann (New York, 1967), 17–40.

I selected the arrangement by chronology and race within each part because I wanted to emphasize how significant our time of birth and our race (and the class to which we are born) are in the way we remember our lives and the lives of others. I wanted to emphasize how these different factors govern which version of history we inherit. I wanted to show the different versions, side by side, through memories of and about female domestic workers in the South. They, more than any other group of workers born between 1880 and 1965, personally experienced and witnessed at first hand the ways race and class governed the lives of people in the South. They were participants in the day-to-day lives of the two sides of segregation.

Certain memories and terms in the narratives are explained further in the headnotes that precede the narratives and in footnotes. The headnotes are meant to point out patterns and topics I heard in the interviews, many of which are not included here. The subjects I address, of course, could be written about in great detail. They are given here only as brief guides to my hearing of the speakers and my readings on the domestic worker–employer relationship. The headnotes are also meant to provide information on the types of homes the domestic workers commuted to and from, and pictures of the types of women who worked as domestics or who remembered domestics.

Within both the headnotes and the narratives, all of the names have been changed. Interviewees were told in advance that names would be changed in order to assure them the freedom to discuss whatever they remembered. Similarly, within the headnotes that precede the narratives, I have sometimes rearranged the descriptions of the women interviewed. The voices, the homes, the clothes worn, the places described are not always those of the speaker in the narrative that follows. In some cases I have substituted a picture of a person similar to the person who speaks.

When I began this project, I had no idea of the years or different stages that would be required to complete it. I believe now that I was inspired in a very personal, perhaps too personal, way by my own childhood memories. If I had known at the start how often I would feel that my own memories of childhood were distorting not only my understanding of the past but also my ability to change my understanding of it, I probably would not have undertaken this task.

As I began, Adrienne Rich's brief comments on black domestics and white female children in the first edition of her book *Of Woman Born* seemed to me an adequate reason to proceed. Rich wrote:

As a child raised in what was essentially the South, Baltimore in the segregated 1930s, I had from birth not only a white, but a black mother. This relationship, so little explored, so unexpressed, still charges the relationships of black and white women. We have not only been under slavery, lily white wife and dark, sensual concubine; victims of marital violation on the one hand and unpredictable, licensed rape on the other. We have been mothers and daughters to each other; and although, in the last few years, black and white feminists have been moving toward a still-difficult sisterhood, there is little yet known, unearthed, of the time when we were mothers and daughters.[5]

And yet, in Rich's revised edition of this book she herself calls her earlier view overly personal. She felt, in retrospect, that she did not "give enough concrete sense of the actual position of the Black domestic worker caring for white children. Whatever the white child has received both in care and caring, the Black woman has given under enormous constraints."[6] I hope, however, that, by interpreting her first remarks as a literal charge, I have worked against this tendency to be too personal. I knew that if I was to "unearth" the memories of white children grown up, I must also at least try to unearth the memories of black domestics.

Many of my own personal memories, of course, affected the interviewing, editing, and selection of interviews for inclusion. I have therefore written about portions of my childhood in some of what follows. This seemed a fair way to show the part I played in the interviews and the editing and to reveal parts of myself that I asked others to reveal.

Soon after I began, I became aware of a number of recent historical and sociological analyses of the subject.[7] As a result of these works, my knowledge of the history of domestic work increased, and so some of my interviewing and editing changed. And of course, as I learned more from

5. Adrienne Rich, *Of Woman Born: Motherhood as Experience and Institution* (New York, 1976), 253.

6. Adrienne Rich, *Of Woman Born: Motherhood as Experience and Institution* (10th Anniversary ed.; New York, 1986), 255.

7. Recent sociological studies include Robert Hamburger's *A Stranger in the House* (New York, 1978), an oral history of northern domestic workers; a chapter in Bettina Aptheker's *Woman's Legacy: Essays on Race, Sex, Class in American History* (Amherst, 1982) in which she explores domestic work within a Marxist framework; a work published by the Center for Research on Women at Memphis State University—Elizabeth Clark-Lewis' *"This Work Had a' End": The Transition from Live-in to Day Work,* Southern Women: The Intersection of Race, Class and Gender, Working Paper 2 (Memphis, 1985), which treats domestic workers in the Washington, D.C., area from 1900 to 1920; Judith Rollins' *Between Women: Domestics and Their Employers* (Philadelphia, 1985), on the relationship of domestic workers to their employers in the Boston area in the 1980s; Linda Martin and Kerry Segrave's *The Servant Problem: Domestic Workers in North America* (MacFarland, N.C., 1985), on domestic workers from 1940 to the present; and scattered publications of the Department of Labor and the National Committee on Household Employment. Historical studies include David M. Katzman's *Seven Days a Week: Women and Domestic Service in Industrializing America* (New York, 1978), which looks at the period 1870 to 1920, and Daniel E.

each interview, interviewing and editing also changed somewhat. I came to see that the data Mary Yelling and I collected represent a body of work that could be useful to many scholars, as well as useful in other, more analytical work on domestics that we or others might undertake.[8] In this book I present my first findings, a compilation of those stories that seemed most representative of southern domestic workers and their employers.

Many of the interviews speak of strongly felt divisions in southern society. Yet, what joins these women together is that they are from the same place and have lived at roughly the same time. Many of them spoke of strong ties with their homes and of a preference for life in the South. Many of them recognized the importance of this place, the South, in their dealings with and memories of each other. They recognized their connections to one another by geography.

The Frenchman Alexis de Tocqueville, writing of early America, observed this bond of a shared place and anticipated some of the problems it would bring to a people split along racial lines. After describing "an Indian woman, a negress, and a little white girl" in the woods of Alabama, he wrote: "I had often chanced to see individuals met together in the same place, who belonged to the three races of men which people North America. I had perceived from many different results the preponderance of the whites. But in the picture which I have just been describing there was something peculiarly touching. . . . A bond of affection here united the oppressors with the oppressed, and the effort of nature to bring them together rendered still more striking the immense distance placed between them by prejudice and by law."[9] "The effort of nature" to bring together these women of different races who live in the same part of the world makes it inevitable that their memories, though quite diverse, will come together to help us achieve a more complete view of the past.

Sutherland's *Americans and Their Servants: Domestic Service in the United States from 1800 to 1920* (Baton Rouge, 1981). Literary criticism includes only one book-length work: Trudier Harris, *From Mammies to Militants: Domestics in Black American Literature* (Philadelphia, 1982).

8. The tapes and the transcripts of them are housed at the Newcomb College Center for Research on Women at Tulane University, New Orleans, and almost all are available for use by scholars, though the names of the interviewees cannot be revealed, since they were guaranteed anonymity.

9. Alexis de Tocqueville, *Democracy in America,* ed. Henry Reeve, revised by Francis Bowen and Phillips Bradley (2 vols.; New York, 1945), II, 336.

Part I

Complex Bonds

As a southern white child growing up in the 1950s and 1960s, I often heard race relations explained by first comparing the South with the North and then referring to the connections between white people and their black servants. White people in the North, I was told, cared for blacks as a group. But white people in the North did not know blacks, and did not care for them, as individuals. In the South, I was told, we did. And those we knew, especially the black female domestics, we loved and treated as if they were family.

Examples were cited from various generations of servants. Many grown-ups seemed to remember house servants who remained loyal to their former masters after the Civil War. And there were also the more immediate examples of the black maid who stayed late to help a sick white child, the black maid who had sewn a special Mardi Gras costume for a white child whose mother was dying, the black maid who visited her former employer every day in a nursing home. In return for such acts black servants were granted special forms of help from whites. Their wages might be supplemented by regular gifts of cast-off furniture, clothing, and food. Some of their children's education might be paid for. Their legal or medical problems might be addressed by highly regarded professionals. They would be cared for in old age, perhaps allowed to live rent free in houses owned by former employers. This system worked, I was told, because these were good blacks who worked hard and because good whites made sure that they were taken care of.

Yet, when I looked around at the lives of the maids I knew, I did not always see that the whites' care or affection for these black women made their lives noticeably better. In particular, I remember a feeling of sadness that their houses—which I, like other white children, might visit—seemed very substandard. No lovely Persian rug given away because a better one had been inherited, no slightly faded, hand-me-down chintz curtains could cover up the fact that these black women lived lives of poverty.

Probably because I came of age at the time of the civil rights movement, I retained this image of poverty alongside the other image of the benign workings of the segregated South of my childhood. Still, the stories told me by whites and the pictures of these women's houses coexisted in my memory for a long time before I actually put the two versions beside each other and asked what the composite picture was. In many ways and for many people, several such versions of the lives of black domestics have been so widely influential—each in its own way so vivid and central to the separate cultures of white and black southerners—that a single over-all picture is difficult to achieve.

For example, in one of my first interviews a white woman stood with one hand on her hip and the other hand pointing up to a portrait over her mantelpiece and said to me:

> See that little girl hanging up there? That was Grandmother. And she had a slave named Annie. Well, Annie came with Grandmother when she got married. They came from South Carolina and they lived here. Her mother had died when she was a little girl and she was an only child and she was devoted to Annie.
>
> And when the war was over, the Civil War, Annie was right there in the house with them. And of course, they had everything stripped from them. They didn't have anything. They were poor.
>
> All right. Annie went out and got herself a job and brought her pay home to help buy the groceries, to feed the children in the family for Grand-mother. And Annie is buried in our cemetery lot right now. She was part of the family. She stayed with the family all the rest of her life. And she went out when everything was gone, to get work, and brought money home to help Grandmother.
>
> Now that's true. And how do you explain it? And Annie is buried in our cemetery lot right now. . . . You go and you find it.

I did find Annie Johnson's grave in the cemetery. On her gravestone are her name and her dates of birth and death. There is nothing to suggest that she was anything other than a member of the family except that her last name is different from those on the other gravestones within the small fenced plot. But I wondered, in response to my interviewee's question, whether this woman named Annie Johnson herself ever questioned that she was part of the family and whether anyone else in the family ever questioned it.

The following week I asked my paternal grandmother some of the same questions about her memories of domestic workers. My grandmother was not one of the adults who told the stories I heard in child-hood. A woman from a small community in southern Tennessee, she was distant in my youth, seen only occasionally on holidays. Moreover, she was not a woman who saw herself as a part of the old aristocratic South. She was a woman who ran boardinghouses and small stores to make ends meet. Yet she, too, interwove a defense of the past, especially of segregation, into accounts of domestic workers. She drummed her painted fingernails on a white porcelain-topped kitchen table and told me: "After all, there were servants in the Bible. After all, God made them black for a reason."

"What do you think, though, Grandmother?" I asked. "Do you think that just because people are born in the South—say in Tennessee—they should always be made to be servants?"

"No," she said. "That wasn't right. I know it wasn't *always* right. And they weren't always treated right, and the Bible also says, 'Masters be kind to your servants.'"

Then she told me of a neighbor's memory of an instance of "unkind-ness." She told of an "old Nigra" who was beaten by a white man because she "talked back" to the white woman for whom she worked. The "old Nigra" was said to have apologized. But the apology was not enough, and she was beaten so badly that she did not come to work for five weeks. Because of that incident, the white neighbor's family was hated by the black family of the "old Nigra." But the "old Nigra" herself did not hate them. She was too good to hate even someone who had wronged her so.

These two stories together, coming as they did at the beginning of my interviewing, had special meaning for me. They placed in front of me more than the images of my youth. They placed in front of me two divergent stories with their own rationalization of a social arrangement that consistently exploited one group of people. They were two separate accounts, both from the white perspective, and they made me even more curious about accounts from the black perspective.

Like these two stories, the stories that I heard most often throughout the project were those that described individual bonds between peo-ple—between mother and daughter, grandmother and granddaughter, and black domestic worker and white employer. In the details of the stories of these relationships, I found some answers that let me begin to reconstruct—if not an overall picture—at least multiple pictures of the past that had some common basis.

For in the details of these stories and in the emotions presented during the telling, what seemed most vividly portrayed was that the domestic was typically a person who connected southerners—white and black—to one another. I found, in fact, that in the South many people have been brought close to others through the care of black women. And though such care involved a complicated entanglement of memories, history, psychology, race relations, and economics, it also involved maternal love, daily contact, mutual dependence, and attention to the needs and strengths of the individuals involved. All of these facets of the black women's care worked to form a common link among a great many southerners.

For example, the way in which many southern women defined, and often still define, themselves revolves around the care of black domestics. Southern white women are apt to describe themselves in terms of place, in terms of their having been reared in the South and shaped by its customs. Being a white female in the South meant, until recently, that it was likely that in adult life one would employ a domestic worker—a black woman to help in household work and mothering. Southern black women, on the other hand, are apt to describe themselves in terms of race. Being a black female in the South meant, until recently, that it was quite possible that one might always work outside one's home. Being a black female in the South also meant that if one could not find other work, she could always be a domestic worker. In such domestic work, she would, on a daily basis, leave her home and possibly her children to care for those of a white employer.

Thus, for both black and white southern women, place and race are among the most obvious defining circumstances. And for both, place and race have meanings for their roles in the domestic sphere, meanings that both separate them from, and connect them to, each other.

In addition, place and race are topics that generally lead to discussions of childhood. In these discussions the theme of the care of black women is common in the memories of many southern women—white and black. Black domestics were the caretakers of the community—as a result of their sheer numbers and also in a symbolic way because they were women who crossed back and forth between the white and black cultures. Beyond this collective and symbolic role of caretaker, many black domestics were also both biological mothers who worked to support their own children and mother surrogates who were paid to care for white children. It is this latter role of the domestic as mother that has been most obvious in southern culture, white and black.

Lillian Smith wrote eloquently and insightfully about this role. She compared the black mother with the ineffectual white mother who conformed to southern expectations that women should be docile. She presented the black nurse as the kind, comforting, and strong parent, in contrast to the white mother, whom she found lacking in courage, strength, and warmth. Although Smith often overlooked some of the burdens in the lives of black women and some of the strengths of white women, her analysis of how education in racism occurs first through the black domestic was certainly confirmed in the interviews. She traced the dishonesty, and the duality of hate and love, in southern life to the white southerner's relationship with the black domestic. About her own relationship with a black domestic, she wrote: "I knew, but I never believed it, that the deep respect I felt for her, the tenderness, the love, was a childish thing which every normal child outgrows, that . . . I, too, must outgrow these feelings. I learned to use a soft voice to oil my words of superiority. I learned to cheapen with tears and sentimental talk of 'my old Mammy' one of the most profound relationships of my life. I learned the bitterest thing a child can learn: that the human relations I valued most were held cheap by the world I lived in." Smith, like many other white writers of the South, felt that the black domestic was forgotten or misplaced in the memories of white adults, forgotten particularly in her role in mothering both races.[1]

In the writings of blacks, the domestic is also seen as misplaced, though in a different sense. It is the black domestic who mothered white children who is most often attacked for making alliances with whites. She is stereotyped as a mammy, mistrusted for what strength she does have, and despised for her weakness in conforming with what whites wanted. Such representations have largely overshadowed the black domestic's genuine contributions. As Mildred, the domestic in Alice Childress' *Like One of the Family,* said: "Domestic workers have done a awful lot of good things in this country besides clean up people's houses. We've taken care of our brothers and fathers and husbands when the factory gates and office desks and pretty near everything else was closed to them; we've helped many a neighbor, doin' everything from helpin' to clothe their children to buryin' the dead. . . . And it's a rare thing for anybody to find a colored family in this land that can't trace a domestic worker somewhere in their history."[2]

1. Lillian Smith, *The Killers of the Dream* (Rev. ed.; New York, 1961), 29.
2. Alice Childress, *Like One of the Family: Conversations from a Domestic's Life* (New York, 1956), 36–37.

That domestics have been a central factor in southern culture, then, cannot be denied. Their experiences and the memories of them have woven complex bonds between the white and black people of the South. Through the accounts of these bonds, we can begin to reconstruct the past and thereby move toward an analysis of the multiple pictures of the lives of domestic workers.

Priscilla Butler

Priscilla Butler (b. 1909) speaks of her childhood on a plantation where she was raised by her grandmother and aunt. Her mother, who died early, was a "baby nurse," a specialist among domestics, one who stayed in white homes caring for new babies and mothers for a period of two weeks to three months. Butler's father was a white man, one of the sons of the plantation-owning family. Most telling in her interview is the account of her mother's deathbed request of her father that Priscilla, then nine years old, would not have to "nurse nobody's babies until she nursed her own."

Priscilla Butler would not speculate at length on the meaning of such a promise—on what it might reveal about her mother's hopes for her daughter or on what it might reveal about the lives of young black women who went into white homes. It seems likely, however, that her mother's request had something to do with the fact that she herself had had to care for babies other than her own and that she had had to leave her child to do this. It seems equally likely that her mother's request contains a warning: that young black women who worked within white homes were vulnerable to the worst aspects of the segregated South. Living within the white household, even for a short period of time, meant that they did not have the emotional support of their own families or protection from unfair and even violent actions of employers, particularly male employers.

As Butler indirectly points out, both the possibility of love between men and women of different races and the sexual exploitation of black women by white men have been largely ignored by white women. Butler would say, "You wouldn't want to know it." I believe this to be a correct judgment: though I had read of sexual exploitation of domestics in white homes—*Coming of Age in Mississippi* and *Soul Sister* come immediately to mind—I did not see this subject as something I should ask about, even as I designed the questionnaire.* However, as I heard many references to mulatto women, I began to inquire further. What I came to see was that white women, indeed, usually denied ever hearing of sexual exploitation of black domestics, either within the white home or by the men in the household. They denied it so completely that it was consistently a subject on which I got only a one- or two-sentence response that usually focused on men called "poor white trash." It is my feeling that such a complete denial is probably linked to the fact that most women, to some degree or another, fear rape. White women were told as children that black men were their potential rapists and that only in aligning themselves with white men could they be spared. Thus, they did not want to believe white men known to them, or similar to the white men known to them, capable of such acts.

Black women, of course, could not so absolutely deny such a problem. And

---

*Anne Moody, *Coming of Age in Mississippi* (New York, 1968); Grace Halsell, *Soul Sister* (New York, 1969).

Butler's mother's request can perhaps be interpreted as a warning—a warning if not of rape, then of other consequences involved with going into the white home at such an early age.

Certainly her mother sought to secure for Priscilla Butler a different sort of life. She also made the white men promise that her child "was never to get out in the field." This promise suggests that her mother saw the crippling effects of agricultural labor on children and adults who might be still bound to the plantation in an arrangement that was but a step away from slavery. This promise also suggests that her mother may have wished for her daughter a life that conformed with some of the notions of a "pure lady" by white definition, a definition her mother certainly knew through her labor with new white mothers. This would have been, after all, the hope of many white sharecropping mothers, that their children could leave field work and find an easier life that provided a more just return for their work.

Butler's narrative describes the continued influence of this legacy and her responses to whites she has known as relatives and as employers.

She wore a dark pink housedress and maroon leather slippers with an open heel at the first interview. She sat on a green couch by a loud window fan that can be heard on the tape. Neighbors, grandchildren, and great-grandchildren interrupted her all through the day.

→ ❈ ←

I was born in Escambia County, Alabama, on the old Clinton plantation. My mother was . . . You know, it's the funniest thing—I can't find no record that she ever was born or that I was ever born. I tried to trace it back, when I got my Social Security.

I guess it might have been some mix-up or because my mother she was nothing but a child when I was born. I don't really know how old she was, because everything I have found out about her I've had to pick up—bits and pieces from what I heard and what my aunt told me. When I was very small, I know she would go wait on people with new babies. She'd go wait on Miz Whoever-it-would-be. And send money back.

And so they all felt it was best that I be with my grandmother. I don't know why exactly. It had to do with me being born out of wedlock and everyone knowing I was the child of one of those Clinton boys—the white people that owned the plantation. But I don't know all the whys of it.

My mother never even told my aunt who my father was. I don't know why. We didn't know who he was for sure until my mother died. I was nine years old then.

But see, when the time come to come out from the cloud and say who was my father, they all come out, him and his brothers. After she died, they all come out.

See, everybody that lived on that plantation, well, whenever one of them died and they got word, well, you didn't have no expenses about the burial. You just go over there and tell the one who had the coffin house, Harry Clinton. He had a houseful of coffins, all kinds and all sizes, and he'd bring the peach tree switch down, and they measured the body and then brought the coffin.

So when my mother died, it wasn't anything unusual for the white man to come down and tell them how to settle the affairs. Well, Harry, the one who had the coffin house, he let his brother know, the one who was my father.

So my father told his youngest brother to come see about me, told Andrew to come. All through my life, Andrew played a major role. He always came for my father. See, my father was old enough to be my daddy, and Andrew wasn't. If my daddy had come, that would have kind of pointed to him. My daddy was the lawyer one in the family. He was considered more professional than the rest of them. They had a lot of boys and everybody knew I was crossbreeded but nobody could lay their fingers on just who it was.

See, that's just the way things had been. Everything is to protect the good name of the white men. But they didn't give a hat about the black women.

But now, getting back to when my mother died, Andrew he came over there. They had a saucer on my mother's chest. They did that in the country, and Andrew thought they had the saucer up there begging for money to bury my mother and what not. He said to my aunt, "Rebecca, you all don't have to beg"—the Clintons called my mother Lizbeth—said, "You all don't have to beg to bury Lizbeth." Said, "Brother Harry got all the coffins, and we're gonna send a horse and cart."

My aunt told him, says, "Andrew," or "Mr. Andrew"—oh, they made you call them Mister when they couldn't even talk!—says, "Well, that's not to bury her, because your daddy has already come down here and told us to see to the measuring for the coffin." Because see, my aunt and my mother had a brother that chauffeured for Old Man D. W., and all the white people loved my uncle, Uncle Joe. I always did think that might be why my father decided to look out for me.

But anyway, they had a saucer up on her chest. Peoples in the country had the idea that if you put table salt or sand in a saucer and sit it on the chest, it keeps the body from purgin'. You ever hear what a purgin' was? That's a form of the body throwing off . . . Sometimes it comes up from your stomach, and you start a saliva and foaming at the mouth. It's what you got in you coming out. The saucer was to stop that.*

Anyway, that day Andrew said to my aunt, "We want you to take Priscilla because we don't want her to nurse nobody's babies until she's nursed her own." My aunt said my mother had asked them for that promise. "And she is never to get out in the field. And whenever she needs something, you come over to the store and knock and you'll wake me up and we'll let her father know." Andrew ran one of the stores on the plantation. In the country they had these stores right on the plantation where you could buy different things.

So after that, I was raised with the best of everything. But I never did want anything to do with my daddy. My husband had to blow on me cold to make me be nice to him. A long time after I was grown and gone, he and his chauffeur came here once the day after Christmas. That was the first time. He always sent Andrew before whenever I needed anything or he thought I needed anything. He started the habit that year. If he came, he'd always come the day after Christmas. And he'd bring a great big old apple box. It's got a tier between the layers, and it had on one side, filled with apples; other side, oranges and raisins that be on little stems.

My daughter was at the door that first time he came. He said, "Is your mother home?" And she said, "Yes sir, Mister." He said, "Don't you ever call me 'Mister.'" He says, "I am your Grandfather, and always when I come here, you call me Grandfather."

He ended up giving them all some money. He gave my husband . . . Sometimes he give him as much as fifty dollars and each one of the children ten dollars. . . . And I always got my share all through the year.

But I still didn't like him. I didn't really hate him, but I didn't cultivate a friendship for him to think that he was on the same level of society as me or that I was on the same level of society with him.

I just don't know why. I didn't feel he was better than me or I was better than him. I felt that the society that I lived in and around, that it didn't want anything to do with me. On account of I was a mulatto, and I guess I blamed him for that.

Even when I was a little girl, I had that feeling of being hurt by mingling up, in me. There was a lot of mulattoes on that plantation, but the womens wouldn't dare accuse those Clinton boys . . .

---

*The practice of placing a dish of salt on a dead body is described also in Ruth Bass, "The Little Man," in Alan Dundes (ed.), *Mother Wit from the Laughing Barrel: Readings in the Interpretation of Afro-American Folklore* (Englewood Cliffs, N.J., 1973), 392–93.

Once, I remember—I guess I just won't let it die—I was standing up on one of the store porches one Saturday. And my aunt used to dress me up. She made my clothes. She would have me the beautifulest clothes. Whenever the material would come in the store, she would just go down there and get what she wanted. 'Cause my daddy paid for it.

Well, I was standing there on the porch—look like to me it was drizzling rain—waiting for it to stop. And somebody said, "Oh, who's that little girl?" I used to have plaits about that long, long plaits coming down to my beltline. And my aunt would . . . If I had on a little red checkerdy gingham dress, well, then I had a big red bow on my hair, a great big one. If I had on a pink checkerdy dress, a pink bow.

So, anyway, they said, "Who's that little girl?" This old woman said to them . . . Her name was . . . I can't remember what her name was. But I hope she done served the time in hell and out by now, 'cause she was an old devil. She said, "Don't you know?" Said, "That's Aunt Grace's old Elizabeth's baby." My grandmother was Grace, and my mother was Elizabeth. She said it in a mean way like that was something horrible to be, like there was something horrible about me.

I can remember they said, "Well, that's a beautiful child." She said, "Well, don't think too much of that," say, "because when she grows up, so's the mammy, so's the child."

I went home to my aunt and I cried and cried. It was something terrible with me, I thought, for her to say such a thing. I had that stigma in me. "So is the mammy, so is the child." I just won't let that die.

Up there, it's just a lot of mulattoes. Here in Mobile I was working for a certain lady one time—this was when it first come that you could go in and sit down and eat hotel food with the white people—and so she told me, "Now you know, we loves you and we respect you to the highest. You raised my babies from the time they been in the world. But you know, I wouldn't want your grandson to marry my granddaughter," and she went on to say what would happen.

I said, "Well, we both feel the same." I says, "You don't want that and I don't either." I say, "But I'm gonna tell you something, Miz Mimi, you and your sister have told me quite a few times about your feelings, or be talking when I'm present. And you're not talking about green people; you're talking about black peoples." I said, "Now I don't enjoy hearing it." I said, "But as long as I'm gonna work for you, I guess I'm subject to it."

I said, "But I'm going to tell you something about my hometown, where I was raised up." I said, "There is a church there, one church there, that the white people go to, and you go over there, you going to find nothing but white people." I said, "But now there's Shiloh Baptist Church there, and there's St. Joseph's Methodist Church, and there's Holy Hill Church." I said, "That's three churches." I said, "Black peoples go there." I say, "And it's just as many people in those churches three time, multiplied by three for that one white church." I said, "But when you walk in those churches, you'll find black people, brown ones, tan ones, red ones." I said, "You keep on looking, you'll find them as white as you is." I said, "You know black man didn't do it."

I said, "Well, what have we had to do? Accept it." I said, "White people would kill black people for not accepting it." I said, "Now no one would like to see it straightened out more than me. To tell you the truth . . . What if I told you today how much mixture I have in me?"

She said, "You always told me you was Indian." I said, "I didn't tell you that. That's your mama said I was an Indian, that I was the prettiest red Indian Creek gal she had ever seen." I said, "She said it."

She said, "Well you knew you wasn't." I said, "I didn't have no reason to tell her what I was." And I didn't. I just let her say it. She wouldn't have wanted to think I had a white father. Oh no!

Well, I don't know if it was rape or money or lust or affection or what that caused the mingling up. I never talked to no one about it in those terms. In my mother's case, I don't know. I've spent a lot of my life trying to know, but I don't. My father felt something to keep up with me, but I don't know why he felt it—duty or guilt or what. I just don't know.

My mother protected me by making them promise I wouldn't have to nurse no babies until I'd nursed my own. Maybe the trouble came in when you were so young and went into the white homes. I don't know.

After I married, see, I moved to Mississippi and was glad to go, and my husband worked there in a paper mill. He made good money and we had two children. But one of the supervisors there told him, said he'd been up North and saw the depression coming and said they were gonna start laying off soon. And said we should move to Mobile because in the city, women could always work in white homes.

So we moved to Mobile in 1930. We moved and stayed with another aunt of mine. Her name was Aunt Caroline. We stayed there until we built our own home. At first my aunt and husband both worked, and I did washing and ironing at home. But then my aunt got a bad place on her leg, and my husband got sick. So I went to work full-time.

I went to work for this lawyer and they paid you ten a week, and oh, that was a lot of money then. But darling! You stayed there. If they wanted to have a conversation around the table, you didn't act sour, didn't rattle those pots and pans. And maybe it be nine-thirty before you'd get out of the kitchen. And oh, my dear, you'd been there since six-thirty in the morning.

They had two children, and one, that little old spoiled Clara, she was a teenager then. I still see her. She used to always get me about working for her, says, "You raised me and I want you to raise my daughters." One of her daughters used to be very nice and was one grade ahead of my granddaughter, and every year she'd send Marian her books down.

But I was glad when I didn't have to work there more. And why I didn't work more was on account of we had a run-in. Because my aunt she needed help getting insurance money from her son dying. They wouldn't pay, and finally, he got them to pay, Lawyer Scott. He put the money in the bank in his name though.

He said he was just taking his 4 percent out slow. My aunt she accepted that. She was raised up where Negroes were supposed to do whatever boss told you, you accept that. She thought she'd get it in time.

Well, a year went by and no money for my aunt. I quit there. And I called on Miz Lucy Meyers. She was a white lady, and she would do all she could for the Negroes because the white people didn't recognize her husband altogether as being white. His mother had had two colored children before she married his father, and the white people, for that, wouldn't let those children go to school.

She asked me about my father's people and who they were and say, "You know, time now to come up and talk straight about it." So she got in touch with Andrew, my daddy's brother. And Andrew called on Lawyer Scott and fixed it.

He was stealing her money! And some of those whites, I don't know! I never felt quite like I could trust any of them. Not even Andrew, who played the dear one, always coming for my father. No, I didn't trust the ones that were family or the ones I worked for, neither one. Now Andrew he died not long ago. He'd been down sick. His cook was named Willie Bell, and Willie Bell let me know about it. She called and said he's been asking for you and asking for you. I kept on avoiding it, till finally my husband said, "Why don't you go?"

So he carried me over there one Sunday, and when I got there, that doctor had just given him some kind of sedative. I was at the door on the porch, and his wife asked me, "What is your name?" I said, "Priscilla." She said, "Ain't Joe your uncle?" See, she didn't know her husband was my uncle, too. She was talking about my mother's brother that I told you all the white peoples loved. I said, "Yes ma'am."

Say, "Well, you the Priscilla he's been asking for." Because Andrew and my father had a sister named Priscilla, too. And says, "You waited a mighty long time to come." I say, "I admit that." And pecans began falling on the house, on the roof. I told her I'd better go so she could close the door and he wouldn't hear the noise of the pecans on the roof. He was right down the hall there.

So I left, and he died that week. Well, I didn't see him, so I never knew for sure if I would have trusted him in the end. We knew each other most all our lives. And I later heard through the grapevine that I cheated myself out of something, some money or some land, by not going earlier. But you know, some days I care and some days I don't.

From an interview with Mary Yelling

Winnie Hefley

Winnie Hefley (b. 1918) also speaks of a rural childhood. Unlike Priscilla Butler, however, Hefley did not have the advantages and the disadvantages of being half-white or of a mother's deathbed request. The ninth child born to a family of sharecroppers, she clearly remembers working in the fields as a child. She also remembers that domestic work offered the only means to leave the drudgery of agricultural work.

Hefley is the type of black domestic that was called "Old School" by younger white and black women. She asked me for help in locating medical treatment for her daughter. She did not ask for this sort of help from the relatives of her former employers. But, she said: "I would have if I felt like they'd help me. You have to know the kind of help people want to give before you ask. That is something you learn in the country coming up."

She told me how she was taught to work through whites to provide for herself and her family. Charles S. Johnson, a sociologist who studied the Black Belt in Alabama during the first half of the twentieth century, observed: "For those [blacks] still living in the country there is, it would appear, one unfailing rule of life. If they would get along with least difficulty, they should get for themselves a protecting white family."*

Winnie Hefley has incorporated this rural means of coping into the life she has lived in the city. As she notes, such country-bred blacks as herself were, in turn, seen by whites as ideal workers. White women in their interviews said that country-bred blacks were more docile and trustworthy than city-bred blacks. A number of white women mentioned seeking out such blacks—"going up the country to get them." And black women, newly arrived in the city and with the look of a country person, recalled being sought out by whites in shops or on downtown streets.

Although a preference for people of the land is found in much American thinking, white southerners appear to have built a unique prejudice toward country blacks. Particularly as urban southern blacks left for the North and West, whites came to idealize country blacks. White women, for example, in recalling an especially fond memory of a domestic worker, would explain her character, often lowering their voices slightly and looking down, by saying, "And she was from the country."†

From Hefley's viewpoint, life in the country was hard and made domestic work in the city appealing. She told me that she was not unhappy in old age, even with "ninety-five-year-old legs on a sixty-five-year-old body."

She walks slowly with a cane, and her hands are swollen and bent from

---

*Charles S. Johnson, quoted in Eugene D. Genovese, *Roll, Jordan, Roll: The World the Slaves Made* (New York, 1974), 118.

†This preference for country-born blacks as servants is discussed further in Part III.

arthritis. For our first meeting she wore the type of closely knit stockings that nurses wear—support hose—and a gray-blue suit with a gold flower pin on her blouse. She offered me small peppermint candies that she carried in her purse.

I was born in Clarke County, Alabama. These white people owned the farm—the land and everything. And they would hire families like my daddy and all of us. We didn't have nothing. They'd give us a place to stay, and we'd farm.

And the man, the white man, he'd share with us food and stuff, and we would wash and iron for his wife. Now my first job would have been working in the fields. And ever so often we would go up, like on a Saturday morning when the lady wanted her yard swept.

But mostly we worked in the fields until we got grown. There were ten of us, nine that lived. I was the next to the last. And we all worked even as children. And then if you got grown and didn't work in the fields, well, you could just work in people's homes. I worked for a lady for a little while. Mostly I just kept her baby for her. She worked at the filling station; her husband owned the filling station.

And then I worked for her grandfather. He and his wife were pretty elderly people, and I just kept house and cooked for them. I had a little house on the place, and I stayed there. My mother and them they lived further up in the country—up in the woods, on the farm. And they kept my child.

She was just a baby about six months old when I left her. Yes, my mother and father took care of her. She was happy with them. And I had to go.

Her father was just a boy. I really didn't want him and he didn't want me, and you know how you'd let things slip and then . . . have a child. He was killed when she was three weeks old. He fell off the back of a truck. It was sad, I guess, but at the time it just seemed like life.

I had her and I loved her, and I could go home on weekends. I could walk up.

I reckon those were my first jobs. And on the first one I believe she was paying me $3.00 a week. It was a very low salary because when I come to Mobile in '42, I was getting $3.50 working for her grandfather.

Since I had a child, you know . . . When the war was, they had better jobs in Mobile, paying jobs and all. So I asked my mother if she would keep my child, I would come and work and help them as much as I could on the farm with making a little more money. I wouldn't be able to go up on weekends. I'd go up maybe once every six weeks. But see, it wasn't so hard to leave. I had to, because my parents were old and they was on the farm and I didn't have a husband and somebody just had to bring in a little extra money. That's what it was.

And so my child she loved my mother, and my mother loved her. So my mother said she'd keep her. And then I went to the man I worked for. I told them that I enjoyed working for them, and I say, "I want to go to Mobile where I'm gonna make a little more money." They said, "Winnie, go on down and find out, and if you don't like it, you know you can always come back." Because you never run off a job. Always talk to them. Get that straight so if I wanted to come back, I could.

And there was a lady that lived in the country, and she had come to Mobile and got a job. So she encouraged me to come and start working at the same place she did. White people, they felt like if you was from the country, you was good and honest, like you came from a family and all like that. She was working for Miz Watts, who was running a boardinghouse. They were paying ten dollars a week and she hired me!

So I worked for Miz Watts from 1942 to 1972. I liked it there. I was the head cook. Salaries, at that time, were pretty low unless you were working on defense jobs or something like pertaining to the war. But Miz Watts was just such a sweet, good lady until I didn't even want to try to work for nobody else.

And by me not having a husband, she helped me with my child, helped me to raise her up. She would give me things for her, and she would make her clothes and send them and give me something extra when I go home to take to my parents and all. And I got a vacation with pay. Everybody wouldn't give you a vacation with pay.

And another thing, I was a diabetic in '64, and she told her doctor about me and my condition and that I was a reliable person. And she wanted them to do everything they could to put me on disability, because I had given her my life's work and everything and I was still able to work some but she didn't want me to just really *have* to work.

In the last days, I reckon about '68, she had her daughters come together and talk with me and she made a will out. She wanted them to sign and witness and everything. She said that I had been so good to her all the years and that she wanted to make a will in case of I wasn't able to work for nobody else or didn't have money or something like that, it would help me awhile till I could see something.

She stayed here until 1974. She stayed until she just wasn't able to live by herself, and if I had not had a husband at the time, then I could have lived with her. 'Cause I married in the sixties. And so I couldn't stay with her and my husband, so she had to leave and bought her a house in Florida, where she would be close to her daughter. Then I promised her I'd come to see her anytime she wanted.

She would send my fare and she would pay me. I would sleep right in the bed at her house, and we'd cook, we'd eat, we'd lay down and rest in the afternoon, and we'd talk.

She passed in '77. And I have the last letter she wrote to me. She wrote that letter Monday morning and . . . I just keep it and I'm gonna keep it as long as I live. She said, "Oh, Winnie, I just wish I could see you. I wish you could just come over . . ." And she told me what was happening. She was feeling pretty good and was eating well and all. And she passed on Friday. Oh, it just killed me! Everytime I start thinking about it!

She was eighty-six, and she was buried in Selma. That's their original home. That's where they all were born, the old people were. So I went up to her funeral.

One of her grandsons he writes me every once in a while. And she have a lot of people here in Mobile if I want to hear from them I could call them anytime. One of her daughters is alive in Florida, and I have her phone number. The other one died. She's the one I went to Birmingham and stayed with a good many times. She was an alcoholic, and I'd have to go up and stay with her.

Now that was hard on her mother on account of she was old. It wasn't hard on me; it was hard on her. Because she couldn't go help her daughter, and even if she did, she couldn't help her very much. She couldn't cook or clean up. When a person get in that drinking spell, you know how they get so unclean. So Miz Watts could send me up there to stay with her, maybe a week or two at a time, just as long as I could stay. Where I was strong enough that I could clean her house up and keep her clean and talk to her and keep her in the house and cook for her. You know, at least give her a plate of food. I'd set it by the door of her room for her if she wouldn't come out. I never could stop her from drinking now, but I was just there with her for company.

And so I did a lot of work for them. I sure did. I'm not bragging on myself, but I have went through that family trying to help people. They paid me. I wasn't working for charity, but I went through most of my life trying to help them. I really stuck with 'em and they did me, too. She would send me Christmas presents. She'd send me money all along anytime that she felt like that I needed ten or twenty dollars or something, I'd always have a little surprise.

After she left Mobile, I just picked up days work with different people.* I worked for some nice people, but with days work you wake up in the morning and you don't know which way you're going.

But I love people. I'm not partial with people. I try to live a Christian life, and the Bible teaches you to overcome evil with good. If anybody treat you mean, you just be nice and good to 'em right on, and then you can break 'em down. They'll get shame, or they'll see something in you. The Bible tell you to hold your peace, and then you don't have to be accounted for, for no fusses, for no quarrels.

From an interview with Susan Tucker

Working days, days work, and *day work* refer to work done by the day, as opposed to a more permanent arrangement by which women would work by the week. It seems that in some areas of the United States all work in which one does not live in is called day work, but among the women we spoke with, work paid by the week and done on a live-out basis was not called day work.

Sallie Hutton

Sallie Hutton (b. 1920) speaks of a strong affection for her white employer that was perhaps born of a common distrust of men. Both women had husbands who were neglectful of familial responsibilities. Hutton's focus upon the failings of these two men seemed typical of other stories that I heard describing discussions between white and black women about their private disappointments with men.

In such stories, however, it is important to note significant differences. Hutton, and all the other domestics who went daily into white homes, were privy to many of the white families' secrets. Such secrets could not be hidden within the private home, and black women, as the invisible good servants, often overheard and saw evidence of infidelity, alcoholism, drug addiction, financial loss, and a host of other problems. With black women, such secrets were safe because of racial etiquette that ensured that what went on in the white home would never be mentioned by a black to another white. These secrets were also safe because until recently white women have not openly acknowledged that such problems exist at all levels of society, especially their own level. White women seem to have felt that they could confide in black women, who lived in a society said to be violent. The white women felt that their black domestics could best understand their problems and comfort them.

Black women may have felt a similar safety in discussing marital problems with someone outside of their own community. Their descriptions of such conversations, however, do not have an intimate tone. They speak instead of men—white and black—humorously as "boys" who were "just playing at life." Hutton, for example, made light of her husband, dismissing him as one of these "not very good men."

Black women revealed less than did the white women in these discussions between the two races, probably out of a desire to remain separate from their employers. Maintaining the distance between themselves and their employers, however intimate the employers might be, ensured psychological separation. This was significant because black women clearly saw that shared gender, and shared secrets, could not erase the fact that most white women did not wish to change a system in which their own standard of living rested upon the cheap labor of all blacks, male and female.

Sallie Hutton seemed to say that though she worked within the narrow social and economic restraints of her time, she nevertheless saw that the affection she felt did not actually join her to her white employer. Like the stereotypical mammy figure, she was loyal to her white mistress until the latter's death. But she also locates within herself a position of superiority from which she pities her employer. Hutton left her husband and supported herself and her children; her white employer did not.

She lives in a house with aluminum siding, a small one-story house with a neatly kept yard. She is known as "the cake lady," in her neighborhood. She bakes for both whites and blacks and makes extra money by catering parties.

My mother and father worked the sharecrop on a big plantation in Monroe County, Alabama. There, there were all these families living, just worlds and worlds of people working for a Mr. Bradford, who owned the plantation.

It's hard to say, though, just how many people there was. I know there would be as many as one hundred kids in the school. On the plantation, there was a Lutheran school that my grandmother had organized. She had the Lutheran superintendent come down and help her. He was white, but we'd have two teachers—black teachers—and the school went to the seventh grade.

It wasn't a bad life, but the crops were failing. I came down to Mobile when I was eighteen. I had married when I was fifteen, and we'd gone to farming, but you couldn't make the money you could in Mobile.

We came, and I've been here ever since. He hadn't; he went back. At first, he was a good husband, but something came over him. I never did understand what, but he got wild after I had my third child. We'd been married about seven years.

And every time I'd have a baby, I'd have to quit work. He didn't like that. It didn't seem like he cared about providing for his home. One day, when my youngest was a month old, I went down and mailed my mama a letter. There was a letter for my husband waiting there, and I started home with it. When I seen it was from some woman, I opened it. She was telling him what a pleasure she had being down here with him. I burnt all the corners on the letter and put it in a new envelope, burnt its corners and mailed it back to her. That was a way to let her know she wasn't nothing. And I left him.

So I always found my own work, and I worked for a number of families. I had a list of them because the last place I worked they didn't want to wait on me to come back when I was having the baby.* But with my husband gone, I didn't have that problem.

The last one, I stayed there, with the Pierces, for twenty-five years. At first Miz Pierce, me and her did the cleaning. She was well then. I did all

*To *wait on* was the term used to describe unpaid pregnancy leave.

the cooking. And then, too, I did the washing and ironing. After she got sick, I did everything and I nursed her. I'd go in the morning, seven to three for the housework, and then I'd work three to eleven, nursing her. And many a night he'd call me at three, four in the morning to come back.

She had to be handled. She was bedridden. Something happened. I don't know what happened, but she had some sort of cancer, and she had nervous spells and was deathly sick. She went down and down.

But she depended directly on me. She called me for everything. Didn't care who was in the room with her—I had to go in there with her and sit. She would get those nervous spells and cry, and I was the only one could console her. I'd just sit down beside her and pet her and talk to her and tell her I was going to be right there with her and not leave her. Otherwise nobody else couldn't calm her down.

I always stayed till she was better. I didn't want to just walk off and leave her, 'cause see, she had nobody. She was all alone, and I felt so sorry for her. I really did. And she didn't have no kind of married life with him. I think that's why she was sick. I do. He was always drinking, and he'd leave her at parties and different things. She told me a lot of different things he'd done, but I never mentioned them to nobody. 'Cause she was such a good person, you would hate to know she was hurt. I couldn't tell now for her memory.

She was a wonderful woman, and she wanted to see, if you were working for her [and] you were nice to her, she wanted to see things better for you. She would try to look out for you.

Sometimes, if I'd go to work and I wasn't feeling good, she'd say to me, "You mustn't work so hard. You must lay down." And she would take me over the bay and I'd go fishing and crabbing and it wasn't bad and many times were very good.

Today, sometimes I dream of her, and in the dream she's always reaching out to give me something. She was that way, and I'm glad I nursed her.

He was another story! I don't know what to say about him. Was he worse than my husband? If you put each one of 'em in a sack, I think they would fall out together. There's a very few good men. It's a very few. He was not one of them. Mr. Pierce wasn't. For the last two years in her life he'd have his girlfriend come stay there—Miz Amy.

But that first morning he said to me, "Miz Amy is in there in the bed and would you fix her some breakfast and look after her until she's able to go home?" I looked up at him and said, "Do you think you're being nice to

Miz Pierce?" I say, "I just think you're horrible." I say, "I'm not scared to tell you about it." I said, "Do you think you're being nice?"

He wouldn't say a word. Slammed the door and went into where the other maid was and told her, "Sallie's crazy out there. Would you take care of Miss Amy and feed her breakfast and things?" She told him, "Yes."

He tried to make Miz Amy leave after the first week. I heard him. But I don't believe he was feeling guilt; he was worrying what the neighbors thought. Having his friend living over his wife! I just thought it was awful having her walking in and out over Miz Pierce like that. I let him know it, and someone else did, too. He got two threatening letters about it. And he presented both of them to me. I told him I didn't write them. He told me to ask the neighbors. I did and they said no, they didn't send them. But I think his guilt was getting him 'cause he wouldn't have asked me to go to these people, would he? He would have gone himself.

Miz Pierce got worse and worse. She died; she's been dead three years last January. And after she died, about one month, I came in there a Friday, and he left a note and a check for the week on the counter and told me when I got through cleaning up, just lock up the house and don't come back, because he was gonna get someone with a car what could run errands. He didn't explain nothing to me or anything.

I took the check and left because I said, well, he didn't pay me what money he owed me. That whole eight years he didn't give me a dime for my vacation. I didn't take a vacation because, see, she was so sick, and he kept promising to pay me but he never give me a dime. But I said if that help him, may God go his way.

Ever since I left there, he's been in and out of the hospital. But that's the way it goes if you don't do right. Miz Amy she's catching it now. Thank God! 'Cause he's been down on her ever since.

I don't care to go back there. I hear from the daughter once in a while. She married and left as soon as she could. She wasn't there when her mother was really sick. But I had a haul with her as a teenager. She didn't want to listen to nobody. But now she's fine. When she comes to visit— she lives out in California—she always comes down here for dinner.

Last time, she said I was her mama now. Said her mama was dead and I raised her anyway. I said, "Well, I'm glad you see it now!" She had to laugh. She said, "Well, I was a bad one, but I done learned some sense."

Her brother, last anyone heard, was on drugs somewhere. But I'll see him at the door down here, too.

Do I hear from Mr. Pierce? Well, I'm not gonna lie on nobody, even him. The daughter, Cathy, she called me the other day and said Daddy told her to call and see if she could check if anything he could do to help me. I told her I certainly appreciate it, but no, I'd rather not him do anything for me. It must be his conscience or something had come up. I told her I was getting on fine with the people I was with.

From an interview with Mary Yelling

Martha Calvert

Martha Calvert's mother is a domestic who since the age of eleven has worked ironing for whites. She is a woman who worked throughout the years her fifteen children were growing up and who at eighty still works. In addition, according to her daughter Martha (b. 1953), she is a woman who taught her children to work and to survive within whatever system they might find themselves.

Like other working mothers, she also wanted a better life for her children. She wanted them to be educated and to hold jobs suitable to their education. She also saw correctly that Martha, her last child, would not allow herself to be relegated to a permanent domestic caste as had earlier generations of southern black women. Martha's attitude is very different from that of the older interviewees, even of those born a decade before her.

In her interview one hears less of both the affection for, and the dependency on, whites. In her interview one can more readily discern certain facts about the nature of domestic work. For example, her remarks make it clear that if a domestic worker works for an employer who does not work outside the home or alongside the domestic in similar household or child-rearing duties, then the job usually becomes exploitative. In such a situation one woman is paid to complete those tasks that society has assigned to another. The latter woman thus escapes social forces that might exploit her by exploiting someone else. Even when the pay is considered good, as is the case here, the psychological response to the discrepancy between wealth and poverty is damaging. For instance, it is painful to leave a small child who is sick to go to work caring for a well child whose mother goes shopping all day.

Such situations arise, of course, because we follow the patterns of life learned from our parents. Judith Rollins, in her work on domestics and employers in the Boston area, found that a woman is likely to hire servants if there were servants in the house when she grew up.* In the South evidence of such modeling is seen in the fact that the behavior of white employers and black domestics tends to be based upon what a woman learned from her mother. Calvert readily sees this tendency in her white employer. Now that she is grown up, Calvert holds a new appreciation of her mother, especially of what her mother was required to do to raise her.

Martha Calvert is the only domestic we interviewed who insisted on being called "Ms. Calvert" by her employer. She is one of the few women to make a distinction between Miz and Ms. She believes the first term is old-fashioned, the second, up to date.

She wears her hair in corn rows. Her two-bedroom apartment is sparsely furnished with a Scandinavian dining-room table and chairs, a child's computer,

---

*Judith Rollins, *Between Women: Domestics and Their Employers* (Philadelphia, 1985), 94.

beds, and a television set. She made chili for our dinner and Irish coffee for dessert.

I was born in 1953, and I'm the youngest of fifteen children my mother had. So you're looking at me, and you can see I'm black and you know I'm from the South, so you know domestic work is something I know about, right? Just given those things about me . . .

It's not what I do now, but I *can* talk about it because of my mother, and my family. And because in between sessions at school and in between jobs, I did [it], too. Like right after my son was born, I worked for a lady awhile. I'd separated from my husband, and it took me eight months to get the job I wanted. So during that time I did days work because it was a way to do something right then. And you paid no taxes, and it allowed me the freedom to job hunt.

This last job . . . It was a pretty nice atmosphere, but I wasn't really geared to that kind of work. My mind is not into it. Technically, if your backbone is into it, you can make good money doing it, because like I was getting thirty-five dollars a day in my hand.*

What really made the difference for me was my child. Having a child, I knew I didn't want to do days work. I had a teenager watching my son, and here I was a thirty-year-old woman watching someone else's kids, cleaning her house, taking care of her clothes while she shopped for a living and organized her credit purchases. That's what she did for a living!†

Now she had a lovely house. It was a joy to clean it. And if you're going to have a place like that, I feel like it needs to be immaculate. So it was no easy job. And everybody in that house had their own bathroom. There were five people living in that household, and each had a beautiful bathroom, right off their rooms. And the mother's bathroom had a skylight and gold fixtures and a jacuzzi and a dressing room beside it with all her closets. Her bathroom suite, I should call it. Some people's apartments wasn't like her bathroom!

And beautiful antique furniture. The kids even had beautiful antique furniture, and just each, a little animal farm of little stuffed animals—

*About three-fourths of the domestic workers interviewed chose to have a "reported income" with Social Security withheld. It is still common, however, particularly among older black women and day workers who often collect Social Security, supplemental security income, or forms of welfare assistance to prefer "money in the hand."

†"To shop for a living" means to lead a life centered around buying material goods as opposed to working either within or outside the home.

every kind imaginable. And every night they had to remove them stupid stuffed animals, and every day I had to put them back on the bed! Now, with me, those kids had to make up their beds.

She told me when I first came that one of the kids was spoiled. So I told her from Jump Street, I say, "Hey, if your kids talked to your other maid any kind of way, let me know now so I will not waste your time and you will not waste my time." Those were my rules, and the main thing was any of the sass have to go.

The main thing was the sass. I always saw whites as having a lot of sass. I always somewhat resented the people my mother worked for. I heard about the sass. And I couldn't understand why some woman that called my mama—and I could tell by her voice, she got to be younger than my mother—called Mama by her first name. I got a spanking in the first grade for that—because I corrected a white lady that called my mama Joanna. I told her, "You sound the age of one of my sisters, so I think my mother's name is Mrs. Perdue to you."

And my mama heard me. She said I was being disrespectful to the people she worked for. Now she didn't really satisfy it for me, because I thought the people were disrespectful to *her*. What it came down to was one disrespect doesn't deserve another.

Seems like from the cradle, I resented the way white people behaved towards her. Because she taught *me* to respect older people and then I just saw disrespect for her. I thought, oh, white people basically don't respect older people. That was an idea that I had because, well, my mama seemed older because she had gray hair from day one as far as I was concerned.

And in a way it was something that I always was mad with her for not doing anything about. Because, hey, I don't care what the circumstances . . . Right now if I was to lose my job, I would go back to my little list of people I could work for, so that I wouldn't lose any stroke in my income, go right back to days work, but I'd keep the dignity in it.

But of course, those were different times. I was the baby, and there's fourteen before me. My mother brought up fifteen kids to finish high school, mainly ironing clothes. She did that, and as a child I don't really remember being poor. I mean, she cut corners, but we always had a nice life and we always had food, and I'm talking pre–food stamp days. Now I know my sisters were older and had jobs and helped, and I know I was always surrounded by other kids that didn't have as much as I did.

But I didn't know we were poor till I went to college. And I remember my grant didn't start till September, and my mama paid for my summer semester in $333 in dimes and quarters. She had a shopping bag full of that. She'd saved it that way. And I was impressed, but I knew we were poor.

I was the first one to go to college. She walked me right out of the line at high school graduation and right onto the bus.

You know, for my mama, I was a dream. I was a menopause baby. And I can remember when I needed a little money, I'd baby-sit in high school, and she wasn't too keen on it. But there was one family she let me go to because they behaved so nicely to me. They were really nice people, and they did all the little kinds of things. Like at Christmas, you got the little fruit baskets. But she had this idea about what I was going to be, and one thing I wasn't going to be was a domestic. I came along at a time where, yeah, it looked like it could be possible that a black woman could be more. She worked for me with that in mind.

Now, I do know that she had no time for herself. Time for herself was out of the question. She had a sick husband, a bunch of kids. She got up four in the morning, cooked breakfast, got them out, and got herself out. And I used to remember that she'd come home in the evening time tired. But, seems like I got enough of her somehow.

She specialized in ironing. She worked for a bunch of wealthy people. And sometimes, near Christmas, I know, she'd work for as many as ten houses a week. We'd get to know these people, hear about their families, their little business.

And it's a secret, but if you're changing names and it will be disguised, then, I'll tell it because it's an interesting part of the way things are set up now: my mother works now. She's eighty, and she irons clothes five days a week.

The reason my mother would have a fit right now and I'd probably be disowned if she knew that I was setting up telling somebody is that they would cut her checks. The reason she's working now is because her checks are not enough and because, I think, she would die if she didn't work. She has always worked, and I don't think she knows how to sit home all day.

She won't be listed in any of the great books anywhere, but I think of her as great. And I think now she has a lot of pride in herself and her accomplishments.

No, I don't think she always did. When I was coming up, that was during the time when a lot of the sit-ins were going on and trying to bring about change. It was a needed time because there were people *like my mother*—doing a real hard job and not getting credit. And even though, during that time, she didn't go along with everything that was going on, it changed her. You can see a change in her. Now she travels. She does things that before she thought only white people did.

Still, today, working in private homes, there is always the contrast of your life to their life. You wondered did those two ends ever come together.

I thought about my mother a lot at the last job because I had a child then, too, and I wondered about what she wanted for me that she would see at these white people's houses. I'd love to have a little room for my son like these people had for their children. And sometimes—I didn't get spiteful, but here's how I'd think about it—I'd be at this lady's and she's out shopping and her bratty little kid is giving me a pain in the neck and my kid is home sick with a teenage baby-sitter. It gets frustrating!

It made me send that kid to bed without lunch, 'cause I should have been cuddling my own child instead of listening to hers while she went out shopping or on a fund-raising committee. Raising funds for what? I never did find that out, and they were forever raising money among a bunch of people that one person could write a check and cure the whole problem.

And with this lady I had to listen sometimes to such worthless garbage. She came in one day and said how her friend Ann and her husband make so much and they only pledged a thousand dollars to the charity and she is just hurt and devastated because that is her good friend. And to make matters even worse, she went to her masseuse, and he couldn't take her then, because he had just been called out on a home assignment. Then to make matters even worse, she couldn't even go get her hair done, because it was Monday!

And I'd feel like telling her, "You know what I could do with that thousand dollars? Let me tell you what a good charity I am." And see, my mama probably had to listen to worse than that.

Now, this white lady and I sometimes, we would have a normal talk, as if we were just two women. Not too often. She would rise above me the minute her mother or the thought of her mother came, because her mother taught her how to look for a domestic and how to take care of your help. My mother didn't give me any of those lessons. She wanted better for me.

Her mother didn't approve of me. My employer, she introduced me to her mother as "Ms. Calvert." And I know they had a talk about that, 'cause they called *her* "girl" Lena. But her daughter was younger than me, and if I'm gonna call her Ms. So-and-so, she's gonna call me Ms., too. It's as simple as that. We'll be on first names, or we'll be formal. However you want it, but it's gonna be the same, 'cause that was one of the things I've had all my life to know.

From an interview with Susan Tucker

Gillian Kushner

Gillian Kushner (b. 1961) has lived most of her life with her mother, a sales clerk, and her grandmother, a domestic. In her narrative she speaks of her grandmother, whose courteous, kind, and responsible ways have made her a mother figure in the home of her white employer.

Both the black and the white women we interviewed spoke of the role of the domestic as a mother surrogate to white children. This role was, of course, particularly important in homes where the white biological mother was absent, as in the white home described by Kushner. But it was important in other homes as well. The idea of the black woman as the more instinctive mother was central to the imagination of many southerners. After the Civil War white people retained little of the plantation life-style, but they did retain power over black people and the ability to hire domestics at low wages. The domestic, in turn, became a symbol of the Old South. Thus, the stereotype of the mammy remained. Black women caught in the entanglement of race and economics, in turn, realized that to retain their jobs they must sometimes act according to this mother image.*

In response to whites and to their own maternal feelings they, too, often saw themselves as the "more instinctive" mothers—both to their own children and the children of whites. They did not wish to be cast as mammies, and they did not perceive their child-rearing as romantically as whites did, but they did see themselves as warmer and more balanced in their approach to children. They felt that white women "didn't know how to love children" or that "white women didn't stay around to know how."

Gillian Kushner is not especially introspective about this role. Although she realizes the historical precedent of her grandmother's labor, she speaks without anger. Typical of her tone is an evenhanded description of going into the white home as a younger child after school. She accepts the fact that to go into the white household meant sitting down in the kitchen and talking with or helping her grandmother. She accepted the confinement of blacks to the kitchen.† She is a scholarship student who looks upon her grandmother as someone practicing an ancient craft.

They live in a two-bedroom house. Their yard has a chain link fence around it and is surrounded by azaleas. In the middle of the yard is a birdbath. Her grandmother sits on the porch at night. Her mother refuses to sit on a front porch and instead sits inside watching television. Kushner moves easily between the two of them.

*The idea of the black domestic as the more instinctive mother is discussed further in Part III.

†For a discussion of the concept of place in the work of black domestics, see Trudier Harris, *From Mammies to Militants: Domestics in Black American Literature* (Philadelphia, 1982), 16.

Ever since I can remember, we lived with my grandmother. And Maw Maw, I call her, she always worked in a private home. Now that I am older and baby-sit for families, I think about how whites always looked at blacks as being able to clean well, cook well, and that was it. That was all they thought blacks could do.

And with my grandmother in this one family, they also looked upon her as a mother image. Their mother had passed away with cancer, and so if they needed anything, they would come and tell her. They call her Maw Maw, just like I call her Maw Maw. You know how you see maids that been there for years. She's like that. After their mom died, she took a lot of control in their house and over their lives. She had to do what was right for them, and she tried just like she tried for us. If they needed her to come to school for them, she would go to school for them, or if they was sick, she would take them to the doctor—that sort of thing.

And it seems their father, Mr. Lindsey, over the years he changed towards her, too. In the beginning, I guess, he didn't treat her as an equal, but as the kids started growing up, he got used to the idea of her importance. Before, they had a good relationship, and if she needed something, she could ask him, and if they needed something, they could ask her, but it was still that she was black and they were white. Now they seem more equal. He'll talk to her more, and they go more places together. I guess when a person gets older, they start to appreciate life just a little bit more, and that's what he is doing now.

I used to see them a lot, because I used to go there after school and wait for Maw Maw to go home. I would just go over there and sit down and talk to Maw Maw or help her.

I got *my* first job when I was fourteen. And I baby-sit for about three families—one black and two whites. And that's interesting, too, to look at the differences and the ways they raise their children.

The black family, they had two kids—ten and twelve. When I was raised up, if you were ten and twelve, you wouldn't have a baby-sitter. But they weren't typical. The kids were like progressed a lot faster than some kids their age, and yet they were also treated as if they were younger in other areas. Pushed in school, but like at home, not pushed at all.

The next job was with a white family that was very nice. She's not the typical white person. A lot of black people look at white people as snobs, or they think white people are rich and everything. She was an average person, though, and she'd talk to me a lot, and she made baby-sitting fun, and you felt good about her and her kids. She didn't look at me as being black, and I didn't look at her as being white. It was just a friendship.

The other white family were real society, and they didn't have a home atmosphere. The kids and the parents are racing and running against each other. Either the mom is out to lunch and she comes in and fixes dinner and then goes somewhere for drinks and the father comes home and goes out for drinks somewhere else or some story like that. And you feel kind of sorry for the kids because their parents are not putting enough emphasis on their life. The children are growing up to be snobs. Their mom doesn't care or is not interested. The maid really raises them.

I didn't mind being there. It made me like the other two families more. It made me hope that I can always look at people where I can understand what they're talking about and not look at their color. The kids at the really rich house always just considered me their black baby-sitter. And when I got a better job, the other two were real happy for me, but these ones just said, "Oh no!"

Overall I was raised to believe you got to make your independence, though, some kind of way. When you have a job, any kind of job, you have a little status of "I am going to make it." I think that explains why people that don't like domestic work still do it.

I never, though, really understood why white people needed someone to come clean their house 'less they're just so busy that they can't clean it up. I guess a lot of white people wanted their houses to look a certain way that blacks could make them look. And they wanted to keep blacks in a position where they had authority over them.

But like Maw Maw cleans up, Mom works in a store, and I'm going to college. So even though my grandmother cleaned house, it didn't matter to her. She had a job, and she wants to see her children not do things that she's doing and to have money. That's what this whole thing is—money.

In private homes today, I wonder how do whites feel about the blacks that work for them. I came upon something in a book, a story where this guy was telling someone, even though you have this white friend giving you stuff, when something goes wrong . . . like the whites do with the domestics . . . how do the blacks feel when something happens really wrong and the whites don't help?

From an interview with Mary Yelling

Leigh Campbell

+→≍█≍←+

The following narrative is based upon the angriest interview I heard. Most of this anger springs from the fact that Leigh Campbell (b. 1914) has lived in different parts of the country and feels misunderstood by those people she calls northerners.

Her ideas, however, are not unlike those of many other white southerners who express less vehement anger, but nevertheless clear disdain, for the North. The "North," in fact, has become to such southerners any place not within the former Confederate South—whether Connecticut, Colorado, or wherever. Such disdain draws upon the Civil War, Reconstruction, the different economic systems in the different sections, and the national criticism of the segregated South. The steady migration of southern blacks away from the South from World War I to the 1970s also, until recently, contributed to this constant rivalry between the South and the North in the minds of white southerners.

So it is that southerners like Leigh Campbell enjoy telling stories of how blacks in the North felt a kinship with white southerners.* Although such stories are most often used in defense of segregation, they are still valid observations. People from similar backgrounds do get along better and do recognize within one another mutual obligations, and this is true even of people who have between them many other grievances. In short, whites and blacks from the South were accustomed to each other—accustomed to the forms of speech and the codes of decorum each prescribed for the other.

In addition, it is difficult to move from the culture of one's early life into another culture without defending something of one's past. A person in a new culture is singled out and often called to explain his or her past. And that past, out of context as it were, becomes more consciously linked to the person's sense of identity. It is no accident that southerners out of the South often justify the South as if they are justifying themselves.

Leigh Campbell certainly felt she was defending her self-image. She defended southern culture by noting its emphasis on courteous behavior between all people. She carried this defense further when she spoke of the love between whites and their black servants.

Such responses seem not uncommon among southerners out of the South. These responses, in turn, are generally met with a labeling of such "love" as paternalistic. Yet, the memory of loyalty and affection between white employers and black domestics cannot be dismissed by such labeling. Like Campbell, Eugene Genovese, the great historian of slavery, comments on such bonds, albeit in a very different way and about a different era. Genovese notes that incidents in

---

*The preference of black domestics for southern women as employers is also discussed in Judith Rollins, *Between Women: Domestics and Their Employers* (Philadelphia, 1985), 219–22.

the aftermath of emancipation showing deep loyalty of slaves to their masters, though not as frequent as whites wish to believe, should not be ignored: "Three strands run through these incidents: a compassion for others born of their own suffering; the recurring idea of mutual obligations in an organic relationship; and a new sense of having the strength to reverse traditional roles within that organic relationship. . . . It was no fault of the blacks that their choice of generosity and compassion over retribution and vengeance did not prove adequate."*

It seems that black domestics often made such "choices of generosity and compassion," and Leigh Campbell chose to remember them. She is angry that others have tried to make her change her memory.

She is more aware of her anger than others are, because she has moved back and forth between the North and the South. Such moves have led her to be unusually introspective about her past. Robert Coles, the psychiatrist, interpreted the advice given him by a black father about the necessity for such introspection in this way: "One cannot leave one world and go into another without misgivings, regrets, confusion; and when the point is to find out how the two worlds are coming together (at least a little bit, if ever so tentatively) then one ought indeed go back and forth."†

I am from the same "worlds coming together" that Campbell is. It is only my age that could make me a foreigner to her. But she saw this gap as a huge one. As she spoke, she often paced. Sometimes she would stand up and walk to the edge of the glassed-in porch. Then she would sit down again, often leaning forward, moving her arms about, pointing into a large yard where a black gardener was working. She is a friendly woman, well known and well liked in her community. She offered me ginger ale and cheese straws.

⊷᠅⊶

Now my husband said I shouldn't talk to you. I told him you were coming and he said, "Well, you just as well keep your feelings to yourself." He said, "Nobody is ever gonna understand it, and we cannot explain it." He said, "You remember how it was. We all know how it was, but *they're* not going to understand, and they don't want to understand." And he said, "You're just wasting your breath" and "Just keep your feelings to yourself." He said, "Nobody will ever understand it, and we'll just die knowing that, and the next generation will never understand."

But it makes me so mad that I want to talk, because we did know so many of them and they did love us, too. And we loved them. We were always together. Like our house when I was growing up was just this side of where all the blacks lived. My mother and daddy had built a house

---

*Eugene D. Genovese, *Roll, Jordan, Roll: The World the Slaves Made* (New York, 1974), 133.

†Robert Coles, *Farewell to the South* (Boston, 1978), 378.

there, and my aunt lived next door. And we had Joseph and Callie that lived there, too. Joseph took care of the cows, and Callie would work, too. And they had a little girl named Lillian, and Lillian used to come and play with me all the time.

Then, there we had Geneva, and her mother was our slave. She was Mammy. I've got a picture back there of me and Mammy. They took it for her. They wanted to get a good picture of Mammy.

And Mammy's granddaughter died here just the other day. She was written up on the front page of the newspaper. She'd been a teacher for so many years, and she was named for my sister Anne. And I was talking to a co-worker, a black woman. She said, "You know, they've got a picture." She said, "I don't know where that picture is now, but I've seen it so many times, with the little white girl and Grandmother Beasley." She was a friend of theirs. And I said, "Well, that's Mammy and me."

And Mammy . . . Oh, she had the sweetest cheeks, and we used to crawl up in her lap and just pat her and pat her and just love and kiss her. And after I was grown, we lived down the street, and Mammy would ride the streetcar out to see us. I'd see Mammy coming, and she was coming to spend the day with us, and we were just thrilled.

She always wore a red or blue head handkerchief. And we always went to Georgia every year. I guess this might have been before I was born, because my sister Anne was eight years older than I was. Anyhow Mammy always wore a head handkerchief, and they were going to Georgia to see my uncle. Mammy got herself all dolled up to go down to the train station to get on the train. She had on her white apron, and she had on a white head handkerchief, and she was going to sleep in the pullman like they were. And so Anne saw Mammy with that white head handkerchief on, and she said, "Mammy, you take that thing off your head. I don't like it." And she cried so that Mammy had to go open her suitcase and get a red or blue head handkerchief to put on her head, 'cause Anne just didn't like her mammy with that white handkerchief. She cut up something terrible because she wanted her mammy just like she wanted her, like she knew her.

And Mammy's daughter, like I said, worked for us, too—Geneva. All right, there's another example. When I was grown and married, we were in Rome, Georgia. My son was a baby, and my mother had such a fit because I was there with no help. And Geneva had moved to a town near there. And Mother woke up one night and thought, "Oh, I'm going to write Geneva. She's in Culpepper and that's not far from where Leigh is."

This was during World War II. So Geneva came over. Got a friend to drive her over or . . . I don't know if she rode the bus over or how she got there. She came, and she got a girl to come to work for me—Laura, who I had letters from for many years after that. And Laura had a little boy my son's age. We lived in an apartment hotel, and I never did see the little boy, but she was always telling my son about her boy. And she worked for me till we left there about two years later.

Geneva got me Laura, and she, Geneva, would come over when she had a ride, and the doorbell would ring, and there would be Geneva. And she'd say, "All right now, I've come to spend the day"—now this is Mammy's daughter—"I've come to spend the day and I'm going to take charge of the baby. I'm going to do this and I'm going to do that . . . make you a pie" and so on. And she would say what else she was going to cook me . . . maybe some of her rolls or something. She was a first-class cook. And she'd say, "All right, you just get lost and go." She would come over there and do that, and she did it because she loved me. She was just a member of the family and, you know, she wouldn't let me pay her.

I mean it was just a way of life and there was no hard feelings, no hate. I think Jack Kennedy is the one that started this word *hate*. There was never any hate in anybody's heart. We just accepted each other for what we were. And I never had any feeling of anything else. They were just part of our lives, and they were black and we were white, but that made no difference. They loved us and we loved them, and I can say that very sincerely that I know they loved us, too.

Of course, they brought the children to work sometimes. Of course. And another thing they did, and it was the way and accepted—they toted.* They toted during the old days, I mean, before the depression. We had dinner in the middle of the day, two o'clock dinner, and they gave the cook what she wanted to feed her family. She would always tote something home.

And one time Octavia, who worked for my sister for so many years, was there, and I said, "Octavia, I want some more rice" or something. And my brother-in-law he said, "Remember, the cook has to eat." I said, "Well, my father used to say, if the cook don't take care of herself before she puts the food on the table, it's her own fault."

So they toted. They got plenty. They'd carry a basket, or sometimes like they'd take it in a tin lard can or something like that. I don't know why

Toting was the practice of taking food from the employer's kitchen as a supplement to paid wages. It is discussed further in Part IV.

they quit. They thought if they said they didn't tote they'd get more money, I guess.

Now times have changed. Things will never be the same. We loved them. They were all good cooks or whatever they did, they usually did well. Which I think is important today, because there are so many like Sabrina. I think Sabrina would be better going out and being a domestic than trying to be a secretary. That's Octavia's child that she raised. I don't think she's qualified to do that, but she wants to get out and do something like that. Well, Octavia . . . I think Octavia would much rather Sabrina learn to be a good domestic.

Octavia, now, she always worked for us, too. She worked for my family and for my sister, and she raised my niece. She is just a member of the family, and we all love her. It was just a way of life, and there was no hard feeling and no hate. And I think they were happier then, and now all of 'em trying to think that the white man hate 'em. I never hated one in my life. Who started that hate business? Jack Kennedy? Or was it Bobby Kennedy? Or was it some other Yankee earlier?

I think the image that is tried to be painted about the southerner and the black person has been entirely wrong. We lived in Philadelphia once, after I was married. And I had a maid, Dorothy. She worked for a lot of nice families in Philadelphia, and she worked for me two days a week. And when we left to come back south, she said, "Miz Campbell, I want to tell you," she said, "I have never worked for a family whose children treated me with the respect that yours do." And she wrote me letters to that effect. I wish I still had them.

And the day we were moving, this neighbor of mine she came over, and she said she wanted to have me for lunch but she said, "I just want to tell you . . ." I had Dorothy helping me. She said, "There's only one thing, I will have to say that you're going to have to sit at the table with Dorothy because I'm going to have her for lunch, too."

I said, "Well, that's all right." I said, "That doesn't bother me a bit in the world." We just didn't do that—whether the servant was black or white. That used to burn me up, those northerners would think the servant had to come and sit down at the table with them. I said, "Well, the president in the White House is served by blacks and whites, and he doesn't have them come and sit down at the table." They're there in the capacity to serve. Now isn't that true? They couldn't understand that. She would not dare have me come over if she didn't have Dorothy sit down at the table with her and me. Well, that was all right. We just would have done it differently—taken her sandwich over to her while she's working or sat in a different room. But they just don't understand.

And Rosa, that was another one. She worked for me when my oldest boy was still pretty young. And "Rosa," I'd say, "Rosa, we're going over the bay and spend the day, and you go on and do what you have to do." Nobody watched the clock, and she would leave when she was through.

Or I'd ride her home. I'd take her to pay her water bill. "Miz Leigh, I've got to go downtown to pay my water bill. You mind taking me down?" I'd take the kids. We'd drive down and pay the water bill, maybe the gas bill, just things like that. "I've got to stop by the store. Would you let me get so and so?" she'd ask.

And we'd come over the bay. All right, I was young. I probably had no idea what I was going to have for supper when we got home. We'd come in that house, and Rosa in that kitchen had made . . . She'd gone to the store, walked up there, gotten turnip greens and maybe fixed turnip greens and cornbread, black-eyed peas, or sweet potatoes. She would pay for it out of her money. She knew I had to feed the family. She knew when we came back, she'd get her money. Now, wasn't that wonderful? Because she loved us.

And I used to take my son to her house when I'd have to go do Junior League volunteer work. He'd play the record player there. I've got a record right in there, right now, I went over the other day. She'd play the record "Christ, My All" and some others. They're old-timey records. And he liked "Christ, My All" so much that I've still got it. She said, "Well, you can have it."

She might have a little boy from next door come over and talk to him and play with him. He loved to go to Rosa's house.

You see, we loved them dearly, and my daughter, when we were out in California, she got the idea that they thought the southerner hated the colored. She said, "Mother, I don't understand it." She says, "Why do they say that we from the South dislike the colored people?"

You're not supposed to use the word *colored* anymore. It's supposed to be *black,* but half of 'em aren't black anyway. Why do they want to be called black? "But," she said, "I can't understand why they keep telling us that, when I can think of only Octavia and Rosa and this one," and she named the ones she knew. She said, "What are they talking about?" She says, "We love them." And we did.

From an interview with Susan Tucker

Mary Patricia Foley

As late as 1945, it required only half as large a family income to employ a servant in the South as it did in other parts of the country. The South had long been known as a white "housewives' utopia."* Mary Patricia Foley (b. 1938) correctly links what she calls this "specialness" to the labor of black domestics. The abundance of maids available to work at low wages made for southern white women a relatively elite life-style that was often called special, aristocratic, or "old southern." Interestingly, many white southerners also use such terms to describe black domestics, to include them in a fantasy of themselves as special people. Over and over I heard the appearances and demeanors of specially favored black domestics described as aristocratic or royal.

In such descriptions white women are ascribing to domestics a dignity within situations that were often degrading. But such descriptions have been a traditional means of semantically dealing with blacks who do not fit the stereotype of a low-born person.

I had a sense that Foley was also aware of some of the semantic means whites have contrived to speak of the past. She did not want to talk long. A professional woman today, she is unusual in that she does not employ any household help. Most southern women with a high enough income still seem to do so.

She seems not so unusual, however, in other ways. Leaving the interview, she said that she thinks about inequality, "but not a lot." Like her, many of the educated white women of the South are conservative in their views on feminism. They are conservative, perhaps, because any study of gender inequality would at least implicitly address the full equality of all people, which in turn would challenge attitudes toward race and class as well. On a less philosophical but nevertheless important level, the educated white women of the South, unlike such women in other areas of the country (who spearheaded the formation of feminist groups), are perhaps less inclined to support change, because their traditional roles within the family have been easier ones that have not blocked the road outside the private sphere. The traditional roles of many white southern women have been, instead, "special" at the expense of black women.

This, too, seemed a topic Mary Patricia Foley would rather not discuss. She was very busy, and we did the interview late on a summer night at her office. She has fair skin and blonde hair. She wears silk blouses and navy blue suits.

*C. Arnold Anderson and Mary Jean Bowman, "The Vanishing Servant and the Contemporary Status System of the American South," *American Journal of Sociology,* LIX (November, 1953), 223.

I was born to what I suppose one could only describe as an old southern family. The stereotypical kind—that had the maids and so on. And I always felt that we were very special.

Things about us were old: the furniture, the house, the town, and there was also this talk of the family as being old—a sort of heritage, I guess you'd say. Of course, we didn't have a lot of money. I mean, we always had things, but we were expected, after we made our debut, to marry well enough to make it on our own.

In childhood a part of that specialness I felt, I think now, had to do with the maids and cook. They made you feel like you were in some movie, being waited on and all. And for a long time, up until about three years ago, Delores still made me feel that way.

That was the maid I used to have—Delores. And Delores had worked for my mother. Everybody's dream, I know, to have a maid who used to work for your mother. I have a friend who lives here now from Connecticut, and she says everybody here who has a maid has one who has been in the family for years. She says she doesn't think the normal kind that one just hires exists. She says she feels like an odd mother not to have such a person for her children. But of course she's exaggerating. Good maids who want to work are rare these days, for everyone.

But Delores . . . What was even more interesting about her is that she was the daughter of the washwoman my grandmother had. And Delores and her sister would, when they would bring the wash, stay and play with my mother, as little children. And then when Mama was about thirty and Delores was about twenty-nine, she came to work for Mama. She stayed with Mama for twenty-three years, and then she came to me for ten years. After Mama died, she came to me.

And then when Delores died, I was so sad. I don't know of any death that's grieved me so. As time went on, she really became a source of strength to me, like a mother.

And she could do everything. She could cook and she could cook anything. In the early days—she supplemented her income by catering parties. Imagine working until three or four o'clock and then going home and cooking for forty.

She had a lot of energy. You wonder how. And she worked for me right up until she died. By the time the children were older, I didn't have her permanently anymore, but my uncle got her a job in the school and she was just so happy there. And she would come to me on her days off. They found, though, that she had cancer, and she died within one year of knowing.

There was another maid that I really liked, too—another one Mama had. Her name was Claudine, and she died in about 1955 so I didn't know her as long. Nobody ever saw where she lived. She didn't want us to come see her when she was sick. But she was tall and very black and had an aristocratic carriage. For some reason, though, Claudine didn't work for us after a while. We came to a parting of ways with her.

But I loved Claudine. She was the one, when Mother said, "Claudine, you know you must make Miss Pat learn to clean up after herself." Claudine answered, "She ain't never gonna have to clean up after herself!"

Well, I have had to clean up after myself. She would probably get a good chuckle on me today. Now I don't have any help. I tried two after Delores died. One, Clara . . . If it wasn't nailed down, she'd ask you for it. She scouted around the neighbors for old toys, and if she saw some curtains up on the top shelf or some clothes in a bag, she would say, "If you don't have any use for that, I'll take it." It was just most irritating.

The other one came, the first thing she said was: "Well, I don't eat ham. I don't eat bacon. And what I have to have is something for my high blood pressure, lean for lunch." This was when we were paying them $3.30, and I thought she ought to bring her own lunch. I only had her two days! It was like if I don't get rid of this black person, I'm going to die.

I do the housework myself now. And you know, I visited with some friends out in California last week, and they—they think nothing of vacuuming the whole house themselves. And I realized it's not so unusual a thing to do. The only difference is I'll never vacuum the whole house without thinking of Delores or Claudine.

From an interview with Susan Tucker

Sarah Kingsley

The domestic whom Sarah Kingsley (b. 1942) remembers most clearly acted in place of her mother after the latter's death. Thus, the narrative that follows speaks of the other side of Gillian Kushner's grandmother's role.

It is interesting that Margaret, the domestic, told Sarah not to announce to people, "This is my mother." Margaret must have felt a mixture of feelings at hearing this remark. She might have felt that this could have well been literally so—that black women domestics were sometimes sexually exploited by their white male employers. She probably saw, often enough, half-white children. She might have felt that she did not want to be typecast as a mammy. Or she could have felt deep sadness on hearing Sarah's remark—sorrow that Sarah had no mother and sorrow that she herself lived away from her own children.

Such a mixture of feelings occurred not infrequently in the lives of black women who went into white homes. Going between the white and black communities, black domestics also recognized that as servants to white households, they were allowed to go places other blacks were not. Black domestics, thus, were singled out by whites, but they were also reminded that this singling out was not because of themselves, their character, or even often their work. It was because they were attached to whites. David Katzman discusses this role of the black domestic in the South, noting that some parks even displayed signs reading "NO NEGROES ALLOWED EXCEPT AS SERVANTS."* The uniform—marking the status of the black woman as part of the white household—ensured this sort of convoluted acceptance.

Weddings, however, seem to have been an undefined area within these unwritten laws. Black domestics were invited as guests to white weddings and came as guests sometimes dressed in clothes like other guests. This might present a problem. In our interviews both black and white women remembered insults to blacks not dressed in uniforms. Two white women remembered that specific instructions had to be given so that favored maids could attend as guests and not be turned away at the door for their lack of uniform. Kingsley remembers such a wedding.

The interview was an emotional one, with sudden gasps and crying at the memory of Margaret, the house where she lived in the city, her children in the country, and her kindness to Kingsley.

Sarah Kingsley's husband, an activist, laughs derisively when he hears she is going to be interviewed about Margaret. "It will only be a book about the faithful darkies," he tells her. But she decides to do the interview because "it is something no one ever talks about."

She lives in an older, renovated home with a screened porch and immac-

*David M. Katzman, *Seven Days a Week: Women and Domestic Service in Industrializing America* (New York, 1978), 188.

ulate and shining wood floors. She and her husband decided to remain in the South even though he still receives threats from the Ku Klux Klan. Her voice has the lilting speech of some upper-middle-class southerners—half British, half southern.

My first memories of a domestic? In fact, I have a carriage in there, a wicker carriage just like the one I remember sitting in. And my nurse, her name was Daisy. I remember her taking me to a playground, which had a picnic table. This is where all the nurses took the children in the afternoons. We stopped at a little corner grocery and bought a Pepsi. We had two paper cups, and I remember she put me on top of the picnic table and let me pour. And no one had ever let me pour anything before. I could not have been older than three.

And she was there until I was seven. She had cancer, but I wouldn't say she was old. She would be about fifty or so. We didn't know she was sick. She was sort of discharged for feeling one way about a thing—I don't know what. This is all I can remember. I never discussed this with anyone, but my memories are that she was sort of discharged. She was not doing something she was supposed to be. And then, I think—I just sort of always picked up on something—that maybe my mother had some guilt feelings about her.

I was the youngest child in three, and there was nine years difference between my sister and me, and then my brother was two years older than my sister, so Daisy was all for me. And we had a cook and a maid and lived in a big old house. I don't really remember anything about the other help.

But then we got Margaret and Carrie. They came when I was about ten, and they did not work at the same time. Carrie was the maid, and Margaret was the cook. Margaret, the cook, cared for a little mentally retarded girl in the mornings, in another white family. And she would leave there at like two in the afternoons and come to us and cook dinner. And Carrie, of course, was there in the mornings.

Margaret had nine children. They didn't live with her. They lived in Mandeville with her mother. She did not approve of her children living in the city. You know, looking back on it and knowing now what I know about the civil rights movement, it was all tied up. She just felt her children were safer in the country. And my only real recollection of her children is of the last child that was born. It was evidently the only time she was pregnant when she worked for us, and I was fifteen. All her children, though, were born fairly close together; her oldest, seems to me, was sixteen. But the reason this is so vivid to me is that it was right after my mother died. And when my mother was laid out—she was laid out in her home—Margaret was talking to Carrie, and I can remember I was in the kitchen and I knew something was wrong. I asked Carrie, and she said it was bad luck for a pregnant woman to go in the room with a corpse. And Margaret, of course, went in. I don't think she was superstitious like that, but they discussed it and I knew about it.

And then one day during the following summer, Margaret said she was in labor and would I take her home. And I drove her and walked her back to her little shanty. The next morning I went to check on her, and the baby was stillborn. No one had been there with her. I remember she said one of her husband's drinking friends had come in and he had gone to get the midwife. And I think she got up and got the scissors to cut the cord.

She came right back to work. She seemed . . . grateful, in a sense, that the baby was stillborn. I mean, as grateful as any woman can be when a baby is stillborn. I always thought, you know, that her other children were being raised basically by her mother—and her mother was elderly—and that Margaret was worried about her and all of the children, so many of them.

But I think back now. Margaret wasn't very old. She had gray hair, but she was really a young woman. She wasn't any older than forty-five.

But I think in general I knew that she was worried about her children. One child I remember that she was particularly concerned about fell off the back of a truck. He had some brain damage. But the others were fine. They always seemed fine when I would go over there with her. She would buy her groceries in town on Friday night. She'd call on Friday afternoon, and they'd give her the list. And usually her husband would take her, but sometimes he couldn't and I would. He was sometimes in jail for drinking.

They all appeared fine. They called her "Sister," which I always thought was so strange because I felt like she was so much a mother, like she was my mother. I thought, how strange—here she was, their true mother.

She had them all in the city, though. She gave birth to them here. And then they'd go back to her mother. She and Sam lived in town. But see, it was her only means of support, and she had to leave them. And when I think what my family paid her, I am aghast. It seems to me she would make something like two dollars a day, and this is during times that I can remember. And she supported all of them.

Sam had a job, but I don't remember what he did. And I don't think she could depend on his job. Many times he got arrested for drinking and driving. But my dad, of course, had a lot of good ties, and only once did Sam actually have to serve time.

But I think back now to her health. When she came to work for us, I remember her telling me, she had had a slight stroke and had gone blind for about a year. Her life—I didn't really begin to really think about it, about the sadness of it until I married and had a baby and realized the way I lived was so much nicer than the way she lived. I had had so many hard times, and then, too, just being young, I just accepted her life as the way a maid's life would be.

My mother had her first coronary when she was forty-two. I was eleven or so then, but she had had heart trouble. No, I mean I really don't know what she had—there was so much that happened and I was so little. But she had had rheumatic fever as a child and gone through menopause at forty. The Catholic church said you couldn't have a hysterectomy. So, being a Catholic, she went out of the city. The doctor had said, "There's this technique where they do cobalt, and they just zap your ovaries. The church hasn't said anything about this. No one here will know."

And what they did, they just castrated her. Just like two years later, she started having massive coronaries. So my memories of Margaret being there . . . Well, my mother was very sick. And even when my mother was home, Margaret was the one that was always there, always the one I could depend on. I never knew if my mother had gotten sick during the day and had to go off to the hospital, but Margaret was always there.

I think now . . . I could come home and ask her questions about anything—sex or anything. Her favorite expression, one that she used when we used to talk about money was, "If the Lord ain't wanting you to have money, he going to send something your way." That meant that things were the way they were because the Lord didn't want us to have money.

And see, my dad, right after my mother died, went into bankruptcy, and we literally lost everything. The house by that time was put in my sister's name. And my daddy and I moved into a little tiny apartment. In fact, the first few months after it happened, my daddy sent me away to school and he went to live with my aunt.

Then after I came back from school, we moved to a little apartment, me and Daddy. And so we'd always had Carrie to be the maid, but he just didn't have the money, and so I was the maid. Margaret was the cook. She didn't do anything in the afternoons other than cook dinner, and she did some ironing, and I did the other. And she used to say, "Sarah, if the Lord ain't wanting you to have money, he going to send something your way."

And so often in our married life, when we thought we were just about there and then some catastrophe happened, I've thought of that saying. It's almost comforting when something happens, because Margaret's words play back in my mind so. But she had more common sense! She made that period so much easier.

And now, she had always before worn a uniform. But after we moved to the apartment, she didn't. She just wore an apron. And I used to take my dates into the kitchen and say, "This is my mother." And she used to say, "Sarah, don't tell those boys that." But to me, she was my mother. I felt the need to say, "I love this woman."

She stayed until I got married. She didn't go to work for anyone else. She was really too sick. I mean, we knew. I can see her sitting at the table now. We knew that she could hardly do what she was doing. But in fact, she stayed two years after I married. She stayed till my father remarried. She stayed just to make sure he was all right.

And I think now, I don't even know what she really thought of him. I mean, they got along, but . . . By the time we were in the apartment, my sister was living in town again, and a lot of what was going on between Daddy and me Margaret was able to call my sister about.

My father was, is a person who was never able to show his feelings. And, when Mama died, they came like in the middle of the night to tell us, and I cried. And I remember that afternoon I was in my room crying, and he came out. My uncle was with me, who was a doctor, and Margaret. And my father said to my uncle, "Can't you do something to make her stop crying?" And I remember Margaret just holding me.

And I know what he was saying was that my crying was hurting him. But he couldn't say it. And it was not till I was married and living away from home that he was ever able to say, "I love you." But Margaret knew all that. She couldn't explain it to me, but she could at least plant a few seeds so that later I've understood. There was so much bitterness, and I really felt that he killed my mother. I was just sure that in his own way he had. And Margaret balanced out the bitterness, by listening and being there.

When I married, I had my wedding reception at a friend's home. In fact I worked for these people in their store, and I never thought to have to say anything to Margaret about her coming. She came, and she had on a black hat—her big picture hat—and her black dress. And the woman whose home we were having it at said, "Has she come here as a guest, or has she come here to work in the kitchen?" I just remember being absolutely mortified. And Margaret said, "Sarah, I don't mind working in the kitchen." She said, "That way I get to see everyone."

I realize now—probably, hopefully—it didn't hurt her the way it did me. She was used to it, and probably she felt more comfortable drying glasses and talking to everyone than mingling.

After that we always kept in touch, and I would always visit her when I came home. The last time I saw her before she died, we were living in North Carolina, and she came over to my sister's—which was the house we had lived in. We were staying there. And Carrie was working for my sister as the maid, and Margaret came to visit. She wasn't working then. But she insisted that my sister and I go out to lunch, and she stayed there with my two babies.

Afterwards, I took her home. I took her across the lake, and·when I turned around the car, I looked at her and she was crying. And I said, "Why are you crying?" And she said, "Because I'm so happy."

I've often thought about that. I don't know, but I think she meant she was happy because she realized I was happy. I had had some really rough times, and I guess she was really the only person that knew what I had been through. It still makes me cry, you can see, to think how *much* she helped me and of her standing there crying for my happiness, for my sadness.

And I often think of my own work today and how she'd be proud in her own quiet way of me and my family. I often think what my husband does in his work for the rights of poor children might make it easier for her children, her grandchildren.

From an interview with Susan Tucker

Margaret McAllister

When a black domestic works for many years as nurse to a white child, a situation is set up in which eventually there will almost surely be broken promises between the two. Black writers, for some time, have asked the question of what it must be like for a woman to raise children who grow up to exploit her.* Black domestics, for their part, have answered this question, at least to some degree, with such sayings as, "I never met a white child over twelve that I liked."†

White writers have also addressed the theme of the change in the white child's feelings for the black domestic when he or she enters adulthood. To young white children of the segregation era, the black domestic was an equal within the family. Before the rules of segregation were learned, she had been a person worthy of love. But as white children reached maturity, they were taught that she was only half a person, a person of a race that remained children. She might have been singled out as different from other blacks, but the childhood view of her as fully adult would never be recaptured.‡

There were, however, times when the white adult remembered his or her affection for this woman and sought, I believe, to recapture some of the equality known or dreamed of in childhood, to undo some of the rules of segregation. Lillian Hellman wrote of such a recapturing in her memories of Sophronia, her childhood nurse. Hellman described her own confrontation of racism through Sophronia and Sophronia's response to the young Hellman's desire to seat herself and the black nurse in the white section of the streetcar. She quotes Sophronia's warning about, and explanation of, race relations, especially the continued affection between white child and black nurse: "I got something to tell you, Missy. There are too many niggers who like white people. Then, there are too many white people think they like niggers. You just be careful." It seems from Hellman's account that Sophronia acknowledged a special affection for the girl but told her, also, that such feelings, because of society's attitudes, were fraught with problems for both whites and blacks.§ One of the problems was, of course, that whites and blacks as adults moved in entirely separate worlds, where they could not speak of certain topics to one another and where they could not, for example, sing at each other's weddings.

---

*See, for example, Jeanne L. Noble, *Beautiful, also, Are the Souls of My Black Sisters* (Englewood Cliffs, N.J., 1978), 75–78.

†This is a statement that Mary Yelling and I remember hearing as children. A character in Alice Walker's *Meridian* (New York, 1976), 105, makes a similar statement.

‡The southerner's perception of blacks as a childlike people is discussed in many works, notably Lillian Smith, *The Killers of the Dream* (Rev. ed.; New York, 1961); Robert Coles, *Children of Crisis: A Study of Courage and Fear* (Boston, 1964); Richard H. King, *A Southern Renaissance: The Cultural Awakening of the American South, 1930–1955* (New York, 1980).

§Lillian Hellman, *An Unfinished Woman* (Boston, 1960), 239.

In the following narrative, these separate worlds are barely discussed. Margaret McAllister (b. 1950) speaks of the wedding as if telling a humorous story. Perhaps on some level it is, but it seems also to be a disquieting memory for her.

At our interview McAllister was soft-spoken, almost as if she was too tired to speak loudly. She was surrounded by plastic pastel tricycles, a Sesame Street piano, and two children who were playing indoors on a rainy day.

She lives in a suburban neighborhood of ranch-style houses, few trees, and young families. In her front living room are her mother's antiques. She told me the front room was never used. We sat in the family room, which was almost stripped of furniture to give the children more playing room. They rode their tricycles on the linoleum floor.

I grew up in Biloxi. It seems silly to describe it, because to me it seemed such a normal growing up. We lived in a nice neighborhood, and we were comfortable. We weren't rich, but we had a nice life. My father was an attorney, and my mother stayed home. And we had Rachel.

She came when I was four. And now, my younger brother—she was there when he was born. And I had two older sisters that she helped raise, too. But the thing I always remember was how close Rachel was to my mother. I mean I think about it today and almost yearn for that sort of relationship. I can remember Rachel fixing breakfast for Mama, and it would just be a poached egg and toast and coffee on a tray, but just the way it looked, I remember. And I remember how she'd take it into Mama's room and sit it on the dressing table.

Today I feel so tired. I have these two children, and I'm pregnant, and I'd love someone to bring me breakfast! And Rachel came every day—well, six days a week—and did that. I can never remember her going on vacation, or anything. She'd go with us on vacation, but I can never remember her away from us for a long time. She came at seven in the morning and left at six-thirty, after she'd fed us and had us all cleaned up.* And so then Mama and Daddy would have their time alone.

The other thing about Rachel I always think of, that was kind of a letdown for her . . . She'd always said she was going to sing the Lord's Prayer at my wedding. That was the thing we talked about, all the way growing up. She'd always sing it around the house, and we'd talk about it. That was her dream.

---

*Long hours were standard for many domestics. The work week was generally set up to allow only Thursdays and every other Sunday off.

Well, when it came time, I just couldn't let her. When I called her, she said, "Oh, I'll get to sing at your wedding!" I got around it. I said, "No, I want you in the front seat watching me." I mean, she had a nice voice, but . . . I didn't want her to sing at my wedding. It would have been real different, for Mississippi especially. But I think I hurt her feelings. It was one of those childhood promises, but you still worry about breaking it.

Oh, yes, though, I still talk to her. All of us are in real close contact with her. My sisters and I take her different things all the time and loan her money if she needs it. And my brother goes fishing and calls her up and takes fish over to her—those kinds of things. All of us feel like we should take care of her and make sure she's doing OK.

She doesn't work for my father anymore. See, my father remarried after my mother died. I was in high school then. She works part-time for someone else, and she baby-sits for all of us, but she's getting older now and doesn't want as much work. See, when my father remarried, she got . . . not really . . . well, I guess more or less she did get fired. And there are a lot of negative feelings towards my stepmother for that.

That hurt all of us, because it was like telling a member of the family to get out and don't come back. We were all pretty hostile [toward my stepmother] because Rachel had been with us all our lives and then Daddy remarried and whammo, she's out. And that didn't seem fair. It was like some stranger came in and just took over and kicked Rachel out, and that was real hard.

Of course, there's two sides to every story, but it hurt us all. And Rachel is real bitter because she feels she's out, so I think that's one reason we try extra hard to keep in touch with her.

And she's alone. She never did have any children or a husband that we knew. She says she was married, but I never saw that side and I never knew of him living with her. It wasn't something she talked about. So I think she looks at us as her family. We're her children.

I guess now that I'm telling it, it seems like I remember a lot of, not sadness, but just times when I felt she was disappointed by me or by us. But you know, those are just the things that stand out. Most of what I think of normally is how good she was and how much we liked her and she liked us.

From an interview with Susan Tucker

Eugenia Bowden

Eugenia Bowden (b. 1960) has memories of the country that make me think of
Faulkner—of the loss his white characters feel when they can no longer be
children and play with their black neighbors and of the very rural South and its
isolated small houses set back in the woods and its infrequent large houses.*
In these large houses little children grow up often with a sense of entitlement,
knowing that the world, as Bowden says, "obliges" their parents' and grandparents' wants and will probably do so for their own wants as well.†

Children born in large houses everywhere grow up with such a sense, of
course. And children everywhere in the houses down the road grow up to have a
different view of life, with less certainty that the world will oblige them. What
appears to have been somewhat different in the South is that these two classes of
children often remained attached to one another, as employers and workers, in
adulthood. The South remained a culture that was much more stable in the
composition of its population than other regions were. Despite migration and
other social changes, these two classes often maintained contact, as Eugenia
Bowden's remarks show, through the black mothers who stayed on with the white
family. The continued contact, in whatever form, alongside the memory of a time
when they were equal as children, seems to result in a sadness and a sense of loss
in the memories of white children, and a bitterness and a sense of anger in the
memories of black children.

Her narrative also brings out clearly a basic duality—not so much that of love
and hate between southern whites and blacks, but that of wealth and poverty, seen
side by side. Placing the wealth of a family like Bowden's alongside the poverty of
the domestic "back on the dirt road," and adding to the picture the publicly
professed democracy, one sees how the figure of the black domestic became
important to white southerners. White southerners like Bowden's family saw in
the domestic proof that it was possible for the two races to live side by side. On
some level, white southerners such as Bowden seem glad if their domestic's
children have left home. At any rate, Bowden, though they are her contemporaries, is not often reminded that things are "different" now. If they had stayed
home, they would not have had the same advantages she did. If she was reminded
of this too often, she might be forced to question further the society in which she
lives, question the connections that exist and do not exist between black and
white southerners. There is a sense of powerlessness about her feelings toward
these black people known to her, a sense that she has been told too many times
that conditions are best as they are.

---

*Irving Howe, "Faulkner and the Negroes," in Seymour L. Gross and John Edward Hardy
(eds.), *Images of the Negro in American Literature* (Chicago, 1966), 204–20.
    †I use the term *entitlement* as it was defined by Robert Coles in *Privileged Ones: The Well-
Off and the Rich in America* (Boston, 1977), 363.

She lives in an old stucco house with an inner courtyard and a small pool. As one walks through the large high-ceilinged rooms, one sees the works of old masters—prints and originals—as well as works of local abstract artists. In the interview Eugenia Bowden spoke quietly so that the maid in the kitchen would not hear.

We used to have a nanny named Annice down at the old house. She's real old now, and she writes all the time. She lives now up in East Feliciana Parish. Her family lives there. But before, she lived with us, so she raised me till I started school. Her and Helen both raised me. But Helen never lived with us. She's been with us since I was born, but she has a husband and two kids, and she lives with them.

And then, too, we have a cook in the country named Willie, a big old fat lady. She's hilarious. She's got all these kids in Detroit and California and New York City. She's always traveling around to see them. It's funny to me because she has this primitive life-style. She just lives back on this dirt road. And here she goes all over the country, but she never really seems to be bothered by the transition.

And she's the type who likes to joke a lot. She was down here yesterday going to the doctor. Her and Helen were here at the house, and they're so funny when they get together, 'cause Helen she's so skinny and here's big old Willie. Helen cooked for me and Daddy, and we were eating some kind of sandwiches or something, and Willie say, "Yeah, you know what you be eating at the farm." Say, "You be eating potlikker and peas and ham or roast." And Helen was just laughing.

Willie used to live across the road from us in the country. She had a shotgun cabin, and I used to go down there and play with the kids when I was little. I remember thinking her house was different from mine but kind of liking it better 'cause there were all those kids around and my house was kind of quiet and nobody else my age. And I always thought they were the lucky ones because they had all these little kids running around.

And we played together for a long time, and then all the sudden things started being different. They didn't ever act different to me, but it was like my attitude got different. I quit thinking of them as being so lucky and started feeling sad for them or something. And I remember one thing that really changed me. We had this piñata. I remember my parents had brought a piñata down there and we were all hitting it. And they kept telling me, "Now, don't you hit it. Let them hit it." And then I think that sort of started my attitude of feeling sorry for them. And I wish I had never done that.

But Willie and her family, too, I've known since I was about three. She probably started working for us then. But she went through a phase where she'd quit or get fired or didn't come to work. And they'd get her back. We had a few other maids then. And we had one white woman. That was just terrible. The white woman was mean and ornery, and she couldn't even cook. I didn't like her. But Willie was going through a phase, taking liquor out of the cabinet or something.

Helen is not like Willie at all. She's much more quiet, and she's real stable. Mama's been so busy ever since I was born with work and all. Everything I've learned, Helen has been like my mother. She's the one I come to when I have a problem or anything I want to talk about or anything I want to know, I go to her. Willie, on the other hand, is funny, and I play around with her, but I wouldn't talk serious to her. But Helen, I don't really think of her as being a black or being a maid. I think of her as like a part of us and somebody to talk to.

I never really remember thinking too much about the way maids were treated. I do remember noticing that they called Mama and Daddy Miz Suzanne and Mr. John, but I've been hearing that stuff since way back, so I didn't think of it. Because like my grandmother she's sort of the Southern Belle. I can still see her with slaves around, the way people act around her—Miz Jeannette, you know. She sort of lives in those days, and when I'm around her, it's just like going back into time. The world sort of obliges her.

And my other grandmother has always had the same maid—since they were really young. They're both so old now, and they both whisper about each other. One will say to me . . . Grandma will say, "Oh, I let Aleta cook. She's too old, but she likes to think she has something to do." And Aleta will say, "Oh, I let your grandmother think she's ordering the groceries, but she can't remember a thing."

Anyway, I was just brought up with it, the way it was. Still, there's a lot of things that made me real uncomfortable—like not being able to eat with 'em and all. I just sort of accept that, too. I guess I questioned it a couple of times, but I never really got an answer, and so I just figured that's how it was.

And I never understood why white people would talk at the dinner table about black people, about race relations, and then there would be black people serving you mashed potatoes or whatever right beside you. I do complain about that. But I sort of compromised and accepted those things when I could and changed them when I could.

I think my family is like that generally—trying to continue to have good relations with these people and not hurt them. I think we tend to know more about them than most people probably do. And we can have help more, because of money. I think just after the amount of time we've had the same ones [that] you get to know them because you know their problems. Like Willie has a lot of health problems, and she's always going to the doctor and stuff. And my parents always take her when she comes down here and goes. And also, of course, I used to know her kids a lot.

Helen, too, I feel, must feel we are OK, or she wouldn't have stayed so long. She has the weekends off. And when she's not here, it is lonely. And I'm always the only one around, and when she's not here, I don't stick around either.

From an interview with Susan Tucker

Part II

Clear Divisions,
Rigidly Prescribed Contacts

In my hometown is a Confederate cemetery, and when I was growing up, boys wearing the gray uniforms of the local military school would march to this cemetery on Confederate Memorial Day. Confederate Memorial Day was on a Sunday in May, and because we celebrated it, we did not celebrate the Memorial Day celebrated by other Americans at the end of May. I did not even know there was a national Memorial Day until I was sixteen years old.

But I often remember the procession to the Confederate cemetery. The "soldiers" were little boys. I do not know how young they were, but several seemed younger than I was, and at that time I was not older than nine. I watched them on at least two occasions from the corner of the street in front of my maternal grandmother's house. I stood with my grandmother's maid, whose name was Mattie Ellis, and I remember her confirming my thoughts of how very young these boys were by shaking her head and saying, "Boys—little boys."

Such a procession commemorating the Civil War showed that the past certainly lived on in the imaginations of many white southerners. It must have seemed grand to the adults who led the march, no doubt recalling the Confederacy in glorious terms. But the grandness is not what I felt about it.

Instead, the parade made me feel somehow uncomfortable and, at the same time, intrigued. It seemed there was some drama going on that I saw but never quite understood. I thought it might have to do with the boys' uniforms. Once one of the boys fainted, which seemed dramatic in itself, and I remember he was held by a little black girl slightly older than I was, until one of the older boys in uniform took over with a first aid kit. Perhaps I felt intrigued because the whole parade seemed unexpected and largely unnoticed. The only adults who paid any attention were a handful of white women who happened to be gardening and might pause in their work, and a few white and black women watching children. Almost all the viewers of the parade were, like myself, children with nothing else to do. I do not remember any men watching the parade except for the boys' teachers, who might stop as they walked ahead or behind.

But I think that I sensed even then that such a march symbolized something out of keeping with the allegiances of southern children. There I was on the sidelines, kept there because I was a girl. I was with a black woman, but I was divided by race from her and connected instead to the white boys. The street on which we stood led to the Confederate cemetery, but it also led into a neighborhood that in my youth became predominantly black. I felt somehow embarrassed at all of these divisions between, and mixtures of, black and white. I wondered how they could just march right through there. I felt that they embarrassed me, and I also felt afraid for them. Yet I also knew that I was supposed to feel grandeur and loyalty instead.

Mattie lived just four or five streets away from my grandmother. In later life I would think of the way to her house. As I went farther into her neighborhood, I saw more people sitting outside—on porches, on stoops, on boxes in the yards. There was more activity—more people in evidence. They tended to congregate around stores and houses. I remember small grocery stores where one could buy cookies out of a clear plastic jar and also what we called penny candy on a stiff cardboard rack. There was one house where we were told never to stop. At this house, black grown-ups bought drinks. But for me the most famous mystery of the neighborhood was the question of which white woman often went to this house. I remember overhearing Mattie and another maid talk of her, but they were careful not to speak her name. In this neighborhood there were also more dogs than in ours. They scrounged about for food and were called yard dogs. They lay in the gray dust of the yards, which had little grass.

Mattie liked going home, and my sister and I liked going there with her. It seemed somehow an adventure, and looking back, I see that this was because such a visit entailed both curiosity and fear. Things were different in the black neighborhood, I'd been told. There were knife fights and men who might try to do something wrong. We were never told exactly what. But we were told, "Be nice to the little colored children," and sent off with Mattie by my grandmother with just a wave of her hand.

Mattie held our hands and walked more quickly than she did on walks in my grandmother's neighborhood. Her voice called out more loudly, more forcefully to people we met. Both her tight hold and her changed voice told us we were in another world even though we were only a few blocks away from home. But we were good children, and we understood that we should not mention that things were different. Instead, like my grandmother and Mattie, we should act as if everything was as it should be.

An experience in early adulthood that made me remember the road to Mattie's house occurred when I was twenty-one and living in Paris as an "au pair girl." I lived in a little attic room on the seventh floor of a building that contained the apartments of eight families. The family for whom I worked lived on the third floor, and every night after I had cleaned up the kitchen, I would carry a large plastic pitcher of hot water to wash with up the backstairs to my room. I began to think of Mattie again as I climbed these steep, curving wooden stairs. I had to go quickly because the light switches on this back stairway were the type designed to save electricity. The light would go off after a few minutes, and I had to reach the top of the stairs and the switch for the hall light before the stairwell light went out. But going up, I always felt a sense of relief, a sense that this way up the stairs was the way to my own sanity. And I have often thought that is what Mattie must have felt as she went home from our house.

Several aspects of my work of minding the French children made me think of the black domestics of my childhood. Many of my duties and much of my interaction with my employers were similar to those of black domestics within white households. I was fairly isolated, seeing only an occasional American. At times I felt myself a child because I did not always understand the language and could not take part in true conversation as an equal participant. At other times, I realized the power I had from this position, for I could easily neutralize family discussions. It was the first time I had thought of my early college readings of James Baldwin and Franz Fanon in a personal way. I remember sitting at the dinner table many nights with four of the children fighting. Madame and I sat at either end of the table—two females who planned our day around these children. I remember that on the nights when the children were especially annoying to Madame, I could ask ingratiating, distracting questions. To them I was unusual: they had never before had an American, and they thought that because I was from the American South, I lived in a backward culture not far removed from frontier conditions. They pitied me.

To Madame, her four sisters, and her mother—all of whom lived in the same building—I quickly learned that I could say things in French that I would have felt silly saying in English. I remember, for example, that I could say liltingly, "Je vous en prie," something that translates roughly to a response that crosses "You are welcome" with "I beg of you." I could anticipate their needs and know when they needed a cheering word. In the beginning of my stay there, I felt that I could behave in such a way because speaking another language requires that one imitate, that one act. But I also came quickly to realize that the deference I gave them had another quality that would more aptly be described as mocking. And I knew that I had learned to imitate, learned to act, learned to mock, at least in some ways, from black domestics. I heard in my words their voices.

As a southern white child, I had been given similar mocking deference and had heard more convincing deference given to white adults. Moreover, I knew that between worker and employer many uneasy feelings existed that were masked within the deference and pity they gave each other. As a southern white child, I had played near the park benches where black domestics sat. I was quiet enough that they let me overhear their complaints, their moans about white employers. I knew, then, the mutual distrust, even contempt, that could exist between the privileged and the unprivileged. And I knew how their voices changed when they spoke among themselves. At twenty-one, I was only six years or so away from overhearing such conversations, six years away from the half-privileged world of the child who overheard both sides.

Of course, I knew, each night on the stairs, that another day was over and that my work there was only for one year. I knew that I was really still privileged. I was there by choice, and I was in transition.

Still, I suddenly realized something of what Mattie's happiness had been in going home. I realized that for her, too, another day had been over. More important, she was returning to a community that was her own. There, she had her own language; we heard this in her changed voice. And there—but this we only barely glimpsed—she took off her mask, a mask that all black domestics, to some degree or other, wore in white homes.

Certainly, such a journey back to a home of one's own and such a lifting of the mask were crucial to the psychological survival of all black domestics. Moreover, such a journey can be seen as symbolizing the most important way that black domestics themselves reshaped domestic work in the South after the Civil War. After the war, they chose to live away from their employers, and in so doing, they placed themselves at some distance, literally and figuratively—from their employers.

In the years immediately after Appomattox, they moved away from live-in service so decisively that the live-out system came to predominate throughout the South. Although the pattern of blacks living away from whites, particularly in adjacent housing, had been set during slavery, live-in servants were still desirable in the post–Civil War South.[1] The moves of black domestics away from their employers, or their insistence in never moving into the homes of employers, then, can be seen as conscious acts to create or retain a form of control over their lives.

Thus, though they worked long hours, they separated themselves and their families from white families. What they also did by such moves was to restructure domestic work so that their private lives were not open to perusal by whites. To some extent, then, they adjusted, in their favor, the resources of each side in the power struggle between the races, for while they remained privy to the secrets of whites, whites knew little of black home life.

Much of the heavy psychological burden of the female domestic worker, after all, lay in the fact that she was seen by both blacks and whites alike as a mammy figure. By insisting that they return to their own families, they broke up the myth of mammy in a small but not inconsequential way. Such an act provoked numerous discussions in newspaper articles on both servants and blacks. David Katzman cites a congressional hearing in which the lack of servants willing to live in was noted. In this testimony a Mobile banker and industrialist noted that blacks "think it is more like being free to have their own home and go to them after the work is done."[2] Elizabeth Clarke-Lewis asserts that the transition from live-in servant to day worker among Washington, D.C., workers occurred not in response to technology and architecture but "as a matter of choice prompted by the women's desire for less restrictive employment."[3] It

1. See Daniel E. Sutherland, *Americans and Their Servants: Domestic Service in the United States from 1800 to 1920* (Baton Rouge, 1981), 34, and David M. Katzman, *Seven Days a Week: Women and Domestic Service in Industrializing America* (New York, 1978), 198–99.
2. Katzman, *Seven Days a Week,* 198–99.
3. Elizabeth Clark-Lewis, *"This Work Had a' End": The Transition from Live-in to Day Work,* Southern Women: The Intersection of Race, Class and Gender, Working Paper 2 (Memphis, 1985).

seems likely that the domestics in Washington, many of whom had migrated from the Deep South, had experienced or witnessed the benefits of live-out service.

Whatever the number of domestics who actually made such moves, twentieth-century literature places emphasis on such decisions. Zora Neale Hurston, for example, expressed her view of separate living quarters as representative of freedom and choice in her novel *Their Eyes Were Watching God*. Janie, the main character, is raised by her grandmother Nanny, so called by Janie because the white children of Nanny's employer call her that. Nanny does not change her name or her job, but she tells Janie: "Ah done de best Ah kin by you. Ah raked and scraped and bought dis lil piece uh land so you wouldn't have to stay in de white folks' yard. . . . Ah wanted you to look upon yo'self."[4]

Katherine Anne Porter in her story "The Last Leaf" shows the reaction of white people to the moving out of the elderly domestic Nannie. Nannie, who is ready to die afer her white mistress dies, asks if she may move to a vacant home away from the big house. Although the white children, now adults, are "surprised, a little wounded," they let her go. Porter writes: "She moved away, and as the children said afterwards to each other, it was almost funny and certainly very sweet to see how she tried not to be too happy the day she left, but they felt rather put upon, just the same."

Although she dresses the same and even comes to visit and work occasionally, "she was no more the faithful old servant Nannie, a freed slave: she was an aged Bantu woman of independent means, sitting on the steps, breathing the free air." Porter shows the message the change of address brought to the white family's perception of Nannie: "The children, brought up in an out-of-date sentimental way of thinking, had always complacently believed that Nannie was a real member of the family, perfectly happy with them, and this rebuke, so quietly and firmly administered, chastened them somewhat."[5]

In the narratives that follow, some of these early ways in which black domestics separated themselves from their employers by such spatial and psychological divisions in the southern landscape are recalled. The ways of crossing over these divisions are recalled as well.

---

4. Zora Neale Hurston, *Their Eyes Were Watching God* (1937; rpr. New York, 1978), 37.
5. Katherine Anne Porter, "The Last Leaf," in *The Leaning Tower and Other Stories* (New York, 1934), 60–61.

Nancy Valley

I learned of Nancy Valley (b. 1888) through a woman at a senior citizen center that I visited in hopes of finding women willing to talk about domestic work. The center is one that serves both whites and blacks, but when I was there in 1980, they still divided themselves into two groups—whites on one side, blacks on the other.

They did not know quite where to place me. I felt strangely similar to the way I had felt as a child with a domestic. I felt very young among these old, old people. When one of the black women took over, grabbing my arm and making me come with her into the kitchen, I felt both relieved and too pale. She sat me down on a long church pew next to the wall in the kitchen. She gave me some peach cobbler and queried me for two hours.

She told me that no one there would talk with me about domestic work. "All of us worked at domestic work in homes, at one time or another. But it is not something we will talk to just anyone about," she said. Only after a lengthy history of my life did she warm to me. But she could still not imagine why I wanted to talk to people about domestic work. I told her about Mary Yelling, explaining why "at least one black lady seems to find the topic of domestics interesting." As I spoke these words, I realized how hard I was trying not to let the fact that the center seemed so racially divided interfere with her perception of me and yet how the old ways that blacks and whites interacted remained so much in evidence as we talked. I recalled a friend's mother telling us in childhood that black females were not called ladies—they were called only women.

"I do know of one lady who would be willing to talk," she said. "But you call her and you tell her. I knew her long ago. And you set it up. But then you send the black lady. This lady is old-timey. She trusts white voices before she trusts black voices on the phone. In person, she might let fall out more to a black person."

Nancy Valley is the person to whom the woman referred me. She is senile. She does not remember either Mary Yelling or me—my voice on the telephone—from one day to the next. Nevertheless, her interview shows something of the old ways of the South.

Hers was a family, like so many others, with a desire to educate the children, a family who centered their lives around the church and hope of the hereafter and who passed such ways on to each new generation. Valley is the daughter of a mother who lived in with her employing white family. Her father, on the other hand, worked as the sexton of a black church and cemetery and isolated himself from the white community. His father, Nancy Valley's grandfather, was a white man whose family left the area when he died. Family legend in Valley's family mentions the attachment of this white man and black woman but does not explain it.

Into her talk Valley interweaves her belief in God and these silences about things that were not explained, just as she was taught to do. Yet, she can display a strong voice, a determined voice that rises when she gives directions and rises even more when she speaks of providing for her son's education.

Her house is unpainted, raised above the ground, on which water stands after rain. On the small front porch is a large, white wrought-iron bench that takes up the entire area and stands out against the weathered boards. Her former employers gave her this bench from their yard when they moved. At the interview she was barefoot and wore an unironed pink linen dress. She had a broom lying against the door frame, and she told how she once chased away an intruder with this broom.

⊹⊱✠⊰⊹

Well, I'll tell you, I worked the best of my life. I went out when I could. But now I'm retired, and I just thank the Lord for all the time he's kept me on earth. I was brought up that way. I was christened by a minister of Big Zion, and I went through life thanking God.

My parents? Well, my father was sexton of the cemetery out here in Summerville. It was the colored cemetery out here. He buried the people.

And we lived out here; this was in the country then. And my mother worked for a family by the name of Abraham. She lived on the place, and she raised those children for them.

So I stayed with my grandmother. See, my mother's first child was a girl. Second was a boy, and he died, and after that she made up her mind she didn't want us. She just got her heart set on that baby boy. And so I always felt like an aunt of mine was more like my mother. She and my grandmother raised us.

My grandmother was nice but very strict. My father had been born to her up in Greenville, Alabama. His father was white and she was colored. So my grandfather had owned her and my father, but he never did marry nobody else—nobody. Well, things like that you didn't really have explained. They were just there. Instead you were explained to about God. Put your dependence on the Lord. And now that's what I did.

My grandmother and aunt made a good life for us. They worked for white people washing and ironing. And then on Saturday and Sunday we always had a good time. On Saturday you'd wake up singing. And honey, they'd start washing their own clothes before daylight.* They had to be cleaned right—boiled and then hung up.

That was chore number one. Then the next thing they'd do was the

---

*Saturdays, and occasionally Sundays, were washdays for black women—days for them to wash the clothes of their own families.

scrubbing. They had a mop that was made with a slight angle to it, and it had eight holes cut in it and a long handle. You'd push that thing on the floor, and you'd throw red clay dirt on it, on the floor with some of that concentrated lye. You'd scrub the floor and then rinse it. Then you'd scrub the water bucket and gourd. Then you'd scrub the chairs.

Sunday we'd have biscuits and maybe big-foot gravy or, if my daddy was helping the white people planting, maybe some hominy grits and salt meat. They'd give him extra for setting out some sweet potatoes or something. Big-foot gravy was just a little bit of lard, all white gravy.

And sometimes there'd be fish. They'd put out baskets on old Mr. McCarthy's land—water baskets. And everything can go in it, and sometimes they'd find a dozen fish in the basket. Doing that, they had to be careful Aunt Mary didn't see them. She was an old colored woman who worked for the McCarthys and she told them everything.

Then my grandmother would have us at church, and we'd be as spick-and-span as we'd jumped out of a bandbox. You going to go to Sunday School bright and early and in pettticoats my grandmother starched with cornmeal. That's the way our free time was, and we were happy.

My father sent us to Emerson Institute, the private school for blacks, and we all worked in homes to pay for the tuition.* And then when I finished, I never cared to teach school, so I worked in these white people's homes. I had one child to live and one died, and a husband I don't even care to think about. I worked for my son, to send him to school. I wanted him to go to Emerson and to Talladega. He graduated from Talladega, and he lives now in Detroit, Michigan.

Well, I worked for one family for over fifty years. It happens like that—you just keep on with them. I'd be working there still if they had their way.

They had two children that I raised. The mother had them, but I raised them. The boy, when I first started coming here and not staying on the place, I had to bring him home with me—for he went to hollering and so on and didn't want to stay with them. I'd bring him home and have a bed put up.

And the girl, I thought I'd seen her grown and my work was over when she married. But no! She was going to have a baby, and she said that she wouldn't go to the hospital unless I went. So I had to go to the hospital with her. I had one bed in the room, and she had a bed. And when the baby was born, the nurse told me, "I'm going to do something that ain't

*Emerson Institute was a school operated in Mobile from 1865 until 1926 by the American Missionary Society.

been done before." Said, "You got a lot of experience, and if she's that close to you, why, I'm going to let you cut the cord." The first navel cord I ever cut and tied was hers. Then I came home with her—showin' her how to bathe her baby and get along. I raised that one.

I stay home now and I would tell you more, but I get things all mixed up, so I'd rather not. Just with that whole family, I worked all the time, till I got too old. I didn't have no hours there, 'cause anytime I went, they wouldn't even let nobody else work but me. Such is life!

From an interview with Mary Yelling

Cecelia Gaudet

Cecelia Gaudet (b. 1897) speaks of divisions within the nonwhite communities. In particular, she speaks of the Creoles of Mobile and her link to these people as a fair-skinned person of African, Native American, and Caucasian descent. The Creoles in Mobile, like the Creoles of color in New Orleans and Charleston, were descended from French, Spanish, and African settlers. They often enjoyed a higher standard of living than did other persons of color. They, like the better-off blacks, often employed domestic help.

When Creoles did enter domestic work, they usually did so as seamstresses, caterers, baby nurses, and midwives. In these positions they could maintain a degree of independence, coming and going into white homes according to a schedule they controlled. Their place was different from that of other nonwhite workers—psychologically, because they were valued for their skills and creativity, and also physically, because their work required them to enter the white home in a specialized capacity, sometimes by the front door and sometimes into rooms generally reserved for family. Seamstresses, for example, had weekly appointments in private homes and might sew anything from underwear to wedding gowns. They generally had drawers reserved for them in the family parlor.

But such work offered more than independence and respect; it was another means by which black women redefined domestic work. By choosing to do this kind of work, married women with children could arrange things so that much of their work could be done at home. When asked, some Creole women I interviewed would say they had never worked, and only much later would I learn that they had actually earned money but had done so at home.

Cecelia Gaudet spoke of these women of color who did these special kinds of domestic work. In the course of her discussion, she identified class divisions within the nonwhite population. Class is very important to her. She asked questions of me designed to see if I was of "the better class."

I had a sense that she did not want to believe that her mother was black and that many years went by before she resolved this conflict in her mind. But she hinted that the advice of her grandmother—"You're either white or black; you're either one or the other"—was helpful in that it made her feel that there was less ambiguity about racial identity than she had previously thought. In recounting this story to me, she also spoke of her early memory of streetcars that had not been segregated.

When I asked her why segregation became more rigid and why the Jim Crow laws were passed and enforced so strictly, she gave me two answers. "There were low-class blacks coming in from the country," she said. And she added, "White people, they want everything their way."

She can also remember having her head shaved when she had typhoid fever and her father's protest that her hair would not come back straight. She showed me a picture of herself with straight hair. In this picture she is eight yars old and wearing an organdy dress. The photograph is enlarged and sits in a large gold oval frame. She had a white British gentleman friend carry it out to me as I sat in her living room. She has the antiques of her grandmother and aunt, and probably also much of their ingenuity, strength, and prejudice. Her gentleman friend told me that he was certain that "there is royal blood in her somewhere."

I'm a Spanish War baby! My father he signed up to fight, but he never did go. He was just seventeen years old, eighteen when I was born. My mother and father both was teenagers.

And from right after I was born, I was reared on my father's side. I was raised by my grandmother and my aunt. My grandmother worked with the doctors delivering the babies, and she also worked with sick old people in their home and with other people in their home. And my aunt was a seamstress. She'd go to people's houses and sew. They'd have a room for her—with a machine. And she would make everything— bride's dresses, design them and all, christening gowns with all that lace—and all the slips and panties for girls.

My grandmother she was also one of those Creole cooks. She used to do parties, weddings, christenings, Thanksgivings. She'd go to big fine jobs like that, and sometimes she'd be gone two or three days cooking.

My father he was mostly a bookkeeper and things like that. So my people on my father's side was pretty well-to-do. And I was the first grandchild and the first great-grandchild, so they just gave me everything. They didn't buy anything—they made all my clothes because they didn't want any of the other children to have anything like it. And when I was young, they had a horse and a buggy and a nurse!

I was with my father's family because see, my daddy crossed over!* My mother was colored, and I was born out of wedlock. But they took me, my grandmother and them. I was the first grandchild, and my grandfather used to say he might not live to see the other ones, because he was in bad health, and he wanted it fixed in the courthouse where I would carry his name. So I carried his name.

This was up in the country. And my grandfather died. That left my grandmother and her children—four boys and in the middle, a girl. And me. So my aunt was for coming to Mobile, because they were very smart.

*Crossed over means to have crossed between the races in some way. For example, it could mean "passing" as white or black, marrying someone of another race, or, as here, having a child by someone of another race.

My grandfather had educated them all, and my aunt she said they had better opportunity to fulfill what they knew in Mobile. Up there, everyone knew who they were. . . . And they could, in the city, go either way, 'cause they were all fair.

So she came to Mobile, and they all followed, with me. I was two. My aunt was about nineteen then, and people would swear that I was her child—my aunt's child. Said that she had me out of wedlock. She said, "No, it's not my child." Says, "It's my brother's child." says, "But I love her like my child."

So it was very funny, when she was on her dying bed . . . I was married and all that. It was in 1930. I went to her bed, and I said, "Auntie, I want you to tell me the truth." She said, "What is it, baby?" I say, "Are you my aunt or are you my real mother?" She say, "Why you ask me that?" I say, "I don't know." I say, "They all told me you wasn't." I say, "But was they telling me the truth?" She say, "Baby, I'm not your mother." Say, "I'm your aunt."

I guess it must have always been something I wasn't quite sure about. See, now down the bay here in Mobile, the Creoles lived in the south part of town. We didn't live down there, but my uncle lived down there. The Creoles—they weren't white, they weren't black. They didn't mix with either group, least some of them didn't. Some of those Creoles they didn't even ride the streetcar. They'd walk because they didn't want to set in the back. And they'd have their own schools, or they'd not go.

But like it was all mixed up—the races, for many people. My grand-mother was Indian and French, but now, she didn't want to be distin-guished as Indian or Creole. She said, "They're ain't but two sets," she said. "You're either white or black; you're either one or the other." But her children, if they wanted, could pass for anything. Me, I was the darkest thing in my house. But I didn't know the difference. Honest to goodness, I didn't know I was black until I was nine years old. That was the age when I learned about colored and white and all.

I had just had the typhoid pneumonia, and I was laying there on the porch. It was in the first neighborhood where we lived that wasn't all fair. The children was there in the street dancing the holy man dance, and that tickled me to death. It tickled me so bad I laughed out. So they called up the banisters. The darkest little girl I ever saw, she said, "Come on down and play with us." And I was so shy. But finally, I made up my mind to go over there and play with them. But it took me a month before I did. I was shy, and I saw they were black children. They were the first ones I'd ever heard say *nigger*. And I was dark, too, and I thought of my real mother.

And then I just realized. Now my grandmother she told me then it didn't matter how dark or light you were.

Cutting the holy man, they called it—that dance. It was just a dance where you crossed your legs and twirled around. I can't remember exactly. I just remember the one that did it the best, she was bowlegged, and that tickled me to death!

But anyway, we had a nice life. We got along nice. They always had a good living. And they sent me and my cousins to the private school for blacks, Emerson Normal and Industrial Institute. It was run by northern white people for the most part. And the teachers had to be a graduate before they could teach and a missionary in a foreign country before they could come down here. And all the teachers lived in big dormitories, and they weren't allowed to go on the streets by themselves. Like the nuns used to be, they had to go two by two.

I started work when I was fourteen years old. This lady had had a baby that my grandmother was helping with. And she asked my grandmother could I come out there and stay with the other children. I made a dollar a week all summer. I worked with the same people until I graduated.

Then I worked for Dr. Standish and them. He was a doctor, a prominent doctor. A friend got me to work for them—a colored girl. They had raised her up and married her off. They raised her. Seem like her mother had died when she was working there, and they took her. She slept right in the room with Miz Standish. And she married right in their parlor, and she used to work for them. Folks used to have separate bedrooms in those big houses. And rumor always was he had another woman, and Miz Standish kept this girl in with her to make sure he wouldn't come in to her. Well, but she married off, the girl who worked there did. And then when she began to have children, it got to the point where it was too hard on her, and she recommended me.

And now they were rich. Miz Standish, she was *fast* rich. She showed me the picture of her place, where she was from. She had one of those big old antebellum homes with big columns. Said they had the big cotillion balls and things there back in those days.

Oh, she was fast rich! And she was hell to work for, but she was nice to me. She was crazy about me. She picked me. She bragged across the street to the lady that she had the two best-looking people working for her. That was me and the cook.

And for her big parties, boy, she had me so thrilled! She bought the clothes for me to wear. She liked to show me off. She had me a beautiful black dress. It was shining, and she had the apron—it was just lace. And the most beautiful lace cap. I was a picture. And my hair was eighteen inches long then and very thick, and she used to like me to wear it in a plait. She took pictures of us, and she liked to show us off.

And the doctor he was very nice. I helped him in the little office he had set up in the house. And he said I was born for a nurse. When I left there, he wanted to put me in school. He said he would pay all my expenses, and he'd buy me a lot where I could build me a house. He said, "If you stay, I'll fix things for you."

But now, couldn't nothing stop me from going to Chicago. My cousin that I was raised with was in Chicago. My aunt she was going to be with him. But she had a very good position here where she was sewing, and she said she felt like what I was doing wasn't much, so they got me to go ahead. I was supposed to go up there to look for a place.

I was there in Chicago for three years. I worked making lampshades, and then I beaded. They were wearing beaded dresses then, and I did that. And I met my husband there and married him. He was a Mobilian, too, but I didn't know him until I moved to Chicago. There were lots of southerners in Chicago. See, when World War I was, that's when they had the free transportation for people to go north. And they liked to scalped Mobile. All that the army didn't have, the steel mills and Chicago did.

Well, I liked Chicago, but my husband didn't. The weather didn't take to him. But both of us, we liked the opportunities up there. And the white people up there—there were some more willing to let black people get along and try things out just like whites, although, now, the streetcars and trolleys were segregated and some hotels you couldn't go in. And then the neighborhoods was segregated, most of them.

But people could get more jobs there, and that started the people leaving Mobile. If you look at the obituaries of the Negroes today, you can see they are scattered from here to there. There's nobody home; children just scattered every which way. They did better by leaving Mobile, them that could. Even those who thought they had good positions here could do better there.

My husband was a boner up there for Swift's. But he heard from his sister that they were losing some of their property here. So we came back in 1924. I got a job working at housekeeping for a gentleman. He had lost his wife, and he had a sister there. She was an old maid, but they were rich, and she never didn't know nothing about housekeeping.

She and his two children and him, they fell in love with me. He said I was a perfect housekeeper and cook. I was like their mother. I stayed there until I bought me a place in town. They lived too far out, and my husband said it was too hard on me to go out there.

Then, for a good while, I just did work here and there. This family I'd worked for some before, her son got typhoid pneumonia. I nursed him. Then, her daughter she got grown and married, and whenever she wanted something special done, then she'd come around me—for serving parties. And when these babies in white families were born premature, well, I nursed them.

I took a little girl—she wasn't but six years old—and I raised her because I didn't have no children of my own that lived. So I took care of her and sewed at home and sold vegetables, flowers, chickens, eggs. And sometimes I'd go out and serve parties or weddings.

But I worked a long time. And I'm going to tell you, now, the majority of people here in Mobile worked. And the majority of them made their living working for white people or washing and ironing for them. Everybody couldn't be teachers, and that was the only thing for them to do. They had to work for white people as cooks, housekeepers, maids.

And it's some people that just done it for a lifetime. It was the only job they had. They done it for a lifetime, from young people till they got old for the same family. They raised the people's children, and they raised the children's children, like that.

And there were a lot of washwomen. Now my sister-in-law did hand laundry. She was a beautiful hand laundress. She went to people's houses and did some on the yard. She used to do it at her house too. She did beautiful work.

But, oh, the pay was so small! I know some people say they got $1.00 a bundle, some said 50 cents and 75 cents. And if they got $1.50, I think that was big money! When I was a child, you could see them carrying the clothes on their heads in baskets—bundled on their heads.

I stopped work when my husband got very sick. It got too much on me. And I said, "Shoot, why should I work?" I worked all my life, and he was getting three checks from retiring. So I came down at sixty-two.

I miss work, in a way. Everywhere that I went, people liked my work and they just turned me loose. They didn't bother me. I never did work for nobody mean. Some people had a hard time because some people was poor, and I wasn't and I was always treated nice.

I tell 'em all: I don't regret a day that I lived. I was raised nice and my people . . . people left 'em money. I won't say they were rich, but they were good livers, and I didn't know nothing about no hard times. I didn't know nothing about being real poor. I say, God just blessed me. But it never went to my head.

And I guess it didn't, because of my grandmother. Everybody said she was more like a virgin! She cared for everybody. She would take our clothes, our material, and make a shirt for a poor little child. And poor people would come by our house. My aunt always had people to come there and do wash and things for her, and when they'd leave there, she'd just have them loaded down, with things she'd given them.

There was a priest that came down there. He'd come eat supper with us. And he said we acted more like the holy family than anyone anywhere he went! Say when he come there, we'd all come in, and say, we'd act more like the holy family! But that's the way we were raised.

From an interview with Susan Tucker

Ella Thomas

Ella Thomas (b. 1908) tells of working in an auditorium in a southern town, and her story provides a good example of the role of the domestic as a go-between. Domestic workers often acted as interpreters of white life to blacks, of black life to whites, and as messengers between these two groups (see also Part V). Such a role was based upon the coming and going of black domestics in and out both sides of the segregated community. In the course of such coming and going, black domestics often aligned themselves with upper-class whites, or upper-middle-class whites, forming alliances that could possibly aid them in the community. Black domestics such as Thomas often spoke of such an alliance with whites whom they described as "good whites." This alliance helped them, they felt, in their encounters with lower-class whites.

Such alliances seem to have been understood by people within the southern community as a whole. Thus, when Tallulah Bankhead, the famous southern actress, came to town, Thomas was singled out among the auditorium staff as the intermediary to work with her. The white supervisor, who was from the working class, did not himself tell Bankhead that a black man could not be in her show. Instead, he instructed Thomas, a black woman, to do so. This was probably so because he, too, recognized the complex alignment of blacks with upper-class whites. He probably knew that only a black woman could possibly instruct someone of a higher socioeconomic background, like Tallulah Bankhead, on racial custom.

Ella Thomas told of an early life on a plantation and the choices she made about her life as an adult in the city. She enjoyed telling which white people she would work for and which she would not. She enjoyed telling how she spoke up for herself.

Her floors are unpainted and wooden. The floor in the living room is partially covered with a piece of linoleum. Between each room, she has hung curtains. She has photographs of her grandchildren on tables and walls. Above her sofa she has a cloth hanging on which are painted portraits of Martin Luther King, Jr., and the Kennedy brothers.

I was born in Washington County, Alabama, in the year nineteen hundred and eight. And I've worked almost all my life. When I got about ten or eleven or twelve years old, I was on my own two feet trying to make a living. See, my mother died before I was two, and my daddy raised me and I had to work. I had to cook. I learnt how to cook when I wasn't big enough to reach the stove. And when I was really little, my father used to carry me to the field with them and put me in a cotton basket and sit me under a tree. You see, my daddy had five of us there, and he done what he could—he and his mother both. They both farmed. In the country, when you're farming, if you soak that farm, well, it went for all you got. That's the way you did in them days. And then whatever we needed extra, we got from working in the white people's homes.

My aunt she worked for the Snowdens. She worked for them ever since she was a girl. Dah, they called her. They called her Dah. It was a name for a nurse in South Carolina, where Miz Snowden was from.*

Miz Sybil she died, and she left those children there for my aunt to take care of. And they had others. They had Jane Phillips. She was the cook, and she was the only one of the house servants that Mr. George had brought from the penitentiary.

See, they'd catch them doing something—whatever crime—and those white people would go to the judge and buy their time. Old Man Will Stone was kin to the Snowdens—Judge Stone—and he'd tell them: "I got a nigger I'm going to sentence tomorrow. You need some fly hands in the spring? Well, you come down, you can buy their time." He would sentence them for money they couldn't pay, and rather than be in the penitentiary, he'd let 'em go work for the white folks.†

I didn't work there. I went to the fields and worked there until I was about twenty-eight. I had married when I was sixteen and had one child, and when she was big enough, I brought her to the city. I came to live with another aunt.

And directly, I started working in homes. I worked a good while. At first, they paid very little. I made on the first job $2.50 a week, six hours a day, five days a week. We from the country, that was still money, and we'd do anything to keep ourselves going.

And they said can't nobody cook a beef roast like me! Or I'd cook stew meat or a cake or something. But that wasn't in my work, you see. I went on domestic work, just to clean and dust and clean the restrooms and tubs and whatever. But if they left the roast sitting out there on the table, they wouldn't have left it out if they didn't mean for me to cook it. But in those days, extra was how you got more—not in money, but they'd give you stuff or they'd tell other people about you.

The good points of that were that you worked by yourself and did like

---

Dah was a term for a black nurse in Charleston, South Carolina. F. W. Bradley, *A Wordlist from South Carolina* (N.p., 1950), 25.

†*Buying their time* referred to the process of using convicts as field laborers or workers in private homes.

you wanted to do and seems like they believed in me. They were working just like me. I always preferred to work for people who worked, and they'd tell me to do what I could do and get ready and go home when my time came to go.

But I got tired of days work. So I left there and went to the school, where you'd be sitting down for a while when the children got in. I worked ten years at the high school when it wasn't any colored out there—it was just white and us maids. We all had different sections to clean up, and I worked the auditorium. All these big shows that would come from out of town, I'd be right there to help fix the stage. A lot of times I'd do the ironing for the show people. I was making pretty good little money from them, that is, if the man who had you on the job let 'em pay you.

Miz Tallulah Bankhead had a show there once, and I done some little ironing for her. She gave me ten dollars. Oh, the overseer like to had a fit! And there was a colored man playing in her show there, and the overseer told me to tell her that that colored man couldn't play. She told him that if the colored man didn't play, she didn't play. And you know, she let him know that her daddy had been a senator up in Washington and put that Bankhead Tunnel through.

And so then, a very sweet lady that I'd known before asked me to work for her, and I worked there till '79. And see, she wanted me to work for her. She asked me, and that's been true of most of the jobs I've worked. And I must have satisfied them, because some of them come to me right now and want to know if I feel like coming out there and cooking a meal or doing something for them. Or just like if something happened around here or something happened in my family, they going to come and see what they can do.

And I'd always tell them the way I could work. See, you ought to always speak out for you—not like those black people in the country. I told them what I could do and what I couldn't.

Now they used to have hardwood floors, and one place I worked the lady had a big old box of this here paste wax sitting on the table and a bunch of rags. I came to work that day, and I just run the buffer over the floor. She say, "I see you didn't put the wax down." I say, "How you intended me to put it down?" She said, "Well, I put the rags up there." I said, "Well, not for me because I only gets on my knees to pray." Is that right or wrong?

And one of them had venetian blinds! I told her, "Well, I don't use venetian blinds, and I don't know how to dust them." I kept arguing about them. So they took them down and laid them on the garbage can. She said, "Do you want them?" I said, "I told you I don't use venetian blinds."

A maid suppose to say how she can work. If you don't never open your mouth for yourself, who going to talk for you?

I done what I could, 'cause I tell you I wasn't born with anything and I figure I'm going to die without anything. And I didn't have the advantage of education, but I could look and see that if I didn't change something about my life, I'd be living just like my aunt lived—fearing the white, doing everything they say. Some people say, oh, you're just independent, but I say I just figured how to get along the best I could.

From an interview with Mary Yelling

Edith Whitney

＊＊ ✺ ＊＊

Edith Whitney (b. 1882) was the oldest woman we spoke with. Her interview reminded me very much of the Old South and of what she calls "the old-timey" servants, especially the washwomen with bundles of clothes on their heads. As I left, she wanted to talk of these women, of how they looked carrying their baskets down the streets and on the streetcars.

A number of other women born before 1930 also mentioned the visual memory of black washwomen carrying bundles or baskets of laundry on their heads. After the automobile became more common, it seems, these women no longer came to the homes to pick up the laundry; instead the white families took the laundry to the homes of the washwomen. At about this time the practice of balancing the basket on the top of the head—which is still done in the Caribbean—seems to have disappeared in the American South.

Faulkner, in a short story entitled "That Evening Sun," remarked upon the absence of these washwomen carrying their baskets. He evoked the memory of an earlier time by describing them.

> The streets are paved now . . . and we have a city laundry which makes the round on Monday morning, gathering the bundles of clothes into bright colored, specially made motor cars. . . .
>
> But fifteen years ago, on Monday morning the quiet dusty shady streets would be full of Negro women with, balanced on their steady, turbaned heads, bundles of clothes tied up in sheets, almost as large as cotton bales, carried so without touch of hand between the kitchen door of the white house and the blackened washpot beside a cabin door in Negro Hollow.
>
> Nancy would set her bundle on top of her head, then upon the bundle in turn she would set the straw sailor hat which she wore winter and summer. . . . Sometimes we would go a part of the way down the lane and across the pasture with her, to watch the balanced bundle and the hat that never bobbed nor wavered, even when she walked down into the ditch and up the other side and stooped through the fence. She would go down on her hands and knees and crawl through the gap, her head rigid, uptilted, the bundle steady as a rock or a balloon, and rise to her feet again and go on.*

Edith Whitney told me that sometimes she thinks she can still see her "old washwoman coming on Blue Monday." The day was called "Blue Monday" for the blue liquid or powder used in rinsing white fabric to prevent yellowing. Whitney said she still did not have a washing machine. David Katzman has speculated that "the Southern preference for hiring servants retarded the development of commercial laundries."† Whitney told me that my step-grandmother, who ran an appliance store, tried to sell her a washing machine once in the 1940s. She saw

---

*William Faulkner, "That Evening Sun," in *The Collected Short Stories of William Faulkner* (New York, 1950), 289–90.

†David M. Katzman, *Seven Days a Week: Women and Domestic Service in Industrializing America* (New York, 1978), 62.

this incident as ironic, since if she had bought that machine, she would not have been faithful to her washwoman. "And here you are asking questions about old Seraphina," she added with finality.

Edith Whitney lives in a house with a circular front porch that has white carved railings and a dark-green floor and ceilings. There are several straight-backed cane rocking chairs on the porch. But we sat inside in a long, wide hall used as the living room in summer. The doors were open at either end of the hall, for there was no air conditioning.

I was born here in Hattiesburg in a house my grandfather built. My mother and father and grandmother and grandfather, we all lived together in a little house. You might like to see it. It's a lovely white cottage, and my grandfather had the date it was built painted in the glass on one of the windows. I have forgotten what the date was.

They came from Rankin County after my mother married. My mother was an only child, and they wanted to be with her. I don't know what they did before. I don't go back that far! They weren't on a plantation, I don't think, though they did own slaves. They were part Indian, though I don't like to say it. My grandchildren all are very proud of that, but we were always ashamed of it.

When they came to Hattiesburg, the slaves came, too. They were free then, but they wanted to be near my grandmother. They found different jobs around town, but every month they'd come to our house to see her. See, I'm 102, so I do go back a little far! And I remember seeing them. They'd cry and tell her all the things they missed from home, and tell her how good she'd been to them. Of course, they didn't have to buy clothes. They didn't have to buy medicine. Everything was furnished to them free, and of course, they missed that. She'd always bring out something for them! I remember those visits.

Here, we always had help, too. I've always had blacks around, and I was always told to be kind to them. I was brought up that way. But now I don't remember anyone in particular. The one I remember the most, Belle, came to work for me in about 1915. And she stayed until she got very sick in 1951.

She was an excellent, kind person and so interested in my children. She lived on the place, and she just catered to them all the time. My daughter—well, she wasn't lazy, but she'd been waited on all the time, and I said to Belle one day, as she was taking breakfast into the bedroom for Louise—Louise was my daughter—I said, "Belle, you're just spoiling Miz Louise." You know they didn't call the children just by their names; they always called them Miz or Mister. But she said, "Well, that's what I'm paid for!"

And my son, she dressed him every morning. She put his boots on and laid out his clothes until he married.

She'd come to us when she was a little young girl—in her teens. And when she was older, I said to her one day, "Belle, have you made a will?" And she said, "No'm I haven't." I said, "Well, you have a house, a lot, and you ought to make a will."

She said, "You know I was thinking about it, and I want to leave it to George." That was my son I just spoke of. I said, "Well, that's awfully kind, but you can't do that." I said, "Your family would say that I influenced you." She was so upset because I wouldn't let her leave everything to George!

And she took such good care of the house here. If it could have belonged to her, she wouldn't have been any more careful about it. She was really a part of the family.

I had another one almost as long as I had Belle—Mildred. And she wasn't a part of the family! I'd forgotten Mildred. She was my cook. The meanest one! She couldn't get along with anybody, especially Belle. The man I had then to do the heavy work, he'd complain so much about Mildred!* I'd go away, and every time I'd come home, he would have written me a note about how he just could not tolerate Mildred! But she made the most beautiful little flowered mints and cheese straws, for parties and all. She was mean as the devil, but I kept her.

When the children had all been gone, though, I let Mildred go. But with the others, we were faithful, and they were faithful to us. With all the help here—the washwoman and all of them—I never had a washing machine here. I don't have one now. I'm not up to date. My washwoman always took it out!

I was faithful to her. But you know it was a shame how we paid. We didn't pay much. Belle only got three dollars a week. Of course, she got everything—all her upkeep, insurance, medical bills—and we always gave them nice presents and things. Always gave presents to their families, too; you felt like you had to do that to stay in good standing. And of course, the pay went up. But we did not pay enough. I don't know why.

---

*Most wealthy people in the South employed a black man to come once a week or once a month to do the "heavy work"—the mopping, cleaning of windows, washing of walls, cleaning of silver and brass, and the changing of the rugs and drapes in summer and winter.

No, I guess we didn't think of higher pay as a form of kindness, or fairness. It is a shame, a shame.

Now they say we owe them and we're never going to finish paying them. That feeling—it's made for an entirely different type of servant! I don't really understand these new ones. I'd be afraid to say anything about them!

But in the old days they were treated well. People today talk about how mean the whites were to them, about how the whites were mean to the slaves. It was a few that were like that, but a good many of them were kind to their slaves. And then later, in my lifetime, they were not mistreated; I mean, some of them were, and some of them were mistreated by the northerners more than the southerners. They place such stress on what the southerners did, but they were worse. Least I've heard, when I was grown.

When I was younger, they didn't talk about ugly things. They thought it was frightening that anyone would be mean to the colored. We would hear, every now and then, some little talk. Our parents would talk about some mistreatment, and they'd be horrified. What was told to us was that we were to be kind to the help. And I taught my children that, too.

From an interview with Susan Tucker

Hazel Lambert

The following narrative contains all the well-known clichés of the "happy days of the Old South"—the plantation, the loyal blacks, the house servants called "Mammy," "Aunt," "Uncle," or a favored nickname. The naming of servants by employers, as discussed in this narrative, deserves attention. The power to name another person, after all, suggests a degree of authority far beyond that of a mere employer. Indeed, it recalls the days of slavery, which centered on the ownership of a person. The fact that a slave was named by his master meant that his very identity was inextricably linked with the master. That such naming continued in the postslavery era speaks of the efforts of whites and, to a lesser extent, of blacks to preserve something of such linking. Whites wished to preserve their power over blacks, and blacks, who sometimes named children after white employers, sought to provide the child with a benefactor within the ruling class.

One servant in the following narrative is even called "Aunt Mammy." Thus, a double name was bestowed on her by whites. Perhaps one was not sufficiently evocative of the Old South. *Aunt* was said by whites to connote respect for the age of any older black woman, whether she was known to whites as a servant or not. But black women generally resented being called *aunt* by whites.

They also resented being cast as "Mammy." They correctly saw that both "Mammy" and "Aunt" placed them within the paternalistic, segregationist order. They also realized that, as one told me, whites "wanted to see an old mammy" in every black woman. The whites' strong preference for an *aged* black woman suggests that mammies were symbolic of the Old South, not just of an older mothering person, and that a white person's memory of such an aged person tells us more about the speaker than the speaker's subject. Herbert G. Gutman, in his study of the black family, has shown that little evidence exists to indicate the presence of many older loyal mammies laboring for white families in the post-slavery era. He points out the young age of most house servants and contrasts this fact to the "erroneous but popular belief about ex-slave women . . . that the typical house servant was an aged 'mammy' who remained in her antebellum place out of loyalty to a white family or because whites had a special concern for such women."[*]

This narrative also illustrates something of the practice of renaming, whereby the employer would arbitrarily choose a new name for a domestic. Renaming, like naming, was a means of regaining some degree of the power over blacks that had been lost with emancipation. Most white women felt that in such renaming, they were acting with no conscious undermining intent, and indeed many said they were only giving affectionate nicknames. Nevertheless, the result was de-meaning in that the servant did not have control over the very basic matter of what

---

[*]Herbert G. Gutman, *The Black Family in Slavery and Freedom, 1750–1925* (New York, 1976), 632.

she was called. Renaming of black domestics by white employers was a fairly common occurrence and is documented in a number of works written by blacks.†

Most black women, like the ones here called "Cookie" and "Aunt Mammy," worked within such a system, manipulating whites to achieve what power they could by being the ever loyal servants. Hazel Lambert (b. 1893) remembers their devotion.

On her coffee table are books about the Orient, southern homes, and antiques. She lives in a small apartment. On the walls are pictures of a large, old southern home where she once lived. As I was leaving, she told me of her respect for Booker T. Washington and the school he started. She remembers opening her house to visiting students from Tuskegee on a tour. She told me they were among the most polite and knowledgeable people she had ever met.

→→ ⋙🕱⋘ ←←

The servants! Oh, they made life so interesting; they were so funny! One of the first ones I knew here was named Cookie. When I first married, you see, we lived at my mother-in-law's, and she always had a cook named Mary, but my husband called her Cookie. And he said to his mother, "Where's Cookie?" And she said, "I don't know. She got sick and couldn't come anymore."

And he said, "What do you mean you don't know what is the matter with her. Don't you think you should know?" Because he loved Cookie. But, "No," his mother said. "She just worked for me, that's all." "Well, where is she?" he said. "Well, you know where she lives. Go find her yourself."

So we walked down to Jackson and Congress or somewhere, and we found Cookie in bed with her stomach out to here. And Mr. Lambert hugged her and she hugged him and she cried, and I was introduced and she looked me over most critically. And then he looked at her and said he was going to call a doctor. And so the doctor came and found a twenty-pound tumor and my husband said, "Now, the best thing is for us to get this tumor out. You know those nuns at the hospital are very nice. They'll look after you, and Miss Hazel and I will, too, and she'll buy you night-gowns and powder."

And Cookie cried and said she hadn't used powder since she was a baby. But she went in the hospital anyway and stayed there a month, and we went to see her every day.

And when she got out she said, "Who do y'all have cooking for you?"

---

†See, for example, Maya Angelou, *I Know Why the Caged Bird Sings* (New York, 1979), 104–108; John Gwaltney, *Drylongso* (New York, 1980), 3, 172.

And my husband said, "Well, Miz Hazel cooks; she's very good at it, and we don't have enough money to pay a cook just now." And she looked at me. I just weighed eighty-five pounds then and said, "That little thing?" But we thought the matter was settled and that she understood.

Well, the second morning we were in our own house, my husband went down to get the newspaper, and there was Cookie on the steps. And he said, "Cookie, what's wrong?" And she said, "Nothing. I've just come to help." And so we said, "Well, we can't pay." And she said, "Who's talking about money?" She was just so grateful. And so she stayed and cooked, and it was good because, of course, she knew everything he liked.

And she stayed with us for about eight years before she started drinking at work. One day I went in the kitchen, and she was drunk and started chasing me with a broom. I ran out the front door and down the street, and she came after me. Just then Mr. Lambert was coming down the street, and he saw me running. He asked me what I was doing. I didn't even stop to tell him. And so when Cookie saw him, she just started sweeping. And he asked her, and she said, "Oh, I'm just sweeping." He said, "Well, come on in the house." And there he gave her some coffee.

But she quit drinking after that and worked for us another few years until one day she had a headache. Robert, the yard boy, took her home on the bus, and he didn't tell us she had a headache, and neither did she. And we were so distressed, because that night she had a stroke, and if we had known, we could have kept her with us. But we had her in the hospital, but there was very little we could do. She was over eighty and she died.

Now, she was an alcoholic, which I think was unusual in Negro women, because they're so religious. And she was religious, too. She sang all the time. But only my husband could keep her from drinking, and only him for a little while.

Now the men, the Nigra men, drank more than the Negro women. I guess that's not much different than white people! But the Nigras thought it was wrong. My husband he used to go fishing and take our yardman Willie. This was another man, after we moved out to the big old house. And one day they were sitting on the bank, and my husband said, "Well, Willie, will you have a beer?" And Willie said, "No sir, I don't drink."

He said, "You don't drink?"

"No sir."

"Well, why?"

"Well, it's against my religion," said Willie.

"Well," my husband said, "we're out here in these woods and ain't nobody around but you and me." He would talk just like they did. He said, "Ain't nobody here but you and me. Do you think that would make any difference?" And Willie was quiet for a little while, and he said, "Well, there's so much trees. I don't believe the Lord can see me." So just little things like that—their funny ways—made life so happy.

And we lived in this wonderful old home and had lots of land about, so we always had at least five servants to help with the children, the house, and the yard. And of course, we always had dogs. At one time I had twenty-seven dogs. Oh, those dogs were my life!

But now the servants they were, of course, devoted to us—some of them. There was a devotion among the Nigras at that time that you'll never get again.

I was thinking about Uncle Thomas and Aunt Mammy just before you called. Uncle Thomas was with my grandfather since he was a boy, and went with him to the war—the War Between the States. Grandfather was a circuit rider. And then when Grandfather was taken prisoner on Johnson Island, Uncle Thomas came home and got a job for two dollars a week. And he brought groceries home to Grandmother. Grandmother said, "Oh, no, that's your money." But Uncle Thomas said no, he'd take care of her till Marse got home. He called him "Marse"—Master—or he called him "Boss."

And so when Grandfather got home, he was a minister in several communities, and Uncle Thomas went everywhere with him. And then his wife was the cook, Aunt Mammy. They were with Grandfather till he died. Then the children—my parents and my aunts and uncles—got together and bought Uncle Thomas and Aunt Mammy a house. One of my uncles had a car and said, "Uncle Thomas, y'all ride all through nigger-town and see where you want a house." But they came back and said they didn't want to live there. They wanted to stay with their white folks. They'd given their lives to them. But my uncles persuaded them to move, and they put the house in Uncle Thomas' name and all. And when they died, of course, we buried them in the family plot.

Now, you see, today the Nigras they behave so differently. Well, they've been so brainwashed. Somebody like Jesse Jackson getting up there and hollering at them has convinced them to not act normally. They expect everything to come their way. Now a servant that I've had eighteen years, the other day . . . It was she that got me thinking of Uncle Thomas and his devotion. She was talking about how all the maids on the bus are wondering what Mrs. Olson left her two maids that she has had for years and years, to take care of them.

I said, "What do you mean? She's been paying them for all these years; she's furnished their houses with furniture from her own; she paid them whether they came or not. When they came and stayed just an hour, she gave them a full work's salary." I said, "What do you mean?"

She said, "Well, they've given all of their lives to her." And she said, "Now I just wonder what's going to happen to me." I said, "What do you mean?" She said, "Well, I've given eighteen years of my life to you, and if you should die, I would just be left with nothing."

I said, "You got your Social Security." She gets that now. I said, "For what I pay you I could get a trip around the world on!" So, she didn't say any more then. But they show you, by saying things like that, they're not devoted, they're not grateful like the old ones were. One minute she's smart as she can be, keeps up, and knows everything about Social Security, all the laws. She's gone to business school. And she can keep my checkbook straighter than I can keep it. They just laugh at me at the bank about it because she does all my banking. Of course, I double-check—now don't think I'm not keeping up with it—but she's the one who does it. And the bank knows her.

And her family, they've all borrowed money. I've gone on the bond, as they call it, for all of them. And they've always paid me back absolutely just on the dot. Unbelievable! And they've all bought automobiles that way; I've loaned them a thousand dollars each, and they paid so much every month. And they're just as honest as they can be. I've gotten jobs for two of them. They do the most beautiful housework you've ever seen.

And I think it is so interesting. In their family they all work. And on Friday night after they get their money, they meet around the dining-room table and put all their money in a pile. Then they get all the bills that have to be paid and deduct that, and then what's left over is divided into four parts. Isn't that wonderful? They're so amazing!

And once, she told me her father said there are just three things you need to know to get along: said, know you're a Nigra, 100 percent black; always say "Yes sir" and "Yes ma'am" to white people, respect them; and always arrive everywhere fifteen minutes ahead of time. So you see, she knows the right ways; [it's] just she gets confused by somebody like Jesse Jackson.

From an interview with Susan Tucker

Corinne Cooke

Corinne Cooke (b. 1897) spoke of divisions in southern society based on race and class in the same way that many other white women whom we interviewed did—with only a slight acknowledgment that either race or class actually exist. The taboo against discussing race was particularly strong. Corinne Cook, thus, couched any mention of it in such words as *kindness* and *specialness*. She has an unquestioning belief that those are the right words to describe how whites behaved toward blacks. She is surprised, almost shocked, that I should ask why something that appears "unkind" might really have been so. She cannot imagine such questioning.

Her narrative also reveals something of how race overshadowed class as a division within southern society. While both black and white women did speak of class in the interviews, they often did so in ways designed to hide such designations. Cooke, for example, defined *poor white trash* from a black person's perspective. She, and others like her, would say, "They were the kind of people blacks would call poor white trash." In so doing, they do not take responsibility for assigning class divisions. In so doing, they enjoy pointing out that certain black people—notably servants—were "better" than "poor white trash." They enjoy telling stories of "aristocratic" blacks who looked down on whites. Upper-middle-class and middle-class whites could then blame race conflict on other whites, but without politically aligning themselves with blacks as a group and without even being consciously aware that it might be logical to do so. They defended their reticence by saying it was impolite to discuss race and class, that such discussions might "hurt feelings."

Corinne Cooke is especially polite. On her lap she had an afghan that covered her aging, shrinking legs. In my childhood she had been much taller. I have known her all my life. She once read me a story from a book called *My Travelship* about the Dutch Santa Claus. In this story some white boys were turned into black boys for making fun of a black person. I do not remember if we discussed the story, only that we read it. When I asked her of her memories of black domestics, she told me stories that I had never heard. She was careful to schedule me on a day when she did not have a black sitter to help her.

I was born at a place called Oakfield, about six miles out of Pensacola. It was in the country. It was considered healthy to go out in the country in the summer, and since I was born in July, I was born out there. Becky lived on the place there. She was an old colored woman who took care of the place in the wintertime, and she cooked for us in the summertime.

It was the old family home, and two of my uncles lived there. They'd built homes out there. And Uncle Phillip, his children had Mammy. Mammy would fix us to go to bed at night and bathe us in the morning when I stayed there. And I wanted so for Becky to be called Mammy, but Becky said no, she was not Mammy—she was Becky. I don't know why. She said she had a hard enough time being Becky. She didn't want to be Mammy! Mammy was buried with our cousins. She's the only one besides the Davises in their lot. And Becky said she didn't care a speck about being buried with us! We thought she was just one of those new types, but we were very fond of her. Becky had had a hard life, I guess. It was an odd way of life in some respects. They were so connected to us, and yet they weren't. Just before I was born, there had been an awful fight where Becky's son was killed, by a white man, the type the colored called "poor white trash." And they said he was killed by a man his mother had nursed, that when she went to get his body, she said to him, "I nursed you, and now you have killed my son." You see, she was a wet nurse.

This is what my mother told me happened. Becky had worked for my uncle and her when they were little. And she had been a wet nurse to many of the white families. She'd had so many children, and she was healthy, very healthy.

So it was odd every once in a while when horrible things like that would happen. They all felt very sad for Becky and Phoebe, her daughter. Of course, they took care of them. They always lived there. There was nothing anyone could do to them, and I was always told that they were special.

When I became a schoolteacher in Mobile, I didn't see them much. The last time I saw Phoebe was in 1946. We were both getting old even then! We just talked about the old place.

In Mobile I just boarded with different people. I lived for years and years with Miz Leila Cabot. And she had a cook come from two till after dinner at night, and the maid come in the morning. She had dinner at night on account of me, so that I could have a hot meal. The last cook she had, I've been to see her. She's dead now, but she was in the colored people's nursing home.

But the white people took care of their servants. Miz Leila left money for that one—Alma, her name was. And Miz Leila used to visit one every week, an old colored woman she'd known as a child. And people often left them a little bit of land so they could live out their days there.

Now my cousin passed away not too long ago. She left five hundred dollars to one that had been working for her since she was sixteen years old. So you can say in your book those servants were well cared for.

And they made life easier for those people who had them. Miz Leila didn't have to worry about growing old. The servants could help. Even the biggest catastrophe, the servants could surmount. Now, I am very old, I have to look about for people trained to be kind and trained to do all sorts of awful things required to keep me going.

When Miz Leila had a stroke in 1950, there was Alma still, and Alma found a colored nurse who had experience with old people. In fact, she found two. Miz Leila's son found a white nurse, and Leila refused her. She was senile, and she would just balk at the white nurse, but she was like a little well-mannered child with the black nurse. She was used to being cared for by the colored people.

From an interview with Susan Tucker

Part III

From Country to City

Eula Mae Rudolph, a black woman who worked long years for my family, had an aunt called Aunt Beck. I remember Aunt Beck as an ancient, thin black woman whom I never addressed by any name. I remember her by the name Aunt Beck only because that was what we called her when she and Eula Mae were not around. There had always been, I remembered in beginning this project, a silence about what we should call her, a silence instigated by Eula Mae and Aunt Beck. Of course, I now know something of what this silence was: it was about the only fairly graceful way to get around being called by her first name. But I sensed even then that it had to do with the fact that Eula Mae respected her too much to have us, little white children, address her by her first name and thus as an equal. She was, in some clearly indicated but unarticulated way, set apart from dealings with us.

Eula Mae had first come to her Aunt Beck's house when she moved to the city from the country in the early 1940s. Eula Mae returned to that house almost every day to visit. I sensed in the way they spoke to and of each other that there was something very special between them, something beyond their actual kinship. They pronounced *aunt* in what we called the Virginia or the New England way, with a broad *a*. And they gave it a different meaning from any of those I knew in the white community. They took care of each other in sickness and in other family problems. They looked out for each other in daily comings and goings. They spoke of each other with what was almost reverence—the way, I think now, that one speaks of one's mentors or one's protégés.

Less intense than the mother-daughter bond, their relationship centered around the help given by an older woman to a younger one, the younger one's desire to repay such help, and, most important, their common ties to a rural past. Many of the black interviewees spoke of similar relationships and the resultant network of sustenance that they found when they came from the country "to stay with" their aunts in the cities.

Such relationships are mentioned primarily in stories of migration, of the leaving behind of rural life and going to the city. These stories point to the causes of such migration, reflect upon the effects these moves had on southern white and black perceptions of each other, and attest to the adaptability of the extended black family.

The cities to which these women migrants went offered a greater number of prospective employers than had the country. This was the foremost reason black women remembered for leaving rural areas. At least until the 1940s the predominant form of labor in the countryside remained agricultural work, which, as the twentieth century went on, became less and less a likely source of financial security. Black women who sought work in these rural areas had fewer choices—both of employers and type of work.[1] In the country, there were generally a few white families who owned large portions of land with whom blacks could enter into sharecropping. These same families employed a few permanent domestic workers—often the wives and daughters of sharecroppers. Poorer whites employed black servants less frequently, primarily out of season to help on temporary projects.

Moreover, the environment of the countryside was one in which those few white employers—their behavior and personalities—were known to blacks. The reputations of those whites also made blacks decide to leave their rural homes. For example, Julia Newman, a white Alabamian born in 1896, mentioned that in two adjacent counties there were only five families who owned land. In one of these families was "a very mean old lady who all the darkies and all the whites knew to be cruel to the help." Two white women interviewed spoke of beatings of black women by whites in rural areas. No one spoke of such incidents taking place in the city.

In the city black women also expected to make a more decent wage. One woman recalled, "Up the country I had hopes, that didn't always turn out, of making $2.00 a week." This was in 1926, the year she moved to the city, where she made $4.00 a week. Those women who worked in the homes of the big landowners in rural areas were often paid only out of

---

1. See the Bureau of the Census' decennial census records for the years 1900, 1910, 1920, 1930, and 1940 for the states of Florida, Alabama, Mississippi, Louisiana, Georgia, and South Carolina. Most black women in rural areas in these states were agricultural workers.

the commissary with food, material, or other items. Rural-born women remembered being paid out of the commissary or in wages as low as $3.00 to $3.50 a week during the 1940s. In the city they could make as much as $10.00 or more per week.

Although the quality of city life did not uniformly result in improved living conditions, the women migrants remembered these higher wages. They also remembered what Jacqueline Jones has called "the greater cultural, educational, and religious opportunities" of the cities.[2] They recalled the excitement of seeing black churches—"built of brick, and two or three right on the same street"—and black businesses. They enjoyed the city's marketplaces, streetcars, and other amenities.

Finally, they often stated that they preferred city life simply because there "they would not have to go to the fields." Going to the fields entailed rising before dawn so that they could work before the sun got too hot, carrying water from a stream or well for washing and cooking at daybreak, and working at a number of other exhausting tasks involved in feeding and sheltering families. City life, with its less tiring work, as well as indoor plumbing for at least some people, electric lights, better transportation, and more and better public and private schools, offered hope of a better life.

Hopeful black immigrants, often arriving literally from the plantations, saw in their moves to the city at least some freedom from the ways of the Old South. At the same time, the conditions under which rural blacks had been raised—with the often brutal punishment they received for not behaving with ritual deference toward whites—made for difficulty in changing the behaviors that characterized the Old South. The propensity of these migrants to act in the manner of Uncle Tom, coupled with legal and economic sanctions against equality for blacks, thus worked against their actually achieving as much freedom as they had anticipated. And such a propensity, coupled with the oral tradition of the rural South, influenced the way whites came to see domestic workers as well as blacks in general.

In the eyes of whites, such backgrounds made country-bred blacks seem unusually sensitive and intuitive. Black domestics from the country were described by whites almost as if they were magical earth mothers setting up gardens in city lots in which they made "anything grow," cook-

2. Jacqueline Jones, *Labor of Love, Labor of Sorrow: Black Women, Work and the Family from Slavery to the Present* (New York, 1985), 75.

ing without recipes, healing ailments with just a wave of the hand.[3] David Katzman and Mary Jean Bowman and C. Arnold Anderson have suggested that the employment of domestics in the South was an urban pattern rather than a universally southern one.[4] But the stereotype of the urban domestic as a sensitive and intuitive person has a strong rural foundation. Thus, the literary tradition of the mothering black mammy was expanded to an urban setting, where it grew to even greater proportions.

The stereotype seems to have expanded as whites in urban areas told stories concerning their own dependence on black servants. These stories were told in such a way as to indicate the class of the speaker as well as his or her place in a romantic version of the past. Whites especially enjoyed telling of the exceptional strength of black female domestics. Certainly, this perceived strength was rooted again in the rural past, in the fact that black women had once worked in the fields, at "men's work." However, a belief in such strength was primarily important because it continued, in both the cities and the countryside, to rationalize the fact that domestics labored under harsh social and economic conditions.

The perceived emotional strength of black domestics is shown in many literary works by both black and white authors. For example, Mammy in Harriet Beecher Stowe's *Uncle Tom's Cabin*, Dilsey in William Faulkner's *The Sound and the Fury*, Margaret in Shirley Ann Grau's *The Keepers of the House*, Lutie in Ann Petry's *The Street*, and Ondine in Tuni Morrison's *Tar Baby* are all strong black women shown in contrast to weak, ineffectual white women.[5] Lillian Hellman in her portrayal of Helen, her longtime housekeeper, says Helen did not think "white people capable of dealing with trouble." Ondine in *Tar Baby* is called "Mother Superior" by Margaret, her white employer. Lutie in *The Street* is the only adult to remem-

---

3. The idea of the black domestic as a foster mother image similar to mythical mothers is explored in Catherine Juanita Starke, *Black Portraiture in American Fiction: Stock Characters, Archetypes and Individuals* (New York, 1971), 125–35; and Richard H. King, *A Southern Renaissance: The Cultural Awakening of the American South, 1930–1955* (New York, 1980), 37, 190–91.

4. David M. Katzman, *Seven Days a Week: Women and Domestic Service in Industrializing America* (New York, 1978), 59; C. Arnold Anderson and Mary Jean Bowman, "The Vanishing Servant and the Contemporary Status System of the American South," *American Journal of Sociology*, LIX (November, 1953), 215–30.

5. Harriet Beecher Stowe, *Uncle Tom's Cabin; or, Life Among the Lowly* (1851; rpr. Boston, 1898); William Faulkner, *The Sound and The Fury* (New York, 1929); Shirley Ann Grau, *The Keepers of the House* (New York, 1964); Ann Petry, *The Street* (Boston, 1946); Toni Morrison, *Tar Baby* (New York, 1981).

ber Little Harry during a crisis in the white family. During the discovery of his uncle's suicide, Little Harry, the white child, is on the floor, crouching in fear: "None of them had given him a thought; they had deserted him as neatly as though they had deposited him on the doorstep of a foundling hospital. She picked him up and held him close to her . . . telling him through her arms that his world had not suddenly collapsed about him, that the strong arms holding him so close were a solid safe place where he was safe."[6]

The black domestic in literature is also frequently shown as a physically strong and robust woman, particularly by white authors. In *Red Rock*, by Thomas Nelson Page, Mammy Krenda hits a Yankee soldier who is bothering the white family. In Julia Peterkin's *Green Thursday*, Maum Hannah is an aged woman, but she can still "wield an ax . . . and the fire in her open fireplace was never allowed to go out." Faulkner's description of Dilsey and the other black servants of the Compson family in the appendix to *The Sound and the Fury* reads simply, "they endured," as if that statement is enough to describe their continued presence while all the Compsons were dying off.[7]

Black writers, on the other hand, show more of the toll that such emotional and physical strength took. In *The Street* Petry writes: "Lutie . . . glanced . . . at the women coming toward her. . . . Their shoulders sagged from the weight of the heavy shopping bags they carried. And she thought, That's what's wrong. We don't have time enough or money to live like other people . . . the women . . . work til they become drudges." And Toni Morrison in *Tar Baby* describes a very exhausted Ondine. Whenever Ondine is not working, she is soaking her feet. As one of the characters says, "Her feet are killing her, killing her."[8]

Katherine Anne Porter, in "The Last Leaf," is one of the few white writers who shows a black domestic growing very old and tired. One of the grown white children, raised by this domestic, recalls: "They had not really been so very nice to Aunt Nannie. They went on depending on her as they always had, letting her assume more burdens and more, allowing

6. Lillian Hellman, *An Unfinished Woman* (Boston, 1960), 245; Morrison, *Tar Baby*, 72; Petry, *The Street*, 48.

7. Thomas Nelson Page, *Red Rock: Chronicle of Reconstruction* (1898; rpr. Ridgewood, N.J., 1967), 125–27; Julia Peterkin, *Green Thursday*, (New York, 1924), 12; Faulkner, *The Sound and The Fury*, 427.

8. Petry, *The Street*, 186; Morrison, *Tar Baby*, 136, 137, 206, 228.

her to work harder than she should have." In her autobiography Lillian Hellman records an exchange she had with Helen, her housekeeper: "Black women get old fast," Helen said. "Yes," Hellman said, "watching white women stay young."[9]

But most white southerners did not think as Hellman and Porter did. Black people, in general, were said to age slower than white people. This belief, in turn, allowed whites to continue to employ aged domestics with little real concern for their welfare. By proclaiming continued strength in black women no matter what the circumstance, white women could ignore the fact that low pay and social injustices worked to keep these blacks at a subsistence level.

One example of this refusal to see beyond the perceived strength of black women can be found in white women's accounts of the care of black children. The white women we interviewed generally stated that all black children were cared for within the extended black family by the strong grandmothers, aunts, and older sisters. Whites chose to believe this oftentimes without asking what child-care arrangements had been made. Once I was told: "She came back to work when the baby was about three months. She left the baby with the old blind grandmother, who always had some little nine- or ten-year-old to help." Why this nine- or ten-year-old was not in school was not considered by the white employer.

To be fair, white women in southern society also operated at a disadvantage, though in a less absolute way. As noted above, the strength of black women was often established by comparing black women with weak white women. The stereotype of the southern white woman suggested that she was a person of almost hysterical weakness. Without their own income, and without skills with which they earned money, they too were often powerless to bring about change. As one woman asked rhetorically: "What could I have done for this black woman except pay her the little wages my husband gave me, and act with decency and respect for her? Could I tell her 'Don't take such low wages.' Of course not. She needed whatever she could get."

White women may have felt that they, too, needed whatever they could get—help with mothering and housework and perhaps even the vision of strength. Since they were pronounced weak, they seem to have looked for other role models. Thus, it is not difficult to see how white women

9. Katherine Anne Porter, "The Last Leaf," in *The Leaning Tower and Other Stories* (New York, 1934), 59; Hellman, *An Unfinished Woman*, 242.

wanted to continue to believe in the strength of black women. If black women could be seen as strong, then perhaps it was possible for all women to attain strength.

Black urban domestics who knew the value of their work to their families, as well as these perceptions the whites had of them, expressed a strong sense of pride in themselves. This sense of pride allowed them a different, but nevertheless related, self-image centered around strength. This self-image was projected both to whites and to blacks.

One role of such self-confident black women was that of guide to younger women, particularly to those younger women newly arrived from the country. The houses of these established black women were often the first urban homes for blacks from the country. The help of these urban women in securing jobs and in generally overseeing the transition to city life for the young rural women was certainly reassuring to their parents. A number of black women remembered that their parents would not allow them to go to northern cities otherwise thought desirable, because no older woman known to them was there. These parents might have heard of the unscrupulous employment agencies that sent domestic workers on jobs in large northern cities.[10] So instead they sent their daughters to the homes of women known to them. These were the women often called aunts, and though they were not always technically the sisters of one of the parents, their kinship as relatives and neighbors, as guardian angels, was unquestioned.

As earlier migrants to the cities, the aunts had brought with them a strong tradition, probably learned in slavery, of helping one another. Time and again in the interviews, there is mention of "keeping a job going" for an aunt, a mother, a sister, or a sister-in-law. Time and again, there is among the black women a habit of defining themselves in relation to the females to whom they are kin and to whom they are indebted.

Within such networks, black women came to look upon both their jobs and themselves with a great deal of humor. With laughter they often spoke of the uniformity with which whites of all social classes seemed to need blacks to take care of them. From such a viewpoint, they were able to look more clearly at the whites for whom they labored, and they found themselves, again, emotionally and physically stronger than white women. In the networks of aunts, nieces, cousins, mothers, daughters,

10. Katzman, *Seven Days a Week*, 207–208.

and finally whole families lay much of the strength black domestics did have.

In the six narratives that follow are the stories of three black women who went from the country to live in the city. Through the stories of three white women, one learns of their perception of the strength of black women.

Augusta Swanson

Anne Moody, in *Coming of Age in Mississippi*, a story of a young black woman's memories of the period 1938 to 1965, notes that black women in the countryside often "went with" white men to earn money, were raped by the white men for whom they worked, or had an occasional white male lover. The children born of such encounters, mulattoes, were then considered black, as young Anne's mother tells her, "because their mothers are black."*

Augusta Swanson (b. 1910) mentions such encounters between white men and black women and speaks with stoical pity of her mother and her mother's life in the country. Swanson, with the help of an aunt, escaped the fate of her mother.

Her aunt was a washwoman who, by working for a number of white families, knew which of those homes she could place her nieces in with some confidence that they would be treated well. The role of the washwoman as a respected married woman who went between the white and black communities and still had time within her own home seemed important in our interviews with black domestics.

The work of these laundresses, then, offers another example of how black women went about redefining domestic work after the Civil War. Unlike cooks and maids, the washwomen were seen as neutral figures who did not owe allegiance to whites. They were seen as more independent of whites than most blacks were, both in their familial arrangements and temperament. The strike of washwomen in Atlanta in 1881 may have helped lead to this respect for washwomen all over the South. Although the strike was quickly halted and though we found only one domestic who had heard of the strike, it does not seem farfetched to believe that some rumor of the Atlanta washwomen's action reached other cities and contributed to the reputation accorded laundresses of being fiercely independent.† Such a reputation may have then been handed down to black washwomen born later.

Carter G. Woodson, writing in 1930 in the *Journal of Negro History*, contrasted the role of the washwoman to the resented "Plantation Mammy." His eloquent words give us some idea of the respect with which washwomen were regarded: "There is in the life of the Negro, however, a vanishing figure whose name everyone should mention with veneration. She was all but beast of burden of the aristocratic slaveholder and in freedom she continued at this hard labor as a bread winner of the family. This is the Negro washerwoman. . . . In the history of no people has her example been paralleled, in no other figure in the Negro

---

*Anne Moody, *Coming of Age in Mississippi* (New York, 1968), 39.
†Howard N. Rabinowitz, *Race Relations in the Urban South, 1865–1890* (New York, 1978), 74–76.

group can be found a type measuring up to the level of philanthropic spirit in unselfish service."*

Augusta Swanson is proud of her aunt who was a washwoman. Swanson is also proud of the life she herself made in the city, particularly of her long marriage, during which she stayed home as her children were growing up, and of her long service to two white families.

Her narrative concludes in a discussion of her domestic work. She accepts, with almost the same stoicism with which she accepted her mother's lot, the fact that whites imposed an arbitrarily low wage and that to get ahead, one could work only "for good whites that had money," whites who gave away presents in compensation for this low wage. To receive such compensation—which Swanson calls "extra"—one had to be "nice." By this, she meant being the self-effacing servant who knows the desires of her employer and who acts within the range of behavior prescribed for the stereotypical southern servant.

To a certain extent, then, Augusta Swanson worked within the system in which she lived. But it is notable that she did not tell her white employer that she planned to marry. She waited until she was already married, so that her white employer could not try to stop her. She was able to live differently from her mother. By leaving the countryside, Swanson was able to exercise more control over the forces that shaped her life.

She has a clear, slow voice. Her hair is very gray, almost white, and is pulled back in a bun and parted in the middle. As she talked, she folded her hands in front of her. Today she lives with a daughter in a northern state, but she spends a couple of months in the South each year, visiting among whites and blacks.

In the country, where I was born, things were very different than what people know today. My mother she farmed, she had cattle—lots of cows—and she rented this land, about a hundred acres, on the plantation of a white family where she lived.

Her aunt, see, worked in the house of the man who had the plantation, a big dairy farm, and he had all these colored people working for him. My mother would rent a portion of this land and have somebody to take care of her garden. It was, there, more like in the family. And Sarah, her aunt, when she died, they buried her right along with them. She lived right in the house with them and never did visit her folks. But that's why they were so nice to all of us and why my mother rented this land and had cows.

I had two sisters and one brother, all half-sisters and a half-brother.

*Carter G. Woodson, "The Negro Washerwoman: a Vanishing Figure," *Journal of Negro History*, XV (July, 1930), 269–70.

Everyone had different fathers. My mother she was not married. My father was white and Brother's father was white, but the others was colored. Because, see, in the country, they didn't have no money, and the only way they could get it was to go with these white men to get a little change. And that's why so many of them had these babies for the white men. Because they'd offer them a little change where colored didn't have nothing to give them. Nothing to help them get along—no money, nothing.

And when she'd tell me my daddy was white and was coming to see me, if I had listened to her, I probably would have had money. But I couldn't stand him. It made me mad when she told me that. He owned a grocery store. And when she'd tell me he was coming over and wanted to talk to me, I wouldn't even come out to see him. I didn't want to see no white man.

The other thing they could do on the plantation to get by was to put the children out to work. And so when I was eight years old, my mother sent me to live with a lady. Her name was Miz May. She wanted somebody to keep her company.

At first, I wasn't big enough to do anything, but she taught me how to read and write, crochet, knit, cook, and how to housekeep. She used to fool me to death. She'd come tell me that the fairy had hid a present, a big surprise, and she'd say, "Augusta, the only way you can find that surprise, you have to move everything, and make sure you general clean, because if you don't, you'll never find that surprise." And so, here I am working myself to death, just moving and dusting, moving, trying to find it. And I never did find it!

But I sat right by her and slept right in her room on a cot, right by her just like I was her daughter. And all I learned was through her, 'cause she would teach me everything right there. That's why I never did go to school.

And that's why I never did mingle. I mean, I never was with the colored much. And I made a dollar a week, and Mother was right there every week to get that dollar. I don't care what I wanted—I didn't get it.

Poor mother. She thought about that little dollar. I guess that helped her. But I'm glad Miz May helped me, 'cause she learned me how to housekeep and how to cook. And I never had to work hard. As I got older, I was mostly the cook and stayed in the house. I never did get out to farm, to work like the rest of them.

She really did a beautiful job, and when I came to Mobile, I knew how to work. When I got big enough, see, I left there. Aunt Cassie she was working in Mobile, and when she came home, we went to visit her. And I told her I was making a dollar a week and if my mother felt like getting it and spending it, she did. To me, it was just one of those things, and I went through with it, but I wanted better.

So my aunt brought a lot of us to Mobile and got us all jobs—my sisters and cousins, girl cousins. I went to work at Miz Nevitte's. My aunt had washed and ironed for these people for years. And they were so nice to her, she wanted to get us there.

When I went to Miz Nevitte, she didn't want to hire me. She looked me over, and she said, "No, Cassie, that child can't do this work." Cassie said, "You take her and try her." And they did, because Cassie had been washing and ironing for them for years and she was a good-looking woman, real fair, and long black hair. All my aunts, mostly, had a lot of hair, except the half-sisters. The aunts looked like Indians. It's pitiful, ain't it, things like that, back in the country?

But I came to Mobile. I was sixteen, and they made me the house-keeper. I worked there until I married. I was nineteen when I married. And Miz Nevitte she cried when I left. She had a fit because I ran away and didn't tell her until afterwards. Then I explained to her about him. I said, "I got to have a man that owned his own home." I married him, and I didn't go back to work for her until I was sixty-two.

I stayed home until the kids got bigger. Oh, I did serve parties, though. I'd have to wear my little white apron, black dress, and little cap, and go and serve those teas. And I made some money.

When the kids got bigger, I went to work for the Lazarres three days a week, then eventually five days a week. I made the grocery list and shopped and seen that the children had their clothes, and cooked.

They took out Social Security, and they paid me well, fifty cents an hour and it went right on up. And they would go out of town for months and paid me night and day to stay there. And each day I'd take the Lazarre children down and fix my husband's breakfast and then go back.

In fact, I was like one of the family. They really trusted me. Mr. Lazarre he was a lawyer, and Miz Anne's daddy was one of the richest men in town—didn't have nothing but money!

But Miz Anne was never happy. Because she drank, I was more like the mother when I was there. And when I left, right now, all of them, they love me more like a mama.

Mr. Lazarre and me ran the house. And I worked there till all those children were almost grown. I say, if you're working with a bunch, you do your job and don't worry about what they do, and it's up to their mama to find out. I didn't never interfere, but I'd see a lot of things I didn't like, and that's when I left there. When something went on that I didn't like, I didn't go back, and today she still don't know why I left.

Then I went back to the Nevittes. There, too, I was the housekeeper. I would write the grocery list, plan the meals. Old Miz Nevitte had a chauffeur and a lady to come in to general clean and a yardman. I paid the people because she was old and couldn't do. And I was the cook.

See, she had a heart attack when I was sixty-two, and I went back to work for her. She had the chauffeur to pick me up and take me to do shopping, mine and hers, and she had a nurse and she paid me a beautiful salary. She left me in her will. Her daughter, Miz Beth, is the one that looks out for me now. And Clarence, the chauffeur, would fuss at me for not having any work. Miz Nevitte would make him clean the bathtub and vacuum. He'd say, "Miz Swanson, you could clean that." I'd say, "Look, Miz Nevitte is paying me, and if she want me to come up and powder her face, pull her hairs, and comb her hair, that's what I'll do."

I didn't do no work, really. She was ninety-three, and I had to just help her—run the house and get her up and help her to get dressed if she felt like it. She'd have the chauffeur to take us riding. She had a wheelchair; they had an elevator to take her up and down and a walker.

That day she passed, that Monday, Clarence said, "Something is wrong with Miz Nevitte 'cause she always wanted to come out here." She didn't want to be in the yard. She was with me, and I had to read off all the old addresses and numbers out of this telephone book, and she made a new address book the day before she died.

And when she died, I was standing right there. She said, "Augusta, if I have a stroke, please don't let Ginny put me in the hospital." I said, "Miz Nevitte, I can't do nothing about it. That's your daughter." "Well," she said, "if you tell them, they won't."

And she said she hoped her yard was covered with flowers when she passed. And it was. She asked me to hold her hand. I was standing there holding her hand, and she said, "Augusta, don't leave me." I said, "I'm not going to leave you." All of a sudden, she looked up and said, "Oh, God, why don't you take me?" She turned my hand aloose, and I thought she was asleep at first. But she was gone.

And I was there by myself. She had a beautiful gold bracelet and a ring and a watch, and she had told me where she wanted me to put them—to lock it, keep the key, and when Ginny comes, give it to her. Miz Beth, her other daughter, laughs about that now. When they came, I said, "Here's the key to the china closet. I put everything I thought was valuable there." Because she had a daughter-in-law that wanted to take everything. So when I gave the key to her daughters, they were so happy. They said, "Augusta wasn't going to let nobody get into nothing."

See, on these jobs I was lucky all the way. I can't say anything but something nice. It's been beautiful.

Of course, at first I didn't get enough money, but other than that, it was nice. At that particular time, it was a certain salary they paid you, and that's what they paid unless they gave you extra for being nice.

I got a lot of extra. For doing and being nice and kind to those kids. And they always treated all my kids just like they treated me. Like old Miz Nevitte, when the kids graduated or something, she'd give me a check.

I just run into luck. But you know, if you meet with people that's used to money and have money, they're going to treat you nice. But you get this poor class, and they get into money, they don't know how to treat you. I never worked for poor class. It was always rich people that had money, so that's why I got along.

From an interview with Mary Yelling

Essie Favrot

It was probably fortunate for Essie Favrot (b. 1910) that, though like Augusta Swanson she was a country-bred black woman, unlike Swanson she was not isolated from blacks as a child. In fiction and in sociological accounts, the black domestics who show the most damaged psyches—who believe the whites' idea that blacks are inferior—are those domestics who live with their employers.* The work at the experiment stations described by Favrot might seem a difficult life for a child, but this work did not link her closely with the ideas of the dominant white class. Favrot displays more anger and humor toward the acts of whites than does Swanson. This ability to express anger, and to laugh at whites, we might trace to the difference in their early surroundings.

Favrot is a woman who, in questioning the ways whites and blacks interacted within the white household, decided to leave domestic work. She has a sense of humor about whites, particularly in her recollection of working for poor whites. She, like other black women, often laughed at the uniformity with which whites of all social classes felt the need to employ blacks. Such a tendency, in the minds of many black women, pointed to the helplessness of whites. Such a tendency also reflected back upon class divisions within white southern society. Langston Hughes, in "Cracker Prayer," wrote of a poor white man's request to God: "Lord, Lord, dear Lord, since I did not have a nice old colored mammy in my childhood, give me one in heaven, Lord. My family were too poor to afford a black mammy for any of my father's eight children. I were mammyless as a child. Give me a mammy in heaven, Lord."†

Essie Favrot is a tall woman who could scoop up my one-year-old daughter with one hand. When I visited her with Mary Yelling, she wanted to know who cared for "this little child" when I worked. Neighbors and friends gather at her house each week to watch football in the fall.

She lives in an older black neighborhood that has both small frame houses and newer brick ones. Her house is a brick one behind the wooden one she and her husband built in the 1940s. A red-clay driveway leads to both houses.

I was born in the country, and all of us worked. We worked mostly on this experiment station. Big farms would send trucks like four o'clock in the

---

*Fictional accounts that seem to show the more pronounced psychological damage among live-in workers are Ann Petry's *The Street* (Boston, 1946); Kristin Hunter's *God Bless the Child* (1964; rpr. New York, 1967); and Toni Morrison's *Tar Baby* (New York, 1981). Among sociological studies, see Judith Rollins, *Between Women: Domestics and Their Employers* (Philadelphia, 1985), esp. 173–78.

†Langston Hughes, "Cracker Prayer," in *Simple's Uncle Sam* (New York, 1965), 124–25.

morning, and all the people who wanted to work would go down there and load up on a truck and then come back home that evening.

I finished out of the eighth grade in the country. But by then my very oldest sister had come to stay with my aunt, and she decided it was time I came, too.

The onliest thing then was for a black girl to do was to get domestic work. So, I worked. First it was just about a two-hour job per day, five days a week for this lady that just had come up to me and asked me to work. I'd go down there to her house, clean up the house, do a little washing, and that was it. Fifty cent a day was what I made. They were poor people. They were probably just about as poor as I was, but the lady worked for a department store!

Then, I think, my brother's mother-in-law told me that this lady needed somebody to keep her kids. So I went there and worked. I was living on the place, and that's when I met my husband. This was in '39, and I remember the salary had gone up to a dollar a day. I was making seven dollars [a week] because I was living on the place. And I worked every day from seven to seven. You worked long hours, but you were making a dollar a day.

I slept up in the bedroom with the little boy. There was a servant house in the backyard, but it was occupied by the cook, which was a male. It was considered his house, but I used the bathroom there.

They were rich people. I guess they owned stock. And when my mother-in-law decided to sell half her land, I don't know why but it came for me to borrow the money. My husband had been working for his people much longer than I had. Anyway I asked them for fifty dollars to pay for the property, and they readily gave it to me. But they said they wouldn't help me to build a house. They had got stung with another maid borrowing from them. We paid the money back right quick, and they were surprised.

After that, I worked thirteen years for the Elliots. Now they weren't rich people. They both worked, and they had six children. I took over the running of the house. I did everything for them—the groceries, the cleaning up, the kids. I did all for the kids—took them to the park, to school, bought their clothes, saw that they wore the right clothes to parties, all that. My neighbors used to laugh because those Elliots were such poor people. Everyone knew they were. I mean not poor white trash—no. Just working people like myself. I was fond of those kids. I still am. I worked for them until my son was born. We still keep in touch. One of the girls just died. She had cancer; that was very sad. And their mother, I worry about her. She's had a hard time. Working for them—since they had all those kids, it was more like family for me there. I feel still sort of protective and maternal towards them. Not like I do my own family, no, but like I would any children I'd cared for that much, watched grow up. I'd help them still anyway I could. I would . . . not go back to work, but I'd help them any other way I could.

After that, I worked days till my son got old enough to go to school. Then I worked for the Helms. I worked there for a while. And they had four kids. Two were up in age, school-age children. And they had two little kids. And I just figured, since I was taking care of her kids and cooking for them, I'd have supper done when they got there and the kids fed and clean. They both worked. And they were so congenial at first. So, when my son started school not far from where they lived, I figured they wouldn't mind him coming down there after school and then going home with me.

But the first day after I did it, Mr. Helms say, "What happened, Essie? Did your son miss his bus?" I say, "No, he didn't miss his bus. It's nobody at home in the evening, so I just took your two children, and when we were on our way back from the park, we picked him up."

"I don't think it's going to be such a good idea, him coming down here. That lady next door . . . Mind you now, it's not us," he said. "But that lady next door don't want him playing down here."

So his wife she thought she could come home early so I could go home early, too. And the next evening she said, "I think I might enjoy coming on home, getting here early." I didn't say a word, because I knew I wasn't going to work for nobody who had two that were not toilet trained and I had to clean both of them up and I had to cook dinner for the whole family and clean the apartment and wash their clothes. I felt if I was doing all of that for her children and her, and mine couldn't come there in the evening, that they could have their job. After she paid me, I said, "Now you be sure and get you somebody." I was headed to my car when I said it. And I left there and never went back.

In the meantime a friend told me Miz Southerland was looking for somebody, and I went up there and interviewed and she hired me. And I found someone to keep my son after school. No, I wasn't really afraid to try to take him again. I just got somebody to keep him—not for my sake, not for my fear it would happen again. But I didn't want him to be shunned, to feel that again. If the Helms felt that way, maybe someone else might feel that way too.

You wouldn't want to work for a nicer person than Miz Southerland. She calls me now "her sister, her brown sister." She was very generous. I'd get Christmas off every year. I'd get two weeks off with pay, all the stuff left in the refrigerator—no sloppy stuff, just food that she had left. And she'd load me down with gifts for the whole family.

This was in the sixties. And it was during the time Martin Luther King was in Memphis settling this garbage strike that he got killed in. And I was sitting down there in her den that day watching the funeral and all that was going on with Martin Luther King, and the thought just occurred to me: I said, now here I am sitting here, and this man is there in Memphis and lost his life trying to upgrade the black people. And I'm sitting here making five dollars a day just as satisfied, and I said, "Lord, have mercy, Jesus, if it's your will, I'm to get out here and do better."

I had been looking in the paper at this nursing school where you go and pay a certain amount of money and take classes and become a nurse's aide. So I asked the Lord to give me a sign whether this school was on the up and up. And sure enough he put a song in my heart, and I just sang and sang that song until I came home. So I studied nursing for two years, every night after Miz Southerland's.

So I had my little diploma in hand, and I went out to the nursing homes to get a job. And no jobs! They told me they were hiring only experienced nurse's aides, but I applied anyway. I thought it might be discrimination, but I figured I'd keep trying. We were used to discrimination; it didn't stop me. I landed the position of the laundry manager.

Now I'm the executive housekeeper at a hospital, and I like it very much—more than I think I would like being a nurse's aide. I have more responsibility. I supervise fifteen people.

But doing domestic work, it didn't affect me too much. It was a job and you needed the money was what I thought. And it was better than life in the country working on those experiment farms. On the whole, when you don't know anything else, you can't snub your nose in the air to domestic work.

From an interview with Mary Yelling

Louvenia Walker

All but one black woman to whom we spoke were active in the church. As historians have long noted, for blacks the church as an institution addressed secular as well as spiritual matters. In the church's teachings on the hereafter, many black women found the means to persevere. To women like Louvenia Walker (b. 1932), the church was often the only established group to which they could voice—in one form or another—their earthly concerns.

Walker at one time wanted to leave the church. Her mother, she said, was too religious, too strict. Yet, in the interview Louvenia Walker spoke of her disappointments in a way that reminded me of what Alice Walker has called "a weary religion-restrained hatred."* I am unsure if her tempering of her anger and disappointment had to do with the fact that she was talking to me, a white person, or if it was mainly a tempering born of having little other alternative. I suspect that it was both.

Louvenia Walker brought from the country her aspirations, the religion of her childhood, and a thorough understanding of the customary behavior between whites and blacks. She spoke of how religion served her within the urban environment and of the need to see good in other people, to overlook the bad.

Perhaps more significant, she finds in her religion values that have helped to counteract some of the oppression and disappointment she feels. She has much knowledge of the whites for whom she has worked. She finds them lacking in a rich spiritual life, in a sense of their own good fortune, and in the ability to see what matters. As Judith Rollins has noted, "the most powerful protections" domestics have against accepting employers' definitions of them as inferior are "their intimate knowledge of the realities of employers' lives, their understanding of the meaning of class and race in this country, and their value system, which measures an individual's worth less by material success than by 'the kind of person you are.'"† Walker, then, feels some sense of superiority over whites. Although she seems to recognize the otherworldliness of the church of her youth, she also told me, "The older I get, the more I think those old people there knew the only way to get by in this world."

Louvenia Walker lives in an unpainted wooden shotgun house. Sometimes we sat in her front room, which has only a single light bulb, hanging overhead and strung from a corner plug. This is also the one bedroom, for it contains the only space heater. On spring and summer days, we sat on the porch. From there we could look across the street to the empty "separate but equal" high school built for blacks in 1960—new facilities meant to ward off integration. It has been abandoned since 1970.

---

*Alice Walker, *Meridian* (New York, 1976), 104.

†Judith Rollins, *Between Women: Domestics and Their Employers* (Philadelphia, 1985), 212–13.

A neighbor child came up and asked her if I am the lady she works for and if I need any other help at home. They talked of me as if I were not there.

I was born in Greenville, Alabama, in Butler County in the year of 1932. I was from a family of twelve girls and four boys, and we worked very hard 'cause my daddy had his own plantation, and that was a lot of work. My daddy, he worked out because he had to work to supply the farm. He worked at W. T. Smith Lumber Company. My mother worked in the fields, and she did washing and ironing or stuff like that for some of the white peoples that lived around the neighborhood. We had our own plantation because my grandfather had been friends with this old white man who let us buy it a little bit at a time at a fair price.

My mother would get up around four in the morning because we had that old wood stove. When I was coming up, we didn't have electric lights—we had kerosene lights. And she would get up and cook breakfast and get my daddy off to work and get all of us children that was going to school to school and those that went to the field to the field.

I was the baby-sitter and the cook in the family. And what my mother would do, she would pick all the vegetables and clean the meat and show me how to keep the water. She would put it on sometimes even before she went to the field. I'd have to keep it from burning. And sometimes she would make bread or something, and I had to keep the stove with wood in it. Then at twelve or one o'clock they would come from the fields to eat at our house, about twenty of them. Those were the people that worked for my daddy, that helped pick the cotton, chop the cotton. 'Cause of us being still small, he had to have more grown-up help.

I was fifteen when I had my first job for money. I was in school, but I did a part-time job baby-sitting for a white family. And I wanted to be a nurse. When I would keep those kids at my mother's, I knew I wanted to be a nurse. I baby-sitted all the kids in the neighborhood and kids of people working in the fields and my mother's kids. And I had one particular little girl—she wasn't my mother's—I always thought of her. She was about two years old, and she cried all the time. She just never was happy. And I often wondered what make a child do that—was it something they were born with, or were they allergic or what? She never did outgrow that crying, and so that's one reason I wanted to be a nurse.

And my teachers up there said I was pretty smart. So when I'd finished high school, Mama said I could leave. The funny thing was she said, "You pick the place you want to go, and we'll let you go."

My first place was in Chicago. Mama's aunt was living there that raised her, and she said I could come live with her. But Mama had grown up in Chicago, and she didn't want me to go there. She said, "You can go to Mobile," my second-place choice. I guess she knew I couldn't come home so often from Chicago.

I came down here in the last part of 1954. And my cousin, an older lady, was here, and I stayed with her. She was doing housework, so she started me with different people. And I kept on. Never did get to go to nursing school on account of I just felt I couldn't afford it and my aunt didn't know where I should go to find out about it. I still regret that.

The ones I was with the longest was the Andersons—the old lady and her son. Those Anderson kids, I worked for them since the youngest was six until he was eighteen. Their mother had died. And they was some good kids in a way. But they had a hard time. I came just that year she got sick.

Those kids they didn't understand sickness or death. Now that's one thing about growing up in the country and maybe just being black. Where your parents go, you go. So you saw sickness, and you went to funerals.

They had to take off their mother's leg. The children would stand back and peep at her 'cause they never seen a lady with one leg before. And one day I said, "Go in there and hug your mother and let her know you love her." I kept on at 'em 'cause they needed her and she needed them. And they finally went in.

She said, "I don't blame y'all about not wanting to see me with this one leg." I'd told the little girl that her mother would get an artificial leg, and the little girl said that to her mother. She said, "I'd rather be dead than to walk around on one leg."

Well, the next couple of weeks he [God] listen to her words, 'cause he taken her away. She wasn't but thirty-one, thirty-two years old. And I think that was the first funeral they ever had been to, 'cause the two older ones came back laughing about how their mother was laying there like she was asleep. And they was laughing at how the people cried and went on. I said, "Darlings, that's not anything to laugh and joke at." I said, "That was a sad occasion."

But now, see, in the country when a person dies, a child's mama and daddy going to take that child to the funeral. When a person die anywhere in the community, you could go to this church and they would ring the bell and everybody know what that tone meant, 'cause they had a different tone between the church meeting and death tone. So everybody rush out to the church and find out who is dead.

And I remember one time they found out my godmother Mary Ethel was dead. She loved my mother, and she always said that if she be the first to go that she wanted my mother to come over and put her clothes out and show the people how she liked to be put on the cooling board.*

So my mother had to go on. She took us with her. I must have been around nine or ten years old. They had to take Miz Mary Ethel, and they had these tin tubs, and my mother and about three or four more womens had to give her a bath. And after they gave her a bath and put her clothes on—well, mens was in there to help lift her—and they put her on this cooling board to the next day. Daddy and them made a box, a wooden box, 'cause there wasn't no caskets. And they would make some kind of little finishing cover and put it in the box.

I'd seen that happen many a time before I was nine or ten. I seen the people sad for the ones that passed and still taking care of them.

But now, Miz Mary Ethel—I remember her because when we were there and Daddy and them was fixing to put her on the wagon, all of the sudden we heard a growling like somebody burped. Everybody started looking around, and it was Miz Mary Ethel that burped! When she went to raise up, we all flew! Lots of grown people ran, too! She'd been in a sort of coma. Some kind of herb she had gotten and taken, it didn't agree with her, and it just put her to sleep! After that we called her the Walking-around Dead Lady!

Well, I couldn't tell those Anderson children that tale. But I tried to help them. Their daddy used to say I was the onliest maid that would get out and play ball with them and try to keep 'em satisfied. He told me that. I feel like if you find children like that, you keep 'em out of a lot of little devilment if you put in time with them. That will give them some kind of interest.

I'd let them help me around the house. I'd tell them it's good, whatever they did to help—which sometimes it would be and sometimes it wouldn't be, but I didn't want to disencourage them. I always loved those kids but after they growed up and got jobs, really they didn't need nobody. Most of the time I used to cook, but they were so busy getting ready

*The *cooling board* was a board or table on which the corpse was laid before burial.

to go out on dates or whatever, I told him, I don't think you need me anymore. He said no.

I used to keep in touch with them, but I haven't heard from them in about two years. I used to feel like they were part of my family, and I felt like they thought the same of me. Now, I don't know. But I miss them just like they're my own. I believe they miss me, but see, young peoples now they do their things. And now, those kids had a lot to get over. They might come back and be my friend one day.

But now sometimes I feel in these white homes, when they got so much, sometimes they don't know really what to do with it. They got to do something that they shouldn't do. When you're the maid, you see the craziness in these whites.

I worked for a lady that was an alcoholic, and she had children, but her children was grown, thank heaven. She wasn't an everyday drinker. She was about a three-or-four-month drinker. For every three or four months in the year, she would drink hard.

She'd come in and just fall out, and scare you to death, 'cause if you never been round people that drink and get drunk, it's scary. I'd never seen it. When I was a child, my father drank sometimes, but we didn't know it. Mama always kept a bed made up for him in the barn, and when we grew up, we found out that bed was for when he'd been drinking. We never saw him drunk.

One time, this lady came in drunk, and she went back in her bedroom. I heard the water running, and it kept on running. I decided I'd better go check on her—maybe she fell or hit her head or something. So I went and knocked on her door and yelled to her and yelled to her. She never said anything, so I opened the door and went on in. She was sitting on the commode just like staring. I waved my hand across her face, so her eyes kind of blinked. I said she's all right, so I cut the shower off and came on out.

About thirty minutes later she came in the kitchen, fell right by me. She had taken a razor blade and slit both wrists. It like to scared me to death. I put towels with ice and tied them around both wrists and called the police to send the paramedics, and called her daughter, and she came. I said, "I can't work here, because one time I might not catch her in time, and somebody find her dead, they might say I killed her." Her daughter said, "Lou, we wouldn't let nobody blame you." I told her, "I'd rather stop working."

She said: "Well, I tell you what. You come to work for me." And then she gave her maid to her mother 'cause her maid had worked around peoples like her mother before.

I'd be ashamed, you know—to have a nice house and be a good-looking lady and do that kind of thing.

From an interview with Susan Tucker

Louise Webster

In the following narrative, Louise Webster (b. 1913) recalls the blacks on her grandmother's plantation and also a nurse she knew in the city. She identified these blacks as instinctual beings who nurtured her in her youth. To show me how reminiscent they were of times gone by, she likened them to the house servants in *Gone with the Wind*.

Gone with the Wind, with its romantic story of the Old South, including particularly its characterization of the loyal and strong Mammy, has also made a lasting impression on many other Americans. Indeed, many writers on domestic work feel that this book and its film version affect the way people from many backgrounds still remember black domestic workers.* The black writer Alice Childress includes an example of this influence in *Like One of the Family*, a book that recounts humorous episodes in the life of a domestic worker. A domestic named Ellie tells her employer that she must quit her job in order to care for her own family. The employer's reaction is so extreme that Ellie is puzzled. The employer cries and moans, saying she had always thought Ellie would *never* leave. The narrator of the story, a domestic named Mildred, explains: "Well the upshot of it was that there was no way that Ellie could explain anything so's she'd understand it 'cause the way Ellie told it to *me*, this woman had read *Gone with the Wind* four times and . . . well, it's just given her ideas."†

Mammy, as portrayed by Margaret Mitchell and Hollywood, possessed a strength of character that appealed to readers and viewers of all races. This appeal cuts across many racial and class boundaries and reflects and reinforces the enduring popularity of the strong black female domestic in American literature and cinema. For whites, she is the mother who loves unconditionally and who forgives all, even those who enslave her. For blacks, the appeal of Mammy lies primarily in the fact that though she is aligned with whites, she is also more savvy and more dignified—more a person worthy of admiration— than are the whites for whom she labors. Jamaica Kincaid, another black writer, explained her own liking of *Gone with the Wind* in her article "If Mammies Ruled the World":

> A Mammy, I think, is different from your mother because while your mother is expected to love you, Mammies love you for no reason at all. A Mammy is fair, loving, loyal, nurturing, supportive, protective, generous, and devoted. . . .
>
> Black people do not like the image of Mammy anymore. . . . What I imagine black people are really objecting to when they disapprove of Mammies . . . is the system that produced those things. . . . Scarlett and Rhett and Melanie and Ashley were not civilized people and that's why they didn't deserve a Mammy. But the worst part of it is, they have successfully ruined for us any ideas about having Mammies. We may not be

*Margaret Mitchell, *Gone with the Wind* (New York, 1936); Jeanne L. Noble, *Beautiful, Also, Are the Souls of My Black Sisters* (Englewood Cliffs, N.J., 1978), 75–78.

†Alice Childress, *Like One of the Family: Conversations from a Domestic's Life* (Brooklyn, 1956), 52.

civilized people either, but I promise you that if [President] Gerald Ford were a Mammy we would all be a lot happier.*

Louise Webster is very happy to remember those servants who remind her of *Gone with the Wind*. We sat in a breakfast room that has a black lacquered wall, a Persian rug on the floor, and silk flowers on the table.

I told my sister you were coming, and we were so glad. There were so many of those domestics that we knew, and they were such a part of our lives—such a marvelous part!

Our old family plantation was up in Clarke County, Alabama, and I used to stay up there with my grandmother. Well, up there they were from all different places. Like I said to my brother the other day, "Oh, Brother, do you remember Nelson?" The best-looking gentleman—very black, but gentlemanly looking and his hair turned white and all. Nelson was a stately, beautiful man! And Brother said, "Well, you know it was rumored up there that Nelson was from African nobility, royalty." And he looked it. His carriage did.

There were others, too, and they each had native things in them that made them special. They all had different things that they did—native and instinctive things—although I don't know if any of that has come down to either their children or grandchildren or us. There are native things in each of us, and certainly you don't want to give them up. Like I said, my southern drawl, I intend to keep it.

But the native black ways—I don't know—they seem gone because the blacks can't work together. That's another subject, of course. The domestics we knew still had the native—the things in them that made them all stand out, become so special. And you knew about these special things because you knew them, knew them well. I had a little black girl up there that I used to play with all the time. She was supposed to be my nurse. We were the same age. She still has a fit every time I get up there. Daisy. She and I would take baths upstairs together, just like in *Gone with the Wind*. And she'd sleep in the room with me.

And they had a creek that ran around back with a little walkway. Daisy and I used to walk along there. Nelson would take us fishing. The blacks there, my grandmother and grandfather wanted them to enjoy them-

---

*Jamaica Kincaid, "If Mammies Ruled the World," *Village Voice Anthology, 1965–1980* (New York, 1982), 54–55.

selves. There was no time limits like today. There was an easiness about life. And you helped each other. You looked out for each other, too. Nelson would reprimand us, and Mother, I remember, if she saw any colored nurse doing something wrong, she would stop and reprimand them.

But now, those people on the plantation I'd see only on visits. We lived in Mobile, and in 1920 we bought a big old house downtown. That was when we met Aunt Cammy. Aunt Cammy Sole Ford was her name. Of course, the others were grand, but no one was like Aunt Cammy. She lived in the little house back of the big house that we moved to. She'd been there forever, and when they sold us the house, she couldn't leave. She just had to stay there. So she came with the house!

And we absolutely idolized her. She was the nurse. She took care of us, sort of, 'cause she was real old then. And if my mother and father went out, we put her in the best chair in the house and all of us would pile on her. We'd hug her and kiss her.

Just recently, we found a picture of her. It's the only one we've got of Aunt Cammy, and I should get my sister to get it out and make a copy of it. She was just ugly, and her face . . . She made you believe in evolution. But we thought nothing of it.

She couldn't read or write. But we would give her a magazine when we'd be studying. She'd sit there with it upside down for hours, just like she was reading it. One of us would go turn it up the other way. And that didn't make any difference to her. It wasn't like you were correcting her! She was just perfectly marvelous.

And she belonged to the Footwashing Baptist Church. And that is literally foot washing. We used to try to get her to church first because then the preacher would wash her feet. But the members washed the others' feet, like they did in the Bible. And we just thought it was wonderful. And she had some kind of white robe thing that they wore. I don't know exactly what, but we saved everything white for her.

We'd take her to church when we could, or we'd pick her up. The church was on Davis Avenue. They used to call it Colored Town. They didn't mind that. They liked having their own town, their own section. But she wasn't going to leave and live there. Not leave her house!

It was a two-story thing with these little steps that went up, and it had a balcony railing, and she had geraniums that just fell all down the thing! And she said, "'Tain't nothing to it. Just put the morning coffee grounds on geraniums." I try it now, but something has happened to the coffee grounds or me, because it is not the same! But she could make anything grow. Course they always could.

And up in that house she had two large pictures, you know, regular portrait size, of two black people—ancestors. They were gold framed. I thought they were oil pictures but my sister said that they were photographs, that they had glass over them. I wish I knew what happened to them.

But I remember exactly how she looked, and I think of her often. She didn't have much hair. She tied it up in tiny little knots. And she always wore a big old apron, and the apron covered way around. She wore simple little old gingham dresses. Mother would buy the material, and Aunt Cammy would make her dresses. But now the cook and maids would wear uniforms. That was the more modern way.

Aunt Cammy . . . She was not modern. She must have been an old woman. I am sure her parents were slaves. But she had lived in that house since she was a young girl. It may have been that she'd come down from the country to stay with some kin. And she adopted us, and she loved that church, and she had some vague kin here. I know that, because when she was very old and very ill, Mama nursed her for the longest time in the little house and took care of her completely. Then when she got where it was impossible, some kin that lived over there on that side of town took her. Mama still went there everyday to see her and take care of her. And one time she got away from those people over there, trying to get back home to her little house. I remember that was sad. She was just so marvelous. None of us would have liked to have not had her in our lives.

Now, the cook we had was named Juliette. She was a dark one, but she was just so Indian-looking. And she lived to be pretty old, too, and she ended up staying in the family, too. And Inez was the maid, and she did everything else. She was about my age—no, a little older, but all of us just adored her. She was this good-looking young, young girl when she came to us, and she learned to press like a French laundress and learned to cook from Juliette.* And later when my aunt was without help and Juliette had gotten old and couldn't manage that much cooking and doing like she had done in that big house, my mother gave Juliette to my aunt. And then Inez moved up as the cook; she had learned so many things from Juliette.

But all of these people were tender and gentle, and they were very

*French laundress was a term that in Mobile and New Orleans was applied to women who were especially skilled at laundering and pressing.

sensitive. They *sensed* things. If you weren't feeling well, they could just pick something up, a rag or something and touch you, and it felt better. They had old-timey, funny ways about medicine, because they were basic things, like salt and soda and potatoes—these were medicinal to them. And they knew more things to do like that, and how to take care of something. I always loved how sensitive they were, how they sensed things, though I still think blacks have a lot of that. It's a sort of protection of themselves.

But that era, for the most part, is gone. They were happy then. So we didn't see the bad sides of segregation. They were learning all the time. They had thousands of years to catch up, and people used to teach their servants as much as they could.*

You know, I think respect for . . . whatever, a different class or a different color, a different age . . . respect is the greatest power I know. I felt that in bringing up children, I had to respect them if I expected them to respect me.

I learned that from the colored. They had such respect for you, even for us children. I certainly didn't learn it as it applied to children from my mother. She used to say, "Well, I can't help you nurse your children. I don't know how; I never nursed you all!"

So I learned that from them. They made the best nurses in the world.

I think now we don't respect the servants in the same way, because they don't respect us or themselves or their work. They don't like doing it, they don't want to do it, and they just want the money.

I can see that they want more opportunities, but I get sad sometimes that things have changed so. I'm very grateful I did know the ones I've known.

From an interview with Susan Tucker

---

*The idea that blacks were primitive people who had "thousands of years to catch up" was one commonly held by many people in the late nineteenth and early twentieth centuries. See Herbert G. Gutman, *The Black Family in Slavery and Freedom, 1750–1925* (New York, 1976), 531–44.

Anne Robertson

Southern white children growing up in households that employed a domestic worker were often helped in the emotional separation from their mothers and given more freedom than children living in families in which the mother was the primary or only care giver. Anne Robertson (b. 1926) and a number of other white women mentioned these benefits to their childhood and maturation. The black domestic was remembered as a neutral figure, particularly for teenage girls. The black domestic, as Robertson says, often became something of a "family therapist" who balanced the psychodynamics of the family.

In addition, many of the white interviewees seemed to be saying that they patterned part of their self-image, particularly their image of themselves as mothers, on black domestics as well as upon their biological mothers. Within such patterning, one can locate many interactions involving gender, race, and class that tell us how white women came to view black women.

For example, white and black women often were said to exhibit opposite characteristics. White women were encouraged to be passive and to hide whatever strength they might possess. They were often taught to fall back upon emotional displays in times of crisis. Black women, on the other hand, were encouraged to be active and to display whatever strength they might possess, albeit strength couched in the stoical acceptance of the traditional behavior dictated for blacks. They were often taught that in times of crisis they should fall back on their own abilities to earn money or do whatever was needed.

Such stereotypes, in conjunction with racial custom, prevented any real reciprocity between black and white women. Yet, white girls, as they grew up, did draw from black women many of their learned behaviors. This was particularly true among those white women who felt most keenly the social changes concerning the roles of women in recent years. It was also true among white women who had to deal with marital and financial problems. White women, in times of change and crisis, remembered the resilience and the perseverance, as well as practical responses, of black women to such problems as child care and money management.

However, just the incorporation of these images did not mean that the cycle of life that usually exists between girls and their female care givers could be completed. White girls could not "become" their black mothers. Instead, white women seem to have wanted to "reproduce" this relationship for their children. This seems to be an important reason why many southern white women continue to employ domestics.* Both for themselves and for their children, they want the balance of another care giver within the family and the familiarity of emulating the households known to them as children.

---

*The influence of the black domestic as a "second mother" to white children needs further study. This brief discussion draws on Nancy Chodorow, *The Reproduction of Mothering: Psychoanalysis and the Sociology of Gender* (Berkeley, 1978).

Anne Robertson touches upon some of this process. She remembers the strong domestics from the country who helped her mother. Her own life was not like her mother's, which had been marked by naps and constant help. She therefore sees the labor of black women somewhat differently.

Robertson has a strong voice with a marked southern accent. On her coffee table were a Mary Gordon novel and *Our Bodies, Ourselves*. On her mahogany buffet were library books, pictures set in silver frames, and a crystal biscuit barrel filled with shortbread cookies.

Did I tell you about when Mother died? She went in the hospital Tuesday night and died Friday in the late afternoon. She was ninety-two, and she developed pneumonia. Well, we didn't have time to set up nurses, and I called Sarah Sells, who'd been our sitter. Sarah came, and she was with Mother in the hospital room when we couldn't be there. Well, on Friday, since I'd been up two nights and the doctor didn't know how long it might be—it might be a week or ten days—I went home to rest. My youngest daughter Lillian stayed 'cause her car broke down, and she took a nap on the cot in the room with Mother and Sarah.

Sarah said the minute my sister and I walked out of the room, Mother closed her eyes and died. And of course, Lillian was the only one from the family with her. I said, "Lilly, what did you do?" And Lilly said, "Mother, if I'm ever in the room with anybody that dies again, I hope a great big black woman is there to hold me." She said, "Sarah just grabbed me and held me and held me and patted me, and held me, held me, and held me."

So these maids you're asking about . . . well, that gives you an idea. They're really a very important part of the network of life in this part of the country. Mother, over a period of seventy years, had three maids and felt very close to all of them. We were always taught that they were our friends.

The first one was Mattie. She was big and fat and jolly, and the kitchen always smelled like rolls and pies. She left when I was about five, and then we had Edwina from that time till the time I went to college. And Edwina would come before breakfast and stay till after supper. And she ate a box of Ritz Crackers every day, and she was jolly, very aware of what was going on, had many marital problems, and always told us everything about them. Lots of times she would come to the house in the middle of the night to get away from her husband.

We still hear from Edwina. She ran away from her husband. She came that last time in the night, and she was terrified. She was afraid he was going to hurt her. And she said, "I'm going to tell Cicero that I'm coming here to work tomorrow, but soon as he goes to work, I'm going to have the moving van come and move all my things out. When he comes home, I'm going to be gone. I'm going to be on the train to New York. But he will call you. He will come by here. He will ask. Don't tell him. Tell him you do not know, you did not see me." So Mother loaned her a little money and she left.

Mae came after Edwina left. Of course, Mother had a yardman to do the heavy work, but Mae did the rest. Cooked a hot meal every day. Went to the store, got the groceries, came back and cooked. Mother never drove. And as she used to say, "I think I've been very smart to manage all this."

The story my children like about Mother and the maids is about Mae. Mae came when I was a senior in high school, and she was there until Mother dismantled, which was nearly thirty years later. Once I had asked Mother to show me how to make corn relish. She always sent so much corn relish over to our house, and everyone liked it so much. So she said, "We'll go with Mae to the farmer's market." And so Mae drove us there and Mother sat in the back and she'd roll down the window and have the people bring her all the peppers and corn and so on. We went home and had a big lunch, and then she said, "Let's take a little nap." So we did and then afterwards, we came downstairs and there was a big pot of relish on the stove. Mother stirred it and said, "See, Anne, there's nothing to making corn relish."

Well, of course, Mae had been the one sitting out in the yard shucking the corn, cutting the peppers, and standing over the hot stove!

Mae is my age, and she came from a small town in Georgia, and she was the most timid, the most self-conscious, the shyest, [most] frightened person when she came to Mother. And Mother befriended her and was really kind to her and taught her how to serve, taught her how to clean—everything. And when she left, she opened a restaurant and bar. She said, "I'm going to use all these recipes." And we've heard from her, too, just recently.

And she, too, had marital problems. I had, from a very early age, the impression that poverty and—two adults working in one household caused problems. I saw it in these maids. But now, Champ was her husband's name, and he had a grocery store. And she opened her restaurant on the other side of it. She's still with him, and they've done OK.

Mother had a wonderful relationship with Mae. I have, on my den wall—and nobody but really my sister and brother would know how much she means to me—I have a picture of Mae on the back steps.

Oh, they gave us so much courage, encouragement, support, and love! I mean, I always think of the maid as being the family therapist. You know, you could go to them and say anything, and they would say, "Oh, bless you, you've had such a hard day." Where a mother might be a little detached or busy with something else, the maid gave the love, the support, the continuity. And if they happened to clean and cook a little, that was fine! Psychologically, they were very supportive.

No, I don't remember what they were paid. I remember Daddy gave Mother seventy-five dollars every week, and that was to pay for the help and the groceries for our family of five and whoever else ate there. I remember when I married in 1950—I remember realizing that they did not make a whole lot. But Mother paid a little more than most people did. I think she paid Mae at the time she dismantled—she paid her about twenty-four a day for six or seven hours. But she said Mae did so much for her that she wanted to do for her. And of course, if any of them needed anything—medical help or clothes or whatever—it was there. I don't recall that the salaries were much, but the nurturing of the persons themselves was there.

It is, I guess, hard for people of your generation to understand. These were people who were in the middle of the depression for a lot of the time I remember, and whose mothers or grandmothers were born just after the Civil War. Both the depression and the war affected the cash flow. But even today, there are two types of people—people who treat people like people, children of God, and people who treat people like someone to serve them. You still have that today.

But now, personally, since 1950, I've had three maids, I'd say, but I never had help full-time. I had Marguerite, Marguerite Mary Taylor. She lives not far from here, and I talk to her really very often. I've talked to her twice in the last two months. She stopped work when she became sixty-two because she wanted to draw her pennies, she said. But she stayed about ten years. I had her two days a week, sometimes three, and she was a very large, very active, easygoing person and didn't worry about a thing—just very jovial. Not much of a cleaner, but peaceful and happy and large and fat. She made good gumbo and fried chicken.

And then later I had Georgia Washington, who I just could live with the rest of my life. She came three days a week while I was working. And I paid her a good bit more than minimum wage because she drove. And I would ask her to come at twelve and stay till supper so that someone would be here in the afternoon for my youngest, again Lilly.

And when everybody had left and I was by myself, I said, "Georgia . . ." And she said, "I know, Miz Anne. You can't afford me. And I need a job so that I can draw more Social Security." She was fifty-nine at that time. And so I got her a job at a seafood place where she still works. She had to have an operation, and they paid for it, which made me feel so good.

And then, even after she started there, she continued to come to our house at four o'clock just three days a week, to be sure I was all right, and if I had company, she'd come and clean up. Or when I would be going out of town, she'd help me get ready. When I went to Europe, she came over and cleaned the brass, the silver, got the house in spotless condition, and she said, "I know that you don't want to come home to a dirty house."

And she's so resourceful. She had garage sales about one Saturday a month, and when I would clean out closets, I would always just give her everything. And she would take it. I'd say, "Georgia, I know there's a lot of junk in there that you probably don't want." She'd say, "Oh, I can sell this."

And she has a very nice house. Her house is about the size of mine—a three-bedroom house and not two miles away. And since she hasn't worked for me, I've always gone by at Christmas to give her a check.

I love Georgia. I really do. All right, this will give you an idea about her, even though she wasn't working for me. When we had the hurricane, I was in Denver with my sister. I had gone out there and we were going to take a little trip. And the news came about the hurricane. Well, the anxiety nearly went out the top of my head—worrying about it and particularly knowing our house is low. The hurricane hit that night. And I tried the next day . . . I must have dialed Mobile numbers for two hours, and they'd always have a busy signal. And there was nothing I could do. Well, the hurricane was on Wednesday, and on Friday morning at six, the phone rang at my sister's. It was Georgia. I had asked her to watch out for the house. "Miz Anne, I walked to your house and everything's all right." She wasn't even working for me then. She was just a sweet, responsible person.

I said, "Georgia, how did you get over there?" She said, "Well, it was hard. I couldn't drive. I climbed over the trees. I climbed over the telephone poles. I walked through everything." She said, "You can hardly get down your street. It's bad, but your house is all right." She said, "There's a magnolia tree on the side of it in the back, but the roof did not break. And nothing in the house is damaged." Now that tells you what kind of person Georgia Washington is. She's really been a grand friend.

And she is very close to her church, as was Marguerite Taylor. They belong to the Holiness Church, and they used to march on certain days, and she would always be passing an envelope, and I would give her money. I asked her one time how she felt about her church, and she said, "Well, I'm saved. I'm a Christian."

I think she meant that she had faith and that things happening in the world now didn't matter so much. I think religion gives them the perspective to keep going. Because of religion, I think, they didn't hate us as much. You know, after being in India last summer and seeing the English from the Indian point of view, that is the only reason I can think of why the blacks don't hate us more. And maybe they're kinder than white people. They must be, because they're bound to have resentment. They really are.

Katy, who worked so long for my in-laws, she was a great person, and I always wondered why she didn't resent them more. In her case it seemed repressed more than in other blacks I've known. She was a cousin of one of those civil rights leaders, but she didn't talk about it too much. She thought they shouldn't be making such a big deal about it all. I thought she had been apparently so beat down—I guess that is the phrase—that she didn't realize she had the right to protest.

My children loved Katy. And they would say, "I want to go to Katy's house today." They didn't even call it their grandmother's. And I remember her at my wedding. We were married at night, and I was just overcome with emotion. Here I was leaving my family, leaving my church, and did I really know what I was doing? And my eyes filled up with tears in the back of the church, and Katy came over to me and dried my eyes and she said, "Don't worry, Miz Anne. We're going to be good to you."

I remember Katy a lot. One time—her house was in terrible shape and she wanted to get in the project, and so I asked a friend of mine who worked at the housing board to get her in right away. And she did. Katy was very happy, but then she died not long after that.

I don't know if my experiences are typical. The only thing I remember as a child, being reared so close to the church, is: "Red and yellow, black and white, we are precious in His sight. We are little children of the world." I really was taught that from the earliest age. I felt these are God's children just as much as I am. They were very connected to us, and we to them. And you have to have black friends—you really do—because they are part of the same community.

We were taught to treat them with dignity. And as children, they helped us, not just our mother. We understood that—that such help was something that was good. Because of them, we had a lot of freedom.

But now, the other one I used to have come baby-sit was Marthalena Davis. And Martha—when my husband would take her home, she would always sit in the front seat. This was in the fifties, and it would embarrass him to death. Isn't that funny? And I wouldn't have even thought anything about it. That shows you how different we are even in our own families. And we're all different depending on who we're dealing with.

Sarah, the sitter who was with Lillian when Mother died, she called me not too long ago. And she had told me earlier that her son, who was a high school senior, had impregnated a girl. And Sarah didn't know what was going to happen. She was so mad with him, and he'd flunked out of school.

I said, "Well, what's happened to Jeffrey?" She said, "Well, he had that baby." I said, "Sarah, are you taking care of that baby?" "No way, Miz Anne."

So here's the nurturing great big loving black woman for us, who's tough on her own. But people are always harder on their own children. I'm harder on mine. Psychologically, these maids balanced the white family. They helped many a white child to grow up in an easier way.

From an interview with Susan Tucker

Ellen Owens

Ellen Owens (b. 1952) tells a story that begins, "I never will forget." This was a phrase heard over and over in the interviews and one most often used to begin an account of some incident that seemed to have been told and retold many times. The way the women spoke in giving these accounts—the gestures, embellishments, and digressions—suggested to me that both whites and blacks have used one another as subjects to create continuously evolving stories to explain the workings of their lives together. These are stories that give factual accounts embroidered with humor, and they probably change as the storyteller decides to add something, leave out something, or vary the order of the telling. In the interviews they seemed to be almost standard responses, particularly to my questions for whites about the perceived strength of black domestics.

Owens, for example, readily told the story she "never will forget" in which a black domestic calls down a white policeman. Such a story gives humor to popular theories concerning the alliance of upper-class whites with blacks. There is a sense, however, that such stories come too quickly to mind. In answering my questions, several of the white women launched into these stories, but halfway through, I could tell from their slowed voices that they were not quite sure they should have begun. They were probably asking themselves if the oft-repeated story was actually racist. The educated women I spoke with were sensitive to saying the "wrong" thing. The taboo against discussing race and a fear of saying something inappropriate (a fear born of changed attitudes toward race) made not just one but two reasons for caution.

For these reasons, a number of white women would not sign release forms. They had told stories that they had heard all their lives; they had spoken as they had heard people speak all their lives. Yet, they heard these stories anew when they realized they would be written down. They realized that we live by unwritten, oral tradition and that such stories do show us as, perhaps, more racist than we had thought ourselves to be. Our unedited words are often those that are most familiar and also those that tell us more than we want to know about the culture in which we live.

Something like this happened as Ellen Owens told the story about the black domestic and the policeman. She quickly turned from this story and spoke instead of her mother's illness and of the black domestics who helped at that time. In other words, she turned to more serious memories, speaking of the strength of black domestics in a more specific, realistic way.

She lives in a house built in the 1940s with closets along every hall and storage areas above the doors. There are many small rooms in her house—a study, two small porches, a breakfast room, children's playrooms. She has always lived a life of privilege, and yet she is very unassuming and defines herself as not different from other southern women.

It's interesting that you're asking about the families of these domestic workers. In my life there was Mama Lou, and what I remember most often about her family was her funeral. I remember her funeral.

I was living in Boston then, and I flew home to the funeral. And I remember that Amelia—her daughter who I had known when I was little—Amelia was standing by the grave. And they had lowered the coffin, and she was just crying. She was just sobbing. Her older sister was named Adele. And Adele said, "Come on, Amelia. We've got to go." And Amelia wouldn't leave. That stands out in my mind—that she just stayed there and sobbed. I was standing a little behind her, and I didn't know how to help.

I suppose I felt that I should have known how to help, that I should have known her better, because I knew Mama Lou all my life. She came when I was about six months old, and she was there until she died. She got cancer and died when I was twenty-five.

And she was always like my mother. That's why I called her Mama Lou. My mother and father both were real busy, and when I was ten years old, my mother decided to become a doctor, so Mama Lou was the one who raised us.

She came every day but Thursday. She came at seven in the morning and left sometimes as late as nine or ten. She was always with us. And even when we'd go on vacation—we'd always, in the summers, go to New England and different places for like a month at a time. (I'll show you a picture of her with me in Nova Scotia)—she always went with us—everywhere. And so she really was just a member of the family. I remember riding on a chair lift with her in Vermont and going to rodeos with her out West and everything! We would never have thought of not taking her with us.

No, I don't remember her missing her girls or sending postcards to them or anything on these trips. I guess they stayed with their daddy, and maybe Adele, the older one, watched out for Amelia. I don't remember that it was ever discussed.

I couldn't be without her! And many, many a Thursday, I'd go over to her house. You know, since I didn't want to be away from her, I'd go spend the day over there and be part of their family.

The only thing I remember—I do remember that her husband drank and I was aware that he was not a very good person. And I also knew that Adele she was not Mama Lou's real daughter. It may be that Adele was his child. The more I think about it, [the more] I think that might be it. I'm not real good at details, but I remember there was something about Adele I never completely understood.

I knew Amelia better. She used to come over and play with me when I was little, and I wasn't the nicest child in the world. We were friends, but I probably had the upper hand, knowing she was my maid's daughter. I said mean things to her, and she never really said mean things to me. She probably didn't feel like she could.

And no one ever stopped me or heard me, I guess. We never talked about race in my family—never. We never talked about me having more than Amelia, either, materially. The only thing said that I can remember even remotely related to the topic was that Lou was our housekeeper— she wasn't our "maid," according to my mother. So I always worry, still, if the word *maid* has bad connotations.

To me, she was perfect! Because she was an emotional person, and she loved me and took up for me. And the thing she used to say was, "You won't be little always." When I'd get mad, she'd say, "You'll be walking out of here before you know it." Whenever my parents would get mad at me or there was a conflict, it's like she would admit there were problems.

It wasn't like, "You've got to live here blah, blah, blah." It was, "Don't worry, baby"—she called me baby—"You won't be little always. You'll have a family of your own, and you won't have to worry with all this." Which is kind of neat! Most people would say, "Now, listen here, you should be thankful for this, this, and this." Her response kind of relieved me.

And she was a pretty strong person. I think she felt a lot of power, probably because she worked for my mother and people respected my mother so much.

I never will forget—a story my husband loves to tell—when we got married, the day of our wedding, as a matter of fact, we were going to a luncheon, and Paul was running late, and he was stopped and got a ticket. When he walked in, he said, "Louise, I'm really upset," he said. "I've just got a forty-dollar ticket."

She said, "Well, we just can't have that on your wedding day. I'm going to call my friend Lieutenant Kelley." He was the chief of police or the assistant or something. She called him and said, "I work for the Stricklands and my future son-in-law was stopped and he was trying to get my baby to a luncheon for their wedding on time. And I don't think he should have to pay it."

And you know, they tore that thing up! She did that all on her own. I don't know which way it worked—whether she had a real input or whether my mother was behind it. But it was her idea!

Now the other maid we had a really long time was Estella Saunders. And talking of Mama Lou's death, I often feel that when Estella dies, I will really lose something. I feel like I have a bond with her that has continued.

She came when I was about five. And she continues to have a tremendous influence on me. I mean, I call her, and she dreams about me and calls me and worries about me and so on. And she is a person who relaxes me. She called me baby, too, and still does, and she says, "Baby, you don't need to worry. You can only take one day at a time."

But in another way, Estella's a real moralizer! When she worked for us, she used to drive Paul crazy. She'd kind of lecture us all the time and tell us how to do with the children. It never bothered me, because I was used to listening to her talk like that. I can remember when I was young her saying stuff that we had to do. She was always real big on mothers, too. We'd say something about Mother, and she'd say, "Oh, you'll only have one mother. That's all you'll ever have!"

But what is interesting is that she really lives out that philosophy. Her mother is ninety-five, and Estella does everything for her.

She saved. . . This is incredible. A year or two ago when she knew her mother was coming to live with her, she wanted to add on a bedroom, onto her house. And she talked to me about it and asked me to find a contractor. And I did, and she told me how much she was interested in spending. Then she told me that at some point when she was working for my mother, she started saving like Christmas money and birthday money. And she's been putting it under her bed all these years. She had almost twenty thousand dollars. She said she's saved every gift she's ever gotten from my grandmother, my mother, my father, everybody in the family. She had it in cash envelopes. Paul was horrified! And it was all under her bed.

She is, well, not smart that she put it under the bed, but a real determined person. Can you imagine saving that money? And she knew she wanted to do that for her mother.

She has a real strong feeling of loyalty to her mother, and had to my mother, too. And I was thinking about Louise—Mama Lou. Both Louise and Estella loved my mother. They both worshiped my mother. I'm sure [it was] because she was good to them. I think they got the same pay as most people—twenty-five dollars a week is what I remember—but Mother paid for everything. She paid for all their medical bills and gave them many, many things. And she paid for Louise's children's education. Estella's children were grown, but Mother had a real part in Louise's children's education. She would call Louise into her room—I can remember this—and talk to her about what the girls were interested in. And when they got out of college, she made sure they had good jobs in their professions.

But Estella, when my mother was real sick—she got where she couldn't eat anything and all the food had to be liquified and she couldn't move—and Estella just *took care* of her. She had a nurse towards the end, too, but for a long time, except at night Estella did everything. And I often think, my gosh, if Estella hadn't been there and I had had to take care of Mother . . . You know, I believe blacks are stronger, at least compared to me. I don't think I could do it physically or mentally or anything else.

And Mother she was pretty demanding. If Estella didn't do things exactly right, Mother wasn't mean, but she would let her know that it wasn't right. It takes such tremendous emotional strength to take care of somebody just all day every day, at their beck and call, and yet Estella just did it with the greatest of ease. She loved my mother and felt like my mother did everything in the world for her. And she was completely unselfish and loving to my mother. I think every moment she helped my mother, she did it just completely unselfishly and lovingly, which I could not have done.

From an interview with Susan Tucker

Part IV

Giving and Receiving

I do not remember much about the giving and receiving between whites and blacks that went on around me when I was a child. Surely whites often gave baskets of food and cast-off furniture and clothing to blacks, but as I grew older, I saw that these gifts did little to change the conditions under which black domestics lived. Still, I never questioned or analyzed the situation. It appealed to me, simply because I, like most people, liked to give. In giving, I felt in some unconscious way that I was in a position of relative wealth from which I could give.

The women who speak in this book were bound to their black domestic or their white employer in many ways, but perhaps the most obvious was in the giving and receiving that went on between them. Giving and receiving were rituals within the domestic worker–employer relationship built upon ancient traditions of interaction between people separated by class. They were also an important part of customary behavior between whites and blacks in the segregated South.

Giving and receiving in all cultures are symbolic acts that carry many levels of meaning. Giving is traditionally considered an act of concern, care, and even love for another person. However, it is also an assertion of one's own superiority, as well as compensation for another act. Receiving means an acceptance of the giver—whether as a friend or as a superior—and an acceptance of the obligation to reciprocate.

Among the foremost elements in each narrative in this book is the giving and receiving of gifts on each side of the employer–domestic worker relationship. Often gifts were central to that relationship. They were remembered and recounted in almost every interview, sometimes with great feeling and always with the idea of explaining how the relationship worked.

Judith Rollins, in her study of domestics and their employers in the Boston area, states that such gift giving falls within the tradition of "maternalism"—a modification of paternalism that takes into consideration the importance of the fact that the employers and domestics are female. Rollins maintains that the function of the domestic worker is "the validation of the employer's class status (and thus the hierarchical class system). And I go further: the presence of the deference-giving inferior enhances the employer's self-esteem as an individual, neutralizes some of her resentment as a woman, and where appropriate, strengthens her sense of self as a white person."[1]

Rollins identifies the gifts given by employers to domestics as expressions of maternalism and finds that they have two distingushing characteristics. First, no return is expected. Second, they are almost always secondhand or discarded articles. She points out that employers choose cast-off, secondhand gifts because these items best reflect the relationship between superior and inferior. And she shows how the acceptance of the gifts (whether or not they are later thrown away) and the domestic's response (which always appears to be one of gratitude) are viewed by the domestic "as another part of the performance necessary to survive in this particular kind of job."[2]

Although I agree with her findings, in the interviews I heard variations concerning giving and receiving that are perhaps unique to the southern pattern. The black domestics whom I heard on tape or spoke with, like those described by Rollins, understood the nature of the giving—its complicated purpose to keep them employed at a subsistence level and at the same time to let employers feel both generous and superior. But the domestics in the South also reacted in two ways not described in the Boston study. First, a number of them refused to accept food. Both black and white women remembered domestic workers who announced, "I don't tote." Toting was, of course, the practice of taking food from the employer's kitchen as a supplement to paid wages or, less frequently, in place of wages. Toting was also referred to as "taking home the service pan." Both black and white women referred to toting as a practice that originated in slavery. Thus, black domestics correctly associated this sort of compensation with a system designed to keep them inferior to wage-earning employees. In consequence, some spoke up against it.

Three white women remembered black domestics who in the late 1920s absolutely refused to tote, making it a condition of their acceptance of a

1. Judith Rollins, *Between Women: Domestics and Their Employers* (Philadelphia, 1985), 180.
2. *Ibid.,* 192, 194.

job that they not be asked to do so. Three other white women remembered black domestics who expressed a sense of disapproval at being offered food in addition to wages, by refusing, for example, to take extra food home after parties in the white household. Four black women remembered asking not to be compensated for low pay with food. The earliest such specification dated from the 1920s; the latest, from the 1960s.

Black domestics also used their own right to give gifts as a means of deflecting some of the psychological oppression they felt from the gift giving by whites. This reverse gift giving seems to have been another way black southern domestics provided a balance in their relationships with their white employers. The fruit basket, a traditional gift in the South at Christmas, for example, was mentioned as a gift given by black domestics to white employers, as well as by white employers to black domestics. A white woman born in the 1920s described how a black domestic would place the fruit basket on the dining room table each Christmas Day: "You'd see it first thing . . . with a big red bow on it," she recalled. White women of all ages remembered being given gifts on birthdays or at weddings or for no special reason at all—because, for example, "she thought I needed it." In being given such gifts, white women were sometimes shamed by black women. As one white woman told me: "I will always remember the canisters that Elvira gave me when I got married. I remember feeling how kind it was of her. I knew she didn't have that much money, and I knew, for example, that the only time we ever gave her or any of her children anything new, all wrapped up in white paper, had been at Christmas. Instead, we were just always giving her something we'd gotten tired of."

When black domestics did not give these literal gifts, they gave another gift, the gift of listening. Their work, after all, required that they know much about the psychological makeup of their white employers. Black domestics knew the intimate details of white lives and could and often did give white women emotional support. This listening became their specialty, and it contrasts sharply with the impersonal gifts of white women—the turkeys for holidays, the cast-off clothing and other household items. In this case, too, black women engineered some balance in the relationship by giving from a position of strength. They believed themselves to be the stronger women emotionally. They saw their emotional support of white women as reflecting their religion and their decency. They saw that they possessed something that was of greater importance than material wealth and white skin.

Such attitudes did help black women surmount some of the psychological oppression, but the fact remains that they led tiring lives as working wives and mothers and were very poorly compensated. Cast-off items coupled with wages may have helped black women to provide for their families, but only at such a level that they could not rise out of poverty. They could not even afford time for much self-analysis about their relationship with their employer. They tended, I believe, to draw themselves inward, to work hard at maintaining their dignity in a very limited and private environment. The nature of domestic work—hidden within the private home, most often without the benefit of co-workers—prevented domestics from achieving any collective power that would have helped them get beyond the established patterns of coping. The social forces that disfranchised all blacks reinforced the established patterns.

Indeed, the giving and receiving that went on between white and black women may have worked to add even greater intensity to the power struggle between the two. Consider the tension created when the white employer frequently gave to assuage her own guilt. The black woman had to respond as if the cast-off gifts were not blows to her self-image. Beverly Guy-Sheftall suggested such tension in her description of the South as a biracial society that resulted in "exaggerated forms of racial and sexual stereotyping." Gloria Wade-Gayles further noted that economic conditions coupled with such stereotyping "created tension between black and white women and, even more unfortunately, caused black women to cope with life as it is, rather than seek to make it what it should be."[3] Thus, black women both deferred to white women to an extreme degree and coped with this deference in traditional feminine ways: by relying on a personal but understated strength, by keeping their children fed and clothed, and by maintaining the connections that existed. Unfortunately, such responses could not pull black women out of poverty, and they worked against the development of a political consciousness. They became almost like cloistered nuns besieged by forces they could only withstand by focusing everything upon their God—hoping, praying, and building in small, humble ways. Only one black woman who spoke with us expressed political opinions.

Most of them expressed some discomfort when they were asked how things could have been different. They argued, for example, that in accepting the gifts, they chose the only possible means to get by. They

---

3. Both quotations are from Gloria Wade-Gayles, *No Crystal Stair: Visions of Race and Sex in Black Women's Fiction* (New York, 1984), 7–8.

defended the system because they saw it as the only way to bring in more for their families and themselves and to maintain their own dignity. They defended this ritual of their childhood, saying that it had been learned from their mothers and, more important, that it was their means of survival and control. Thus, black domestics protected themselves psychologically by seeing only limited meanings in, and results of, the giving and receiving.

But just as often they reported how the giving within the system failed them. They are free to report these failures of the system only because we now live in a society that attempts to enforce minimum-wage laws with some uniformity. In times past they did not have the choice of rejecting gifts as an aid in their struggle for a hand-to-mouth, day-to-day existence. Anyone who has lived on a limited budget knows that a secondhand set of clothes or a free meal help one get by, even if one also recognizes how such gifts reflect upon one's present condition.

White women, on the other hand, protected themselves by not seeing the pattern or the deeper results of the gift giving. They were taught specifically to ignore the fact that, despite the gifts, the social system was designed in such a way that black domestics forever labored at a subsistence level. They were taught that giving assured that some blacks were well treated and that giving was the only acceptable means of behaving with feeling and generosity toward these other women whom they knew to have much harder lives than their own. Thus, in the interviews they defended a ritual of their childhood, a ritual that embodied not only the paternalistic code but also noblesse oblige and charity. They defended what they perceived to be a good in the system, one that perhaps women had carved out themselves. The giving of used items did not involve money and therefore did not involve men, who more often than not controlled the family budget.

Indeed, only three of the white interviewees even hinted that giving had any negative results. Instead, giving comforted the white women, making them feel generous and reducing their guilt. At times, even stealing fell into this pattern of giving. As one white woman acknowledged, she did not mind if a black domestic stole, because "she was an excellent cook, and really, I saw that it must have helped her. At the time, my family was very hard to deal with, and she put up with us. I knew she might stay if she knew I was choosing to look the other way." The response to stealing, then—like giving—sometimes worked to keep blacks indebted to whites and to confirm whites' perceptions of their own superiority.

The mostly unconscious denial by the white women of the negative results and the deeper pattern suggested to me that they wished desperately that the giving would closely bind their black domestic worker to them. Understandably, this wish seemed particularly strong among older white women, many of whom relied upon the same domestic for many, many years. I believe that many of these white women would be surprised to learn that the black interviewees did not feel gratitude for the gifts from their employers. I myself, in choosing the narratives to appear in this part of the book, anticipated that at least one black domestic interviewed would feel a gratitude toward her employer that made for a very close relationship. But I did not find one.[4]

Looking for what my own previous assumption concerning the black women's gratitude and my surprise at its absence might mean, I turned to historical and anthropological accounts of the meaning of gratitude in various cultures.[5] I found the most helpful analysis in Eugene Genovese's *Roll, Jordan, Roll*. Genovese noted that white slaveholders and former slaveholders spoke with great frequency of the ingratitude of their slaves and former slaves. "But just what is gratitude?" he asks. "Why did the slaveholders dwell on it so? And why did the slaves, who showed so little spirit of vengeance and so much kindness towards distressed whites who had hurt them in the past, earn such a reputation? . . . In society much turns on the giving and receiving of equivalences, but where equivalence is out of the question, gratitude enters as a substitute. . . . Between equals gratitude becomes a mediating force, which binds men into an organic relationship. But paternalism rested precisely on inequality."[6]

So the slaves and former slaves did not feel gratitude, and this withholding of gratitude, Genovese found, "drove a dagger into their masters' self-image." By way of further explanation, he cited the work of Octave Mannoni among French colonial people. Mannoni found that dependency, which by definition is created among the oppressed, "excludes gratitude."[7]

4. Sallie Hutton, Winnie Hefley, and Augusta Swanson were the three domestics who seemed to mention the gifts given most favorably. Yet, it did not seem to be gratitude that made them feel close to their employers; the closeness was based upon other aspects of the relationship.

5. Marcel Mauss, *The Gift: Forms and Functions of Exchange in Archaic Societies,* trans. Ian Gunnison (New York, 1967); Barry Schwartz, "The Social Psychology of the Gift," *American Journal of Sociology,* LXXIII (July, 1967), 1–11.

6. Eugene D. Genovese, *Roll, Jordan, Roll: The World the Slaves Made* (New York, 1974), 145–46.

7. *Ibid.,* 146.

Drawing upon Genovese's remarks, one can see that white women, in denying the negative side of their giving, were allowing themselves to continue to believe in an organic relationship between blacks and whites, the kind of relationship idealized in the legend of the Old South. Borrowing Genovese's words, white women may have "needed" a belief in the good of their own giving "in order to define themselves as moral human beings."[8] Like the people of the nineteenth century whom Genovese studied, we are still wrestling with racial issues, and white southerners are still defending the peculiarly "southern" ways of explaining these issues.

But the similarities between the period studied by Genovese and our own era are striking for another reason as well. Like the people of the late nineteenth century, we are in a period in which the compensation for the work of blacks has been adjusted upward. Thus, despite the white women's inability to see a negative side to their gift giving, their response should be considered. Since the civil rights movement, particularly since minimum-wage laws have come to cover domestic workers, some of the giving has decreased. White women have seemed confused and often dismayed that what was once, in the words of one, "a friendly relationship, where you were always giving them something," has been altered.

Evaluated in light of this response, the giving may sometimes have been more than a symbol of white women's superiority and generosity. It might have been representative of their effort to give something roughly equivalent to what their husbands would pay them for such work. Many of the white women we spoke with did not work outside the home and did not have earning power as defined by American society. The gifts did not generally cost money. It was the men within the household who had the money. In a capitalist society, those people without money and without earning power are generally, at least partially, convinced of their lack of self-worth. Thus, the self-image of white female employers—who lacked money themselves, who were dependent themselves—may have been bolstered by their act of giving something else. In the narratives that follow, individual patterns of giving and receiving are remembered.

8. *Ibid.*

Willie Mae Fitzgerald

Willie Mae Fitzgerald (b. 1904) is bitter about whites' gift giving to blacks. She, like many other black domestics, saw the whites for whom she worked as stingy people who did not see their own material wealth, particularly relative to her own poverty. They saw her every day, but they never compared her life with theirs.

She also spoke of her reasons for continuing to work. As in every interview with a black domestic who was a mother, it was her need to provide for her own children that emerged as the dominant theme. Such women typically described their goals as centered on their children: they worked to provide enough food, good clothes, books, and an education for their children. Conscientious mothers, they found domestic work better suited for the flexible schedule demanded by the need to care for their children. Some of them contrasted domestic work with "war work" in the 1940s, a situation in which a mother could never take her child to work with her. They also noted that in other forms of work, if a woman had a sick child, she could not "make up "days later. Also, in domestic work a black woman could "keep her job going" during emergencies or following childbirth by having a sister, mother, friend, or even an older child take over the job in her absence. This practice was the only form of pregnancy leave described to us. These choices were always based upon the assumption of the primacy of a white, male-dominated labor force and upon the historical conditions that made for the privatization of much of the labor of women. But such choices were also formed by conscious decisions by the black women within this labor force to be caring mothers. In her narrative Fitzgerald spoke of such a choice. ·

She also spoke of the bitterness that surrounded such choices. Her husband, for example, did not like her to work. She did not want to talk of him, but I suspect that he felt a complicated rage caused by the fact that he could not provide for the family himself and by the fact that she saw the first white family she worked for in such a friendly light. A number of black women briefly mentioned their husbands' disapproval of their wives taking up the role of wage-earner. Most of them attributed this disapproval to male ideas about the place of women as home-makers. However, two women mentioned their husbands' specific complaints. Said one: "You know, he thought that I could go for help to them that otherwise I might go to him for. I remember when I borrowed money for my oldest child's tuition at a Catholic school, he got all angry." Another said: "My husband never wanted me to work in a home where the man was home. He knew that white men would try and brush up against me, maybe offer extra money, and this was an insult to him." Willie Mae Fitzgerald calls this response "male pride."

She wore a gold necklace and a navy blue jacket over a flowered dress on the first day that I met her at the senior citizen center. She wore a wig every day I saw her.

She lives in a house near New Orleans' Desire project, blocks and blocks of gray cement buildings set down with no trees or grass, near the industrial canal.

Her street is only two blocks from the project, but in her neighborhood there are well-kept yards with fences, locked gates, and large dogs. On my first visit, I knocked on a door to ask directions. An older man said that he had never heard of her or of her address. He thought I was a bill collector. It turned out that she lives next door to him. Her yard is the only one without grass. There are large planks of plywood to step on, so that one can avoid the mud.

I was born in New Orleans. I was born in a house not too far from where I am today, and in 1913 we moved here to the place I am now. And I went as far as eleventh grade in New Orleans schools. I didn't graduate, but I came out of the eleventh grade. I think I got married then. I married young.

I started working after I was married, and my second oldest child—he's dead now—he was eight months old when I got out and got a job. I'd come home and nurse him from the breast. He'd be waiting there. . . . My mama would tease me, "Oh, you giving him that old hot milk!" I had a hard time giving him a bottle, so I had to wean him from the breast.

But my husband stopped that job. He just wanted me to stop, to stay home and see after the babies. I just wanted to work and help. I always did. I always wanted to help my family.

My husband he was just a hard-headed man. He had too much pride. And when things got tough, we had a run-in and we separated and I been working ever since.

But that first job, it was just one of the best of them. All the others—excuse the expression—but they worked the hell out of me. That's why I'm full of cold, arthritis, and everything. I went to work, rain or shine. I met a lady at the hospital the other day, and she was saying that the people she worked for she helped them raise their children, and they liked her and they showed it and they would raise her salary. She didn't have to ask for a raise, and they retired her. They told her she had worked hard, and they helped her get on retirement.

I told her—I said, "Well, you're blessed." I say, "I worked at a place—the last place I worked at twenty-odd years—and they didn't raise my salary." Oh yeah, I thought they was crazy about me. I did. They loved my cooking. They were crazy about my dinners.

But she was—I don't know. When the time came to say you had Social Security, first she put a box in the kitchen. She said, "Willie, I'm going to put a dime in the box, and you've got to match mine—every day." You know, really, that little dime meant more to me than it did to her. So, look like she felt it too, that it was wrong, and she said, "Well, Willie, after this week, I'm going to pay it." She moved that box.

The salaries had went up then. Most people was getting eight, ten, twelve dollars and all. So one day I say to her, I say, "Miz Brown," I said, "things is high now." I say, "And what you pay for meat and bread," I say, "that's what I have to pay, too." I say, "I been working here for a long time." I say, "I'd like a raise." I thought she was going to say, "Yeah, Willie, you deserve it. I'll give you ten dollars."

She said, "I've got to talk it over with my husband." And they ain't talked it over now! I was hurt 'cause I'd worked there and I liked them and I really worked hard.

I stayed with her until I was sixty-seven. She never did raise me! I don't know up until now why she was so stingy. I don't understand that in most of the white folks. I say them white folks worked the hell out of me, and that's why I'm all sick and crippled up now.

I can remember one day I went to work when it was so cold the buses wasn't running. This was for another family, and I was young. I walked to work and I got halfway and I was so cold! I just stopped still and looked back, like I wanted to go back home. My children was small then, and I knew I had to take care of them. I thought of my little children, and I went on to work.

The white people they're sitting up there in their heated breakfast room, waiting on me. "And hurry up," they said when I got there, " 'cause Mr. Quigley got to be to the office." I was frozen. I was just trembling. I ran the hot water on my hands to try to get them warm. She rushed me out to serve breakfast! I felt like cussing, saying, "Damn you, you get back in here and you fix it for once."

I thought of my little children. I stayed. I was quiet. That's how I worked.

You know I took sick on that job with the Browns when I was sixty-seven. I had inflammation in my body, and I just cried like a baby and ached with the arthritis. I went in the hospital. Miz Brown came and saw me and allowed that they had had a birthday and she had a piece of cake to bring me but her grandson ate it. And that was it!

From an interview with Susan Tucker

Melissa Howe

⊷⊱⊰⊱⊰⊷

In the South the number of white domestics has been statistically so small and the number of black women who work as domestics so high that *black woman* and *domestic worker* have been almost synonymous terms. A number of black women we talked with said that, even today, unknown white women approach them in shops or on the street and ask them to work. In the South many white people still take Langston Hughes's words literally: "I am the Negro, servant to you all."[*]

And so it is that when southern white women leave the South, many who hire maids still prefer southern black women. Southern white women feel that they know the type of servant a woman is if she is a southern black. By this they mean primarily that the servant speaks as southern blacks have traditionally done in their deference to whites. White women not from the South probably prefer this behavior as well, for as Judith Rollins notes, "Any hint of competition with the employer must be avoided by the domestic's being clearly non-threatening in all ways."[†]

It may be, too, that in leaving their homes, some southern women, particularly white women, become even more "southern," taking on more and more of those characteristics generally associated with the South. The white employer described by Melissa Howe (b. 1912) seems to have become "more southern," and to reinforce this definition of herself, she wanted a southern maid.

But what is a "southern maid"? Trudier Harris has divided literary maids into three categories. These categories are the southern maids, "who epitomize mammyism"; the transitional maids, who "wear masks evoking the true southern maids"; and the militants, who "wear masks only to bring about violence or never wear them." In her analysis southern maids are those who "generally acquiesce in the paternalistic and place-defined relationship between mistress and maid as it has been shaped by the attitudes and traditions of Southern society." These maids "are more likely than the others to be 'ideal servants,' the mammy figure traditionally identified with southern plantation households."[‡]

Although most of the maids we interviewed would fall into the category Harris called transitional, the employer in Howe's narrative (like almost all the other employers) was certainly seeking a southern maid as described by Harris. What I found most interesting in the behaviors described in the narrative, however, was the extremes—the extremes of the employer's life, perhaps caused by being out of the South, and the extremes of the domestic's life as a result of the harsh realities of her poverty and of the death of her child. These extremes reminded

[*]Langston Hughes, "Let America Be America Again," in Langston Hughes and Arna Bontemps (eds.), *The Poetry of the Negro, 1746–1949* (Garden City, N.Y., 1949), 107.

[†]Judith Rollins, *Between Women: Domestics and Their Employers* (Philadelphia, 1985), 221, 201.

[‡]Trudier Harris, *From Mammies to Militants: Domestics in Black American Literature* (Philadelphia, 1982), 23.

me that the domestic we spoke with who most conformed to the behavior of a stereotypical mammy was a Latin American black who seemed extremely home-sick and, at the same time, desperate to find a place in her new home.

Although the following narrative includes an example of just one employer's paranoia and low self-image, it also shows something of the general psychology involved in the employer–domestic worker relationship. The worker is socially and economically disadvantaged, and these disadvantages bind her to her white employer. The white woman may have material advantages, but at the same time, she may have psychological problems. To alleviate some of these problems, she finds in the domestic worker a willing listener, a confidante, who can, by her very position within society, make the employer feel superior.

Melissa Howe spoke in a monotone about this white woman. That Howe left the white family and did not respond to their pleas to return dramatizes her understanding that no true reciprocity existed and that, instead, her white employer was just "crazy like that."

Howe wore two cardigans, one over the other, and she sits outside even on January days. Her daughter, with whom she lives, said that her mother cannot stand the noise of the children or the television inside. In the living room, one of the teenagers was making paper flowers for a dance. Howe said that they were "always doing something like that" and that she thus preferred the "rotting wood of the porch."

⇢⬎❧⊶

I was born October 28, 1912, in the country. I was born in Picayune, Mississippi. It's up to the north here, I think. I was growed up so fast that I have to think which way it is!

I came down to Mobile when I was about ten years old. My mama and my daddy was separated, and he sent once for I and my older sister. He was in Mobile and was supposed to keep us two weeks and carry us back. He wouldn't bring us back and Mama had to come down and that's why I'm in Mobile today. We all stayed. But him we didn't see much. That's the way that part went.

The first job I had, I was twelve years old. I worked baby-sitting for a lady. I can't call her name right now. She used to work shelling crabs, and she was a white woman, and she paid me fifty cents a week to sit with her baby. Stay at the house, me and the baby, wash dishes and clothes.

See, these white people, soon as they got able, they used to get a colored person to do for them.

Fifty cents and that was it. If you needed the money, you couldn't go get it nowhere else. You had to get the money and take what you could get.

After I got to be grown, I had children, and I worked for two and a half a week to raise my children, because the men wasn't making hardly anything. I didn't make but two dollars and a half, but she was always giving me something otherwise, a piece of material to make a dress, or stockings or something like that. I ain't never worked for no mean white people. Well, all that helped when that was all you could do. All you could do was to take those wages and those extras.

Still, work, work is the hardest thing I had to do in my life, because you *had* to do it. I couldn't make no stand about what I wanted to do, because at that time . . you *had* to take what you could get.

I worked for my children. When I married, I had four children just like that. A girl and a boy and a girl and a boy. And my last boy he's the one that died. And when he died, that's when I left the South.

In '51, see, he drowned, and the family felt like I wouldn't worry about him as much if I didn't stay around here. It looked like I was going to fall apart all this time.

I felt like it was my fault because I told him to start with that he couldn't go—on account of this river—that he couldn't go swimming. But the same day I said it, he went swimming and drowned. I'd come home from work, and the state trooper was there to say he'd drowned.

I wouldn't do a thing. Just couldn't get my mind off it. So my mother and them, they arranged for me to go up to Delaware. I went on a truck where they pick up these people and carry them to the camps, to these jobs in the factories. These canning companies had contracts with these here trucks to pick up these people.

Now, if you stayed on that camp, they let some of you off this Saturday and some of you off the next Saturday. All right, on those off days I started working for these white people.

See, she was a southern lady, and she came out there, and she asked for a southern colored lady to come and wash and iron. And they just took me in, and I didn't have to stay at camp anymore. I'd go to work in the daytime and then be there at their house to work weekends and nights. They didn't have but one little kid, and I'd go there and take care of him and the house and them dogs they'd be raising. They'd be gone a lot, and they wanted someone to stay at the house.

See, she was crazy about me. I don't know why. I was the only woman she ever talked to. She didn't even associate with no female whites. She said she didn't like the white folks around her. She didn't want them in her house—working or being friends either. She said she'd rather look in my face anytime. She didn't even like black people that looked like white people. She was raised in Atlanta, and she said she wasn't raised to have white people around. She was raised to have black people around.

And I, I was in their home just like I was one of them. And I got sick three times and had to go into the hospital, and when I did, she would sit right there. And whenever they discharged me, she came and got me. And she fixed my breakfast, my medicine, everything.

I said, "I'm not going to stay in no bed." I said, "I can get up on one of those stools and put your board up and iron." She didn't want me to do that. And then, they had four cars. They bought me my first car and learned me how to drive.

Well, I just don't know about her. She knew about my son drowning, and she just wanted to help. And she'd say she was southern and in the North and all that, and she had a hard time, and I made her forget it. And so anytime she bought her a dress or hat or anything, she bought me one, too.

I stayed there seventeen years, and when my mother was sick, I came back. But these white people they wanted me to come back. They wrote me and called me and everything and told me if I did come back, they were going to sell that trailer they had on the beach for me, at their beach house, and build a house for me. And she, she was just crazy like that. Because I was from the South, like herself.

From an interview with Mary Yelling

Leila Parkerson

Leila Parkerson (b. 1933) recalls working while a student for white families, which is not an unusual memory for many black professional women of today. To help pay for things that scholarships did not cover, they worked for white families in jobs their mothers, aunts, or schools found for them.* Some were lucky enough to find families in which they were treated with respect. Others were not.

In these jobs, black middle-class college girls were introduced to many aspects of the paternalistic system, aspects their mothers may have chosen not to mention. Parkerson saw firsthand how her attachment to a white family during her father's illness was both essential and unfair. She saw firsthand how a white man could proposition a black domestic, and she heard discussions among whites concerning whether she, a black girl, should be allowed to wear a swimsuit while baby-sitting on a beach open only to whites.

The latter episode was mentioned in varying forms by other black and white interviewees, so that the "white only" beach, like white weddings, was an institution within the segregated South in which the lines were less clearly drawn and in which the inappropriateness of uniforms confused issues. It reminded me that once when I was young, my family also employed a black teenager to stay with us at the beach one summer. I remember that she could swim in the bay but not in the pool of a nearby hotel. The question of why she could swim in one place and not the other was always answered with the formula "That's just the way things are."

Parkerson also learned that southern whites who employed domestics often discussed blacks and even racial inferiority in front of domestic workers as if they were not there. In a number of interviews black domestics recalled being present in adjacent rooms, and intermittently walking through the room where the whites were, as their employers defended the paternalistic system. This practice seems to have been a carry-over from the tradition according to which black domestics, as inferiors, were not thought important enough to worry about what was said in front of them. As well-trained servants, moreover, they were supposed to be deaf to all but words spoken directly to them.

However, a number of the white interviewees recalled their discomfort when such conversations would occur at the dinner table as they were being served by blacks. David Katzman found that the dinner table seemed to be the place assigned to discuss race relations and noted a similar discomfort expressed by a northern traveler to the South in the early 1900s.†

---

*Several black and white interviewees mentioned this practice, which is briefly discussed by Trudier Harris, *From Mammies to Militants: Domestics in Black American Literature* (Philadelphia, 1982), 5–6.

†David M. Katzman, *Seven Days a Week: Women and Domestic Service in Industrializing America* (New York, 1978), 188.

Leila Parkerson has not forgotten what she learned about such customs in her summer jobs. She was visiting her mother when she was interviewed. Outside the house, her nieces were practicing cheers for a football game. She has a northern accent, which they teased her about.

⊷⊰⊱⊶

You talking about jobs? The first ones people had? Well, I used to pick cotton. Yes, when I was about seven, eight, nine years old—pick cotton and pick peas, pick blueberries and pick up potatoes. I think we made something like five cents a quart, which according to the standard of living back there, it wasn't too bad!

We were living in the city then, but we'd go up the country to my grandma's in the summer to do this work. There were seven kids in our family, and my parents would send us up there. I liked it OK, but I do remember that by the time I got in the eighth grade, I didn't want to go up there anymore!

So that's when I started more on the baby-sitting. There being so many of us, we all had to work. My father did construction work, and my mother she worked out later, but when I was young, she mostly took in sewing. And I and my sisters we used to go to school in the day and then keep kids in the afternoon.

I worked out to the Jones' house. And in the summers I'd go with them over to the beach—all summer. For me it was fun being over there. Miz Jones wasn't as southern as a lot of people. She was from West Texas, and her husband was from Mobile. She was kind of way out back then. I was never treated like a servant. I was treated like a member of the family. I would hear her arguing with her in-laws and peoples who said: "You treat that nigger like she's a white girl. Look at her walking down on the beach in her bathing suit. Why she's as black as molasses." I'd hear these conversations, but since they were never directed at me, I'd just kind of ignore them, 'cause she ignored them. I'd hear her setting people straight, so I'd just go on about my business.

And what helped was that I was somewhat of a daydreamer, and while I was with the kids, I kind of dreamed that I was supposed to be there and just a summer visitor like everybody else. And actually, since I was so young, I was different than the servants. Like I said, I was only a kid wearing a bathing suit up and down the beach with the kids I sat with. And I didn't have to stay in the maids' quarters.

But I knew what they had to go through. I'd see them acting real humble. And I kind of felt like I was a little bit odd in that I was not made to stay with them. But still I enjoyed being with the family.

In the winter months I would baby-sit for other people she knew, too. When I was fifteen, Mr. Jones reportedly went broke, and they moved to Texas or somewhere. I remember that well, 'cause Miz Jones brought me clothes to go to college. I went to college at fifteen, and she brought me boxes of sweaters and a lot of nice things. She brought me nicer things than she paid me in cash money!

When they left, I worked more for this Jewish family. They were quite wealthy, and they had a lot of relatives who weren't, but I worked for all of them. Schwartze was their name.

I liked it there because it was a beautiful mansion. I wish I could buy it now. I loved that house. She'd be sleeping a lot, and I'd go up in this man's den where he had all these horses and trophies and things and all these books, and I would read books. Most of the day, I read books when I went out there. The hardest thing I did every day was sweep off the sidewalk all the way around the house!

Then when I worked for Miz Caroline, their daughter, it was about the same thing. Now I did get a job sort of as a maid for a poor white family once. I mean they were so poor till their sink was pink. It was just so dirty. And they had rabbits in the backyard. And the girls used to roll their hair up with paper from the bread. They'd take bread bags and make rollers. They were so poor!

This white lady she had tons of kids. You know, she worked in a dime store downtown herself! And I think her older daughters were working in the theater. They had the kind of jobs then that we couldn't get, but you can imagine how much she was making working in a dime store. And it was a struggle for them to pay me that little twenty dollars a week! All of them had to make it up together to pay that twenty dollars a week.

They had painted wooden floors—gray wooden floors without rugs or anything. And their house was a lot worse than ours! That's when I first found out there are poor white people.

They were poor, but they thought they could afford a maid. That sink I never will forget. I can see it right now. I did proceed to scrubbing it and cleaning it and the toilet the same way. They came home and wanted to know what happened. They couldn't understand how I got it clean, what I used. I got bleach and all the cleaning agents from my mother, 'cause I couldn't stand that dirt there.

It's so funny, though. Every white person, poor or rich, always thought they could give me something. This family even—they gave me an old blouse with stains under the arms, perspiration stains. I took it and dumped it in the nearest trash can on the way home.

And I pass down the street here now, and I remember I used to work for that old fool down there. I never will forget. Old Miz Theilman—she was something else. She was one of the poor in-laws to this Schwartze family I worked for. She didn't have nothing. In fact, she lived in the projects—not public housing, but I call them projects anytime it's a upstairs and a downstairs and lots of people living in the same building. It's a cheap apartment building, but as far as I was concerned, it was a project. Anyway she'd always try to give me food. "Want some watermelon?" she'd say. "Take your mother a slice of watermelon."

That made me detest domestic work. And the more I would work for people and see the books they had, the furnishings, everything in their houses—all nice—I just couldn't understand why we couldn't have this, why we couldn't get paid more instead of just being offered a slice of watermelon or whatever. And even in the case of that really poor family, they had jobs that I couldn't get. I just hated being reminded of that.

I never will forget one time my daddy got sick, and he was over in the hospital, and the doctor wouldn't operate on him, because we didn't have any money saved. There were so many of us, we could never save money.

I was working for the Joneses then. And I called Miz Jones and told her I couldn't come to work, 'cause my Daddy was very sick and I had to try and see if I could help my mother to get some money.

She said, "How much money?" I said, "A hundred and forty dollars is what Mama needs before the doctors would touch him." Now you understand I'm only making $20 a week, so by the time I'd get $140 is a long time. But at any rate, she said, "I'll talk to my husband, Mr. Jones."

So she told him, "Leila's father is sick and has to have an operation, and they won't touch him unless somebody else says the money will be paid." See, she knew the system. So Mr. Jones called the hospital and told them to operate on the man and start right away and don't make no more much ado about it.

I never will forget that. But I'm trying to show you they would do something nice for you when they really felt you needed it. But they wouldn't pay you nothing but these menial wages. Nobody else paid more, and nobody wanted to break the standard.

I told her, "I'll pay for it out of my salary." I was so thankful. But I still knew it wasn't right. The whole system was wrong—because, of course, Mr. Jones never did have to pay a cent. The fact was that the doctors wouldn't touch my daddy until somebody white said they'd pay the money. That's the part that kind of made me say, "Hey, I can't stay around this town and live like this. I've got to do more for myself. I've got to go to school."

I kept on working as a baby-sitter to get me through college, but after that I didn't. Nothing much happened on those jobs. The same stuff . . . But once—you might be interested in this—I only had one white man bother me ever—one. And I wouldn't call his name. But my aunt got me this job. She worked for this rich family, and they had a summer house somewhere. The man he asked her for a nice, intelligent girl to do some baby-sitting for some friends of his. My aunt she was their regular maid, housekeeper, whatever, and she would go with them every summer. The man he would stay in town.

She asked me if I wanted to sit, and I said yes. This man was an attorney—Lawyer X, I'll call him. And she said Lawyer X will pick you up and he wants you to baby-sit for one of his business friends in town.

So he came to my house and met Mama and everything. Oh, he was very big time around the city, and so Mama said, fine. Soon as I got in the car, he said, "Now I understand you're a sophomore in college." I said, "Yes." He said, "You look like a very intelligent girl." I said, "Thank you."

He says: "I want you to sit for my girlfriend. Her husband is in the service, and she's my girlfriend." And he called the name of my aunt and said, "She wouldn't understand this." And say: "If you don't want to sit, I'll take you right back home, and I'll pay you for your trouble. But you can't mention this—I'd rather you didn't mention this to anyone, your mama or nobody else." I said, "OK."

His girlfriend lived right over near here in one of those tacky old two-bedroom houses. She was waiting on the porch there. We saw her. And he told me: "Now I'm going to drive you right up and let you out, and then I'm going to keep driving. She's going to come out the back door and meet me two blocks up the street. You tell her to meet me. And then when it'll be time for you to come home, she'll come in, and you'll walk out the back door and meet me two blocks down in the same location." He said: "I'll be watching you, but I don't want the neighbors to see me picking you up. Or the neighbors to see her leaving with me."

I did that for him a couple of times, and I'll tell you what—that man paid me more money! In fact, he paid me so much money for baby-sitting I got scared! I told Mama. She said, "Well, just shut your mouth. You're in school. You need the money."

I think the first night he paid me twelve dollars and the next time fifteen dollars. Then the next time it was another woman—another one but the same story, a little house and a husband in the army. She had a baby in the cradle that just slept the whole time and all these *True Confession* magazines. I read those. When I decided what kind of job it was, I'd decided to travel light! I mean, I wasn't going to take my school-books in case I had to run, in case her husband came home unexpectedly!

Now the next time he wanted me to sit, it was another woman. But this one she stood him up. We kept circling the block, and she never came out on the porch. Finally he said, "I've been here for two hours." Say, "I'm going to drive out to my house and call her or see if she's trying to call me." I said, "All right."

So we drove out to his house—great big mansion, beautiful place. And I sat in the car and I sat in the car and I sat in the car. He kept coming out and assuring me she was going to get in touch with him and, of course, that I'd be paid.

I said, "Well, I really am bored and tired." He said, "Well, why don't you just come in the house?" I said, "OK."

Well, see, I trusted him. He was a respectable lawyer. And he did not try to force himself on me. But when we got inside, he said: "You know you're a very good-looking girl. How old are you?" I said, "Sixteen." He said: "Sixteen. Only sixteen, and you're in college already?" I said, "Yes." He said, "You're real bright." He said, "I noticed you didn't say anything about the baby-sitting jobs, because had you said it to your mama or anybody, she'd 'a' told what's-her-name, your aunt, and she would not have understood, and then my reputation might have been destroyed." I said: "Well, it didn't bother me. I figured it was your business."

And he said, "Well, let me tell you something about some men." And he told me about himself, where he went to school, how he loved his wife and family, and all he was thankful for. And then he talked about this dark area—these women.

He says, "You know the one you sat for out there the first time." He said: "that was a fifty-dollar job. I paid her fifty. And this one—she's supposed to come here tonight—she's a seventy-five to a hundred job." He said, "Looks like she's about to stand me up." And he called her a ugly name.

And he said: "You're an intelligent girl, and you're old enough. You interested in the job?" I said, "No, I'm not interested." He said: "Why not? All you girls have been touched up by men." I said, "Well, I haven't." He said, "Well, I'm not going to force myself on you." He said, "Do you want something to drink?" I said, "No, thanks. I don't drink." He said, "You want something else—some tea, coffee?" I said, "I'll take coffee." I said, "But I'll fix it."

He started laughing! And then he started talking to me about my college aspirations, what I planned to do and all. He said, "You know, I was going to pay you *all* I was going to pay this one tonight plus your baby-sitting money." He said, "I bet you never made that much money." He said, "How long would you have to work to make that?"

I said: "I don't know. You figure it out. Twenty dollars a week . . ." I said, "But I prefer to continue doing it that way." He said, "You not going to tell me you're a virgin?" I said, "Yes, I am." I said: "And whenever I choose to be deflowered, it would be by one of my own men. So, no sir. Thank you."

I don't know if he was impressed, shocked, or hurt, but he made a big joke out of it. And then all of a sudden he said, "I'm going to take you home." I said, "All right." He said, "I'm going to pay you for baby-sitting."

I think he gave me twenty-five dollars that night—more than I ever made. And when he gave me the money, he told me how influential he was, how important, and if I ever needed anything—if I stayed in the city or if I went anywhere else away, I could always call him. I never had to, but it was almost as if he was apologizing for his rudeness.

That was the end of my baby-sitting jobs here. The end of the summer I went off to New York. I only worked domestic work one day in the North. It seemed different because the people were all away at work themselves. But I don't know. There is a certain stigma attached to domestic work for black people everywhere. When I first came to New York, I was staying with an aunt who was a domestic. She made more as a domestic than I did as a clerk, but do you think I'd give up being a clerk to make more money? No. I wanted a job that was not traditionally associated with blacks, and I didn't want to have to depend on white generosity when times were rough.

From an interview with Mary Yelling

Juliana Lincoln

The following narrative touches on the close relationship between the guilt whites felt and the gifts they gave. Juliana Lincoln (b. 1940), now a professional, remembers and identifies such guilt. She was a young mother when she worked as a domestic, and she remembers her feelings about leaving her children each day and her employer's response.

A number of other black women also mentioned the sadness of being away from their own children while spending most of their days with white children. This situation reflects the socioeconomic and racial structure of the South, which afforded white women help in raising their children at a cost to black women and their children.

Some white women were aware of this cost to black women. As David Katzman has written, "Southern racial etiquette served to ensure highly intimate relationships between black and white." At least some white women who saw black domestics daily knew something of the lives of these maids. White women, for example, remember overhearing calls about child-care arrangements, talking with black domestics about their pregnancies, and being informed about marital discord and family violence. And yet, as Katzman notes, such intimacy "in no way implied reciprocity." To have reciprocity would have implied equality. He noted that even the shared roles of motherhood between employer and domestic worker were denied.*

The shared roles of motherhood were denied almost perversely, it seems, because within this intersection white women came closest to admitting the unjustness of the system. Although white women knew the problems of mothering, they also knew that overt efforts to help black mothers would lead to the upsetting of the white-dominated "housewives' utopia." They preferred instead to rationalize their dismissal of the problems of the black working mother by praising the resources of the black extended family—to recall, for example, "that her children were kept by her mother, in the black way."

In one interview, for example, a white woman told me that she had paid a beloved domestic during a pregnancy leave. She had done so on the condition that the domestic not tell anyone in the immediate white family or black community, since other black domestics might then have pressured for similar consideration. Her requirement of silence illustrates how southern white women, even in cases in which they were in personal disagreement with the system, conformed in such a way that black domestics were denied any collective power.

To be fair, it must be admitted that these issues also reflect the larger issue of child care in general. All child care, after all, has traditionally been provided by women, and it is not and has never been adequately compensated either as a

*David M. Katzman, *Seven Days a Week: Women and Domestic Service in Industrializing America* (New York, 1978), 200–202.

social role or in paid positions. Southern practices form only one dimension of the overall problem of child care.

Juliana Lincoln is a person who sees such larger issues. She is quiet, self-contained, and self-assured. At the interview she wore a white high-necked blouse that buttons in the back and a black skirt. We sat in a swing on the porch of a large pink Victorian house, a meeting place for us both. She does not initiate questions, but she answers slowly and thoughtfully.

++᠈᠊᠈᠂᠊᠈᠂᠊᠉

I was born in Canton, Mississippi. It's north of Jackson and just a little place—very country, and I only lived there about six months. But I know it's home.

My mom's family owned a lot of property right in the heart of Canton. In fact they were always well-known in the area. My granddad was an engineer on the railroad, and they were all educated. They sent them off to Wilberforce to educate them. And then, my mom was the first black woman to graduate from her college.

Now all my dad's family were sharecroppers. My mom and dad were just like night and day. And my mom's dad did not want them to marry. Oh, Lord, he didn't want his daughter to marry my dad! They were from two different schools—one the sharecropper, one the educated one.

But my dad was a pretty man—real pretty, real pretty. And my mom was not. My dad was real fair with beautiful hair and just everything you would want a man to look like. And my mom was very dark-skinned and plain, but a smart lady. She was, and had, everything that my dad didn't have.

Well, it worked out OK. But it was bad in a way. I think my mom kind of grieved over him, 'cause he was just what her dad said he was—just a pretty man, not really a smart man.

But he came to New Orleans with the WPA in the late thirties, and they trained him to be a welder, and then after he got settled, he came back and got my mom and us. I had three older sisters.

There were some federal housing projects, and we lived there a while, and then we bought a home, and I grew up in that home. It was near where my dad's sister lived. Now she was an interesting woman. She started a Lutheran church in their home, like they had on the plantation, and it flourished, and we all go there today.

And so my mom was a kindergarten teacher in the school that was attached to the church, also just like on the plantation. She worked there until she died. She died when I was twelve, when she was fifty-two. So then all my sisters took care of me, and my dad, too.

My dad he always encouraged me to work. When I was twelve, I started and I worked for a white lady that lived not too far from me. I was baby-sitting for her. I worked every afternoon, and she had two small children and one about nine. I remember the nine-year-old because we had a lot in common! It was like we were friends.

I worked there about three years. Then I worked for some people further away, too. At that time we'd get these jobs just by walking down the street. The white people would ride down the street and ask you, "Do you know anybody who want a job or who need a job?" Where I lived, I knew white people in my neighborhood. You know, as a child, it made no difference—race didn't. I never had any problem.

They weren't rich white people, at all. I worked for a lady. She had twins, and she told me when she asked me to work all she wanted me to do—a whole lot of stuff. It sounded like a lot. And when I got there, she didn't have anything in her house but twin beds for those children and a bed for her and a refrigerator and a stove. She didn't have half as many clothes as I did! So some of those whites had maids, and they didn't have anything else.

I didn't ever work for real rich people. Now I know people who worked for them. In fact, I knew a girl that worked for this real rich white lady who adopted a black girl. She adopted the child of her maid. The white lady. And she brought her by our church. I guess she was trying to get her to mingle with blacks, too. She was a pretty little girl, and the lady sent her to school in Europe and bought her all these beautiful clothes. We just all thought she was from another world! The white lady and the little black girl both! I often wonder what became of them.

That was a white world I just glimpsed. But I had a child when I was seventeen, and so at the time I just kept on baby-sitting for the whites who'd ask me. At that time you either worked in a home or you worked in a restaurant, and that was it.

When Johnson was president and all these civil rights things went through, it changed. Some things changed. Well, everything changed. That's when I was able to finish school. Because I went to college in '61 and I had to stop in '62 and save up some more funds and go back again.

I remember one job I had that year—this was the worst experience I ever had. I was working for this lady, and she had two children, and she was supposed to pay every two weeks, and I worked two weeks and she wouldn't pay me. She said she wasn't going to pay me, and I asked her why, and she said I'd better get out of there. And I said, "Yes, ma'am."

I don't know why she did that. She was going through a divorce, and she was just very upset. I think that was why. She wasn't an American. She was a German, and I didn't know what else to do. I cried. I almost died! I'd worked two weeks for nothing!

I work with a lot of whites now. I'm a speech therapist. I notice some whites at work; some are nice and some . . . they want to be, but it's something in them that just won't let them see us as equal.

Some of them feel like blacks should still be just serving whites. And they're having big problems with the younger set. Like my third child is a teenager now, and I can look at something and try to see something else. Well, her group—they don't. They don't see nothing but what it really is, and they just deal with it right then. What is it? It's prejudice. It's unfairness.

Now, though, I don't think I'd be good for your book, 'cause I was so young when I worked for whites. I was just like another member of the family, because I was young. Sometime I wonder did they feel sorry for me? Because they knew they didn't pay well. I remember working from seven to five. Those were the hours you worked. You never worked eight hours—you worked nine or ten. And it was sad because you were leaving your children, going taking care of theirs for three dollars, four dollars, and I guess maybe some made five dollars. A day!

You'd be there just taking *good* care of their children, and yours were probably just somewhere running wild. And one lady always asked about my children. In fact, she would always give me something. She *always* gave me something! So, see, they knew.

That's one thing I don't understand about white people, and I've never come to grips with it. OK, they're suppose to be God-fearing, some of them—good staunch Baptists, good Catholics. And they've treated blacks so bad, and I wonder how they explain that.

They know. Otherwise, why were they giving you so many things? I've had them give me food—meat cuts, whole cows! Whatever.

And I'd stay off work two or three days when I was a teenager, and they'd just say a few words. I guess in *their minds* they said, "Poor young child. I guess she did want to go to a football game" or whatever. They'd pretend they were mad, but they wouldn't fire me or anything. So I always tried to figure God was somewhere in them. But a lot of them, I don't know.

Then I try to look at all sides, and maybe they just kind of got caught up in the swing of things. Because you see mean things. Everyone does, every day, and nine times out of ten you don't do anything about it. You just go on about your daily life, and you never sit down and say, "Well, what am I really looking at?"

Now the younger set they think I'm crazy. But see, they can't even imagine it—can't even imagine thinking about the white people, seeing their side. And like me, I respect anybody. I'll say "Yes sir" and "No sir," and it doesn't hurt me at all. It doesn't make me feel any kind of way. They think that is just out of the question!

And, for example, I have seen them in the mall, walking down the mall. These nineteen- and twenty-year-olds, and they'll do it on purpose, not move when white people get in their way. My daughter one day told me— she said, "Mom, I've watched you walk this whole mall, and you have moved for everybody." And I did it unconsciously. She said, "Have you ever noticed them moving over for you?"

I admit I did it. I moved every time! She said, "I'm not going to move." I said to never move was also unfair. She said, "I'll go around one, and I'll let one go around me." And so I watched her, and you know what would happen? The white people would never move until they got face to face with her, and then they would politely go around.

From an interview with Susan Tucker

Frances Galvin

✦❦❧

Frances Galvin (b. 1897) described her mother's help to the needy in the community. These efforts can be seen not only as an example of a customary form of interaction between whites and blacks but also as a form that was consciously modeled on community work done in larger northern and midwestern cities. The 1890s, the decade of Galvin's birth, began the heyday of the American clubwoman, as well as of the work of Jane Addams and other woman reformers. Other black and white interviewees also spoke about such community involvement. In the South these movements were split along the color line, but they nevertheless influenced the way all southerners thought of serving those less fortunate than themselves.

Within the black community, women's organizations were often the initiators of tutorial programs, food banks, halls of sewing machines, cooking schools, and training schools. Cecelia Gaudet, the black woman who spoke most extensively about such groups, saw them as a charitable, Christian response of the more fortunate. In her view the members of these organizations were middle-class black women who wished to help other blacks who had not been so fortunate as they had. Membership in such organizations reflected class to some degree, but it was seen primarily as a way to help others.

The white organizations, on the other hand, did not have quite the same philosophy. Unlike the black organizations, the white organizations did not see their members as being but one or two steps away from poverty themselves. Nor could they initiate as much of an activist program as could the blacks, because they could not often address the social problems caused by segregation. Although some of their community work was done within their own cities, much of it was not. Indeed, black women who worked for employers who belonged to such organizations often made fun of the white women's efforts, pointing out that these organizations wanted to help the disadvantaged in Africa or some other remote place while ignoring problems at home.

Membership in the Junior League and other white groups seems to have been the main way class status was attained among southern white women. Because working-class whites could also employ servants, the presence of a servant within the home was not as clearly identified with class in the South as it was in other parts of the country. In the absence of this means of class definition, southern white women sought membership in these charitable organizations as a mark of their privileged position.

The whole family of Frances Galvin seems to have had a tradition of activism in such white organizations. Her mother, her sisters, and her female cousins have been clubwomen who emphasized the role of white women as leaders in the community. Galvin speaks of her mother's standing up for blacks in court, of her generosity with food for the hungry, and of her work at the poor farm.

When I interviewed her, Galvin's gray hair was carefully plaited and wrapped around her head. She sat in a rocking chair and told me that she could not afford to run the air-conditioning in summer. Fanning herself, she said that she is of "the Bourbon South, the South now gone forever." It was a chinese fan, held by fingers dry and brittle from age and from gardening chores. On the floor near her feet were two small embroidered foot stools. On the baby grand piano was a picture from the 1920s of her sisters displaying a banner urging women to vote.

My father he had real estate holdings, and at one time he was a silent partner in a tobacco firm. And my mother was a really sweet, wonderful person. She was very outgoing and loved people. She loved to give things away. She'd give away everything she had and yours, too, if you didn't watch it! Which was good in a way and bad in a way. I mean, we were always taught to be very kind. But then, finally, because she was so kind, we all had to go to work later on! You see, we had colored properties, and if they couldn't pay for the houses, I think finally Mother just let them keep them.

And I remember there was one servant, old Willie. Mother found her when she was eating out of the garbage and gave her a job. And old Willie's husband used to say—since Mother was so kind to them—he'd say, "You think Miz Galvin is Jesus Christ." And this Willie wanted to name her little boy after my brother. But for some reason or another, Mother didn't want her to, and so she suggested all sorts of cute names and Willie selected one. Well, word got around that Mother was good at naming. They would come around to our house to ask Mother for suggestions for names.

And see, they all knew her, and she was always going to court with them. They were stealing each other's pigs or something. And she'd go to court with them and help them get straightened out.

Mother helped everybody—black and white! She was just that type of person. She believed in giving. I think women of her time, and mine, too, believed in their roles as people who gave—much more than today, when the government gives. The poor people they were considered everyone's responsibility. They had the poorhouse—they called it the poor farm—that was right over there, right near where we lived really. So Mother took an interest in that. The people could work out there. I don't know what they did with the colored folk; I don't know whether they had a separate place or what. The colored, the ones Mother knew, she helped them because she knew them. She said they were basically good, and she liked helping.

And of course, she helped the servants because she knew them even better and because she was fond of them. And she was fond of them because they helped her. She thought of it—we all thought of giving to servants as a sort of mutual thing. They gave to us, by working and not worrying about if they worked late or whatever, and we gave to them by helping out wherever we could, giving them things, giving them advice.

I'm not sure which ones I can remember, though, to tell you the truth. At one time, I know we had a cook named Erma. And we had Juliana; she milked the cows. And old Uncle Moses was the gardener. And my brother had—well, he was his companion—a little colored boy that lived in the house. He dressed my brother and undressed him and followed him around to make sure he didn't get in trouble—followed him to school and back. And Luvenia was one of ours. I remember her because she used to bring her little girl to work, and I could play with her. But I could play with her just so long. After a while, Mother didn't let us play with them. After you were ten or so, it wasn't considered proper to play with them. That's why so many of them became companions to white children. They couldn't be playmates. Or, of course, many of them went to work doing things like washing dishes at about that time. Anyway, Luvenia and Juliana and old Uncle Moses and Erma and Carrie . . . Old black Carrie the cook . . . we would hug and kiss her and carry on over her. And Aunt Angeline. They called really old colored servants in those days aunt. And I remember there was a half-wit who would walk the streets muttering to herself, and she'd say: "I ain't nobody's aunt. They call me aunt, and I ain't nobody's aunt." But Aunt Angeline was this tall, willowy, light-colored woman, and she carried this huge basket of clothes on her head. She would take them home to wash them.

In later years, we had other washwomen, and we'd take the clothes to them. Their houses they were usually nice and clean—a sort of shotgun house but with extensions. And they loved flowers. You'd always see a geranium blooming in the tin can. Colored people, you know, love flowers, and flowers grow for them so well.

In those days everybody had servants. They were very cheap. And some people, if they'd had them a long time, had servants that lived on the place. But you could never get 'em to live there if they didn't already. They naturally wanted to go home with their own and have fun, and they really did have fun. I remember they used to come down the street singing old-time tunes at night.

They seemed happier than today. Colored, on the whole—I think they had it better then, though most say they didn't. Not with the lynchings, but just with life they had it better. We used to have this woman who would iron for us every once in a while. It was during the time Martin Luther King was in Selma, and I asked her—she was a country Nigra—I said, "You were treated good, weren't you?" And she said, "No, ma'am, I was not." Well, I don't know what she meant. I thought it might not be good to ask.

I just feel like they were happier. They were gracious, and there was work for all of them. They could each have their own little specialty. So many of them could find work in white homes. Now they all want minimum wage, but I think it's better for people to work at all for at least something than to worry about what they'll be paid. It's better for your ego. They're unhappy about unemployment.

And they were all illiterate but they could put things together in a creative way. They said the cutest things. I wish I'd jotted down some of the things they said, because they made sense in an odd sort of way. Seems like they were more illiterate, and yet they made their lives happier than today, when they know more. They created their own little cultures. We didn't look down on it; we were rather inspired by it, I would say.

And now they cry rape all the time. There's always notice of a colored woman being raped in the paper, by a colored man or a white man—mostly colored. And yet I know a maid of a friend of mine. She has had six children, and every one had a different father. And she just told me, "The Lord meant it that way." And one of the children's father got sick, and he came back here, and she nursed him and somebody said, "After what you went through with him, are you going to take care of him?" She said, "It's my child's father." That's the way she figured it. Isn't that amazing? And she's a preacher—she's a Holiness preacher. But that's the way old-time Negroes were. They didn't worry about this rape business.

From an interview with Susan Tucker

Jane Stafford

Jane Stafford (b. 1915) spoke of long years of knowing a particular black domestic whose name was Beatrice. Most interesting to me in her interview were the descriptions of the gifts given, her placement of them as peculiarly female in origin, and her account of a long-standing silence between her mother and the domestic. Although her mother had known Beatrice for over twenty-five years, they did not discuss why Beatrice collected newspaper articles on racial issues; nor did they discuss the articles themselves. Stafford gave no explanation for their silence. Most likely, they were following the unwritten code governing interaction between the races, observing the taboo against discussions of race.

I found in the interviews with white women something of a pattern concerning such silence: the taboo against conversation on race between white and black women and the affection felt by white women for black women were generally mentioned in close proximity to each other. Thus, whereas the code of silence was understood by all southerners, the choice of words by white women—words such as *feelings, politeness,* and *love*—suggests that the white women formed their own female justification to the taboo. Although this justification took into account their own powerlessness as women as well as their concern for black women, the end result of their silence was that they, too, participated in the system designed to keep blacks at a subsistence level. An end to the silence could have brought changes, even if these were just in the immediate environment.

Jane Stafford spoke candidly of this silence, which was observed by herself and her mother. It is clear that she felt that her ideas were more liberal than those of most of her contemporaries.

She lives on an oak-lined street in a stucco house with large verandas on the sides and at the back. Periwinkles and portulacas bloomed in large clay pots near the chairs in which we sat. Against the terra-cotta colored walls ran vines of confederate jasmine.

I *would* like to tell you about Beatrice. Beatrice Waters was her name, and she was really, I would say, a part of the family—accepted for all her quirks and so on. She was with my mother for forty-six years.

And a funny thing that reminds me of that statement—the "part of the family" statement that southerners always say, but it is quite true, really—a funny thing happened at my daughter Mamie's wedding. Her husband, the groom, had invited a schoolmate who was black. His mother, the groom's mother, I think was a little embarrassed. But it was the perfect place to bring him, to us. Everyone was very pleasant.

But during the ceremony, my sister-in-law whispered out of the side of her mouth, "Who's the black?" And I said, "It's Beatrice's grandson." I was just being funny, but that satisfied her perfectly, because it was family.

And the servants, you see, were accepted at places other black people weren't. Even the poorest person had a servant, so of course they'd be at family gatherings like weddings and funerals. They used to say if a southern man had two dollars, he'd give one to the blacks to wait on him. Everybody had servants. It was just the way.

Now Beatrice came to Mother when I was about eight years old. She saw them unloading a lot of new furniture in front of the house, and she just walked up and knocked and asked Mother if she needed help. That's how she was hired—just like that!

And she stayed all that time. She was a little, a very slight little person, and she had a cute little sense of humor, and she could be fun. But she could also be as mean as a snake. She had a real strange side sometimes.

I suppose she didn't feel well. She had a very long day—came to work every day in a starched white uniform at seven-thirty on the streetcar, served breakfast, cooked lunch and cleaned up, and then cooked dinner and cleaned up. Lunch and dinner the other maids would serve.

We had dinner at night, which not many southern people did. But Mother had gotten in that habit of entertaining northerners for father's business. Most southern people had dinner at one-thirty or two, and then the servants would go home. But not us. We'd dress for dinner and come down very formally and sit at the dinner table.

Of course, Beatrice could lie down for a couple of hours in the afternoon. And of course, we were always very prompt because Mother was always considerate of that. She'd say, "Now we can't keep Beatrice waiting." After dinner, Beatrice would get on the streetcar, going home with whatever was left over. Mother always allowed her to take the biscuits or whatever, and she'd go home to her two little daughters.

But I remember her having a much nicer life after Mother moved to the country, because Beatrice could fish every afternoon. Beatrice lived on the place there and went home on the weekends.

She was a very clever person, I'd say, too. She could not read or write when she first came to us. She was from Mississippi, and her family had put her out to work when she was eight years old. I remember her telling me that. And she learned to read and write with her children going to school. That's how she did. She was so smart. Of course, Mother was the kind of person that sat down every Monday morning with cookbooks and wrote out her menus. So Beatrice learned with Mother, too.

You've heard that Beatrice made more than most people? I don't know. She probably did, because Mother was very much for helping the servants. Mother got the first restroom for servants, I mean for the black people, downtown. Before, if they were downtown shopping, they had to go home to their house to go to the bathroom.

No, now, they always had separate fountains. To this day, I can't use the silver—it's not silver, but the silverware the servants use. I think that's just terrible. I know it's just a habit that I have to eat out of silver, because I don't want to eat out of the servants'. Isn't that ridiculous?

The separate silverware and bathroom—that was done because they were a different race. I don't know when it was begun. I expect it was always like that. But of course, a lot of them had syphilis and TB, so there was that, too, that people always mentioned as a reason. But I think it was really a racial attitude. That was something else, though, that Mother did that most people didn't do: she'd always have her servants tested for syphilis. Later they had mandatory testing of the servants, but Mother always did it long before that.

Mother was always very considerate of the servants. She helped Beatrice build a house, and she helped with the education of Beatrice's daughters and took an interest in them. And I remember little things, like when we had a box of candy, she would always send me to the kitchen to give them some candy, and she would say: "Now let them pick it out themselves. Don't be rude and take it out of the box for them."

Another thing I remember Mother said: "Never leave a pocketbook where it would be a temptation to pick it up, steal it." Some people would do it for a trick, as a trap. I know somebody today who does all sorts of things like that to be sure the person dusted the way she wants them to.

And speaking of stealing, there's one little story I wanted to tell you about a maid named Albertine that we had once. Mother had a lot of parties, and we had a downstairs coat closet, and Albertine would meet the ladies at the door and hang the coats in the closet. One day a lady called and said: "I wonder if I left my coat at your house. The last time I can remember having it was at your party three or four months ago."

So Mother asked Albertine about it, and Albertine said she didn't remember anything about it. But something made Mother think that maybe Albertine did know something, so Mother left the house. She was gone long enough for Albertine to go home and get the coat and bring it back, which she did.

So Mother was thoughtful of them and a good manager. She preserved her own standards and yet was kind to them.

Mother died in 1973. She was probably fifteen, maybe twenty years older than Beatrice. In the end, though, they both seemed old, and Beatrice wasn't really the cook then, but she was with Mother to the end.

Beatrice lived on, I guess, about five years. In between that time, I wrote, and we talked to each other and sent Christmas cards and things. I didn't go to see her as much as I should have, but we kept in contact.

But you know, I knew Beatrice a long time, and yet there were sides to her that were never known. She was a lot more distant than most of the help we had. I always called her the old Indian behind her back when she was withdrawn towards me. I would give her a present, and she wouldn't even say thank you.

Or as I was older and married and living right next door to Mother and Beatrice, I used to, every now and then, get in a spot when I couldn't get a baby-sitter, and I'd beg Beatrice to please baby-sit for me. I'd do anything for her, and she'd never do it. And I'd think: Isn't that strange? She's known me since I was eight years old, and she doesn't like me enough to baby-sit for me. But I guess she was afraid if she did it once, I'd be asking her all the time.

And another thing—I thought I wouldn't mention it because I really don't know about it except it was sort of strange. Once when Beatrice went home sick, Mother went over to her room to clean it up. There was like a writing paper box, and on the top, as you opened the lid, there was this picture of Mother's best friend. It was probably something that Mother had thrown away, and underneath that were all these things that Beatrice had cut out of the newspaper about racial matters. We never knew what that was or why. But I know that she really loved Mother, and I know Mother really loved her. As time went on, they used to sort of pat and hug each other, and you didn't do that either in those days.

No, I don't know what they were paid when I was really young. I do remember that when I married in 1938, my mother hired Nellie for me. Nellie lived on the place, and we paid her seven dollars a week. And she'd always get extra if she served a dinner party or a luncheon—both from me and from the other guests. You were taught to leave a little extra for the extra work you'd brought.

Everyone was taught to give them things. Not paying much and yet giving much—no, that wasn't really inconsistent, not for the times. Everybody had been so poor after the war. But they had things to give from the house, and now the women could do the giving. Toting privileges—some people would work for just toting privileges after the war, and maybe a little cash.

Now Mother, I think, when she hired Nellie for me, paid Beatrice twelve or fifteen dollars a week. But Mother was different because she'd traveled and lived other places and even had black friends through her church. Mother paid more than most people did, and she gave the servants things as well.

As time went on, though, people didn't give their best things—as people began to pay more and as the blacks became more insistent. A lot of things—you know, all my children's clothes went to the one I have now. And my clothes, I'd rather give them to her than just the thrift shop, so she had nice clothes. But I always understood that if you were the servant, you wouldn't want to have to count on a hand-me-down. But it makes it easier; it helps them certainly.

A lot of people gave them their clothes, but I don't think they gave them their nicest ones. And people used to say: "Oh, don't give them your clothes. You'll spoil them."

From an interview with Susan Tucker

Marianne Polk

++⁓ᗡ⧳Ɛ⁓++

Accounts of gifts given in return for the proverbial "taking care" were favorite examples used to explain race relations. The narrative of Marianne Polk (b. 1917) provides examples of such giving and receiving and illustrates many of the points noted by Judith Rollins about the maternalism involved in the employer–domestic worker relationship.

Rollins noted, in particular, that because domestic work generally involves the interaction of only two females, it is "measured by both more in terms of the quality of the relationship than the practical work aspects." But she also notes how this form of measurement results in "caring . . . [that] is not human-to-equal-human caring." Thus, "the female employer, with her motherliness and protectiveness and generosity, is expressing in a distinctly feminine way her lack of respect for the domestic as an autonomous, adult employee."* Note how different the behavior of the southern white man toward the black man in Polk's uncle's story is from the behavior of southern white women toward their domestics.

Polk shows us what might be called the typical behavior of southern white women in their interactions with black servants. These white women speak kindly and softly, unlike the gruff uncle. They recall the past as one in which "friendly personal relationships" existed between whites and black domestics. And they recall the past often. Polk, like other white women, tells me later that the interview made her aware of how often domestic workers, particularly old domestic workers, were mentioned in conversations between whites.

Marianne Polk would describe both herself and her longtime domestic as "old school." The domestic is one who still often wears the white uniform. Polk wears tweeds in winter and pinks and greens and navy blue broadcloth skirts in summer. She wears pastel-colored shoes.

Her house is located in an old neighborhood. In the front yard is a cast-iron boy wearing a cap and with one arm extended—on which one could tie a horse. Today these boys are typically painted all one color, usually white. But I can remember such a statue in my grandfather's yard, and in the 1950s the boy was painted in colors. His face was black; his clothes were red and blue.

++⁓ᗡ⧳Ɛ⁓++

I never will forget this story one of my uncles telling one time about the difference between the way northerners treated the colored people and the way southerners did. This colored man was out and destitute and needed something to eat, and he was going door to door, and north-

*Judith Rollins, *Between Women: Domestics and Their Employers* (Philadelphia, 1985), 185–86.

erners would open the door and be very polite and say, "No, thank you." And finally, a man opened a door and just started cussing him and telling him what to do and how he could earn some money. And the colored man said: "Thank goodness. I've found a good southerner."

You see, the southerners treated the Nigras as individuals, and the northerners treated them as a class—I mean, in my mind. And so you've got to think about that. I think now . . . You're asking all about the ones that worked for white families, what they made and so on. Well, I think, for starters, that most of those colored people that worked for families got a lot more than they were paid moneywise. I mean, they were taken care of if they needed to be. They were provided with a lot of food and clothes. And any bad things that happened to them—if they needed money to help, they were given it. It was more of a friendly relationship than I think people will ever know.

I always remember having servants. I mean, I never remember not having them. Now I have Cora. Cora had worked for—had come from Mississippi when she was seventeen. That was where my mother-in-law was from. And Cora came to nurse my husband's younger brother and stayed about fifteen years. Then she got another job and stayed with them I don't know how many years. And then we finally—I needed somebody, and I called her and asked her if she would like to come work for us. I don't know when that was—she'll know when it was. I would say [it was] twenty-eight years ago when she came back to us, and she's been with me ever since.

I don't know how old she is. I ought to know. But I expect she's been with this family forty years or more, and she's really a part of the family. In fact, my youngest son can't go a week without coming to see her.

Nowadays, though, it's gotten too businesslike. Like in the old days, if they stayed thirty minutes longer, that didn't mean anything. Nowadays they're all on the clock and they're—they've got to be paid to the minute, and it's become a more businesslike relationship rather than a friendly, personal relationship.

Like even with Cora, I had to cut down on her hours when they passed the minimum-wage law. I just told her that she'd be making more, and then I cut down on her hours. I guess she does make more, but not a whole lot more than she used to. But she's here less.

Now I was talking to a friend this morning, and she had a maid in South Carolina that was called Florence that they were so devoted to. And she said, "Guess who called me the other day?" She said, "Florence!" Said,

"She just called to tell me she finally finished paying for her house and that I had given her a thousand-dollar down payment on it all those years ago, and she wanted to pay me back the thousand dollars. I told her no way, I didn't want it now!" And Florence may come down to see 'em. She came about three years ago. But it's funny she told me that this morning, and then you're here.

But you see, that type of thing is going out. They're depriving themselves of it now, the new ones are. As long as we've got these old ones, they're still the same. But the younger ones are not going to have the closeness, I don't believe. It's going to be strictly a businesslike arrangement.

And they almost always were given free medical care. And then, of course, they would take food home. In fact, I tease Cora and tell her she won't say no to anything. I give her so much, I said, "someday your house is going to bust." I give her clothes and everything—rugs . . . I mean, I give a rug or curtains, all those kinds of things. And I expect a lot of them she gives to other people, you know, somebody that she knows that needs them.

I should try to find you the poem I wrote about Cora. Some of us had a party for our maids. We just had the ones of us who have had them over twenty-five years, so if you hadn't had them over twenty-five years, you weren't eligible. So we took all the food, and they sat on the front porch, and we served them. They were just as cute as they could be. And we gave them little bottles of perfume and read our poems to them. They had a grand time. They just loved it.

You know, my husband in the beginning said, "I don't know whether that is such a good idea you all might be undertaking." But knowing them as long as we have, it wasn't any question of them being uppity or anything. They just went right along with it. But now they want to do it again.

Anyway, though, they've always been such a part of my life, I guess just—they're just part of your earliest memories and part of your life. And maybe in our family we've been fortunate in having ones that stayed with us for so long. I've felt like they *were* just part of the family.

From an interview with Susan Tucker

Jill Janvier

Jill Janvier (b. 1951) remembers first learning of race through a domestic worker. She remembers asking about the differences in the ways white and black adults behaved, particularly why the black domestic could use only a toilet reserved for her. Other white women remember asking similar questions—for example, why black domestics could not sit in the same booth in the drugstore as whites, why black domestics could not sit in the same section of the bus or streetcar as whites, and why black children could not be taken to the same parks as white children.

Interestingly, white interviewees born before 1930 did not remember asking questions about such differences accorded solely on the basis of race. Possibly they simply do not remember, because they are further away in time from their childhood. Or possibly, before 1930 the custom of treating people differently on the basis of race was ingrained earlier and in such an absolute way that they have no conscious memory of asking. Janvier's comparison of her own questions and those of her children suggests that the latter proposition is true. Certainly, all children must have asked such a question, for it is, as Janvier says, "a child's question"—a matter of natural curiosity and an uninformed observation about what was happening.

Janvier questioned many of the interactions of whites and blacks as she saw them in the domestic worker–employer relationship. But she did not overtly question the giving and receiving that went on between white employers and black domestics. It seems that she was not quite as concerned about this latter aspect of the relationship because, by being born in the 1950s and witnessing the changes since the civil rights movement, she has been able to understand the giving more completely. She did not speak directly of the negative side of giving. For whatever reason, however, she was careful to say that, in addition to hand-me-downs, she also gives items that are not secondhand. She acknowledged the meaning of hand-me-down gifts, and she recalled some that she had given. It thus seems that, though Janvier is aware of the dual nature of giving, nevertheless she does not want to relinquish the power to give. One gives to reciprocate, but one also gives because in so doing, one feels generous. Generosity, in turn, is self-validating as well as rewarded in our culture.

Jill Janvier lives in a house with a screened front porch and wicker furniture. But she is rarely on this front porch, since she leaves early each day to drop her children at a day-care center, then returns with them at night. They often eat in a local café, where one can leave her a message.

Do you know how some southern women of our age will automatically tell children to call them Miz So-and-so—Miz Susan, Miz Jill? Well, as a general rule I don't like that. It sounds so cutesy. But now I have my children calling their baby-sitter Miz Jane. I do because I just feel like, my Lord, this lady is older than I am and they shouldn't just call her Jane.

With my children, this is the first time I've been able to afford a maid. My children haven't been around black people as much as I was as a child. And they are beginning to ask questions about them.

It was different for me because from the time I was born, there was a black maid in the house. And as I got older, say eight or nine, I do remember asking questions. I can remember asking Grandmother one time why Verity had to go outside to go to the bathroom. They had a bathroom out under the garage for the help, and I didn't think that was fair. I don't remember her answer, but it was something to the effect that it was just the way it was.

But now, noticing the physical difference between black and white—I don't remember that. My son is five, and he said to me something about somebody being black. We were at my sister-in-law's house. Her maid's name is Belinda, and he said something like "I like that black Beli." I said, "What?" Finally he said, "I like that black Belinda." I said, "Oh, you like Miz Belinda?" He said, "Yes." And I said, "Oh."

I was upset. I don't want a whole other generation of that—of always noticing and remarking on the difference between black and white. And yet, I said to myself, you idiot, he's not retarded. Surely he's going to notice the difference. I guess it's like noticing trees are green. But noticing race has so many other connotations, and I guess it's just going to be there from now on. Which seems so early to me. I don't want it to be how it was for us, and yet I don't want them to see blacks as foreigners the way northerners do. I don't really know how to respond, because I certainly don't want to make an issue out of it.

Now in my house my mother always had help. And then my grandmother lived next door, and she had help. My grandmother's cook that she had until about two years ago came when I was born—Verity. And then whoever it was she had before that she had for at least twenty years, if not longer. So I grew up not only knowing the ones who were there but also hearing stories of ones who'd been there before.

Now Verity didn't live on the place. But the other one, she and her husband did. Grandmother had a garage, and above the garage were two apartments. So they say! I wouldn't call them but two rooms, 'cause, like the bathroom was downstairs in the garage and it was just a toilet and a sink. It's not like there was a tub or shower. Course, it could have been years ago. I don't know. But it was not very plush. That's for sure.

There were two rooms, and she and her husband lived in one, and another man who worked as a sort of chauffeur and yardman and the heavy-work man—he lived in the other one.

But the cook, her husband was a no-account. He never worked for them. I guess he did nothing, to hear Grandmother talk! Nobody liked him, and they were real relieved when he ran off one day.

They had no children, so she moved in the house and lived in the back room. It was a lot bigger than the garage room. It's the size of a nice bedroom. But there again I know she had to go outside to go to the bathroom. I know that for sure because even the ones in my generation had to do that. That was what I'd asked my grandmother about. That's just a child's question. I'm sure any southern white child that had help in the family asked it.

The other one we had was Lucille. Lucille she still works for my mother some—and Grandmother and my brother and my cousin. She just kind of splits up her days with everyone now. She has seven or eight children, and they used to come over. I remember watching TV with them, and I remember they would go to Detroit all the time and stay with their aunt. But we'd still give them our clothes that we'd outgrown. I remember I would pile them up and tell her if there was anything that she wanted, if anybody could use it, to take it. I still do that. As a matter of fact, I'm getting ready to ask Jane tomorrow if she'd like to have three never-been-worn Vanity Fair underwear pairs that don't fit me.

I loved to go home with Lucille. Every now and then we used to ride the bus home with her. That was a big treat for us, a big highlight. We'd go to her house and play for an hour, and then Daddy would stop by and pick us up.

Lucille had to stop work this summer, and Verity stopped work two summers ago. Well, in Grandmother's opinion they're just being lazy. I don't want that to reflect ugly on my grandmother. I promise you she is a wonderfully kind person, but she has this odd idea they're just being lazy.

Now Verity she got sick. She started having dizzy spells, and they put her in the hospital for tests. Nothing ever showed up. Her children, who, according to Grandmother, have never paid her a bit of attention, they wanted her to quit. And so Verity did. And poor Grandmother! I mean Verity's been working for her for thirty years, and Grandmother was ninety-four at the time, and she felt let down. And to make matters worse, Verity never even called. Her son called and said, "My mother won't be coming back to you anymore." Which, that part, I do think that was kind of strange. But I'm sure Verity was afraid to call. I mean, Grandmother is not the domineering type of person, but yet she expected certain things. And Verity was always the stereotype servant. I mean, she never opened her mouth except when spoken to. She was very polite, very subdued, very reserved, so I'm sure she was too timid to call Grandmother herself.

But Grandmother is sure that those children have talked Verity into being lazy! It's not like Verity is young herself. She's probably seventy-eight!

And the same thing happened about Lucille, who works occasionally for my mother and who worked for Grandmother two days a week. Lucille had to have two cataract operations. She had them this summer, and like, she was scheduled to have them in July, and end of May she stopped working—four weeks or so before she was going to have the operation. Well, everybody in the family thought that was terrible. "She's letting Grandmother down," they said.

I said:"Hey, y'all, this woman's getting ready to go have an operation. She may not *see* again. Let her enjoy four lousy weeks without working." They feel like that's letting them down! To them, neither Verity or Lucille have any right to do that. Now with Lucille, for me, it was perfectly understandable. Verity's case I'll admit is odd, but still I can understand what might have happened. I think she called Grandmother last year on her birthday, but neither of them mentioned that Verity had been sick.

These relationships—they're more odd than marriages. They seem to have a real strong bond to each other, and yet there is this undercurrent of the mistress-servant relationship. There's a lot of tension even in the best of them.

But now, like with Lucille, *I* don't feel any kind of tension. I could call her and tell her anything, and she could do the same for me. But it's not like she's ever worked for me. She did come and live with me for a week when my first child was born, to help me take care of him. But other than that, it's not like she's ever come to work for me.

To her, I'm just another child she's raised. Shoot, I don't know what I would have done without Lucille! When we were in our twenties, we used to have lots of money problems. And when I'd take Lucille home from Mama's or Grandmother's, we'd stop in the grocery store. She'd go buy me rib-eye steaks and all kinds of little delicacies with her food stamps! Little treats once a month!

But that makes me think of how the black and white relationships in the South got all confused. You never really knew who was taking care of who, and in a lot of cases you still don't. And it seems to me that the black maids often were generous to the white families, particularly to white children, like Lucille towards me. To me that generosity has something to do with dignity. It's saying: "Hey, I'm not beholden to you. I can help myself, and not only can I help myself but I can help you."

From an interview with Susan Tucker

Part V

Knowing the White Folks, Knowing the Black Folks

Long before southern white and black children ever went to school together, many of them were known to each other through black domestic workers. Black domestics, in their journeys from home to work and back again, went between the two sides of the segregated community on a daily basis. Black domestics were participants in the intimate lives and rituals of both races. Black domestics became, therefore, interpreters who explained white life to blacks and black life to whites. Through black domestics, many black children heard firsthand accounts of the ways of "the white folks," and many white children heard similar, though usually more censored, stories about the lives of blacks.

The function of these black women as interpreters of the different cultures is often illustrated in southern literature. Calpurnia in *To Kill a Mockingbird* might be considered exemplary of the literary black domestic as go-between. For example, Atticus, the white father and community leader who employs her, asks her to go with him to tell a black woman that her husband has just been killed. Furthermore, it is Calpurnia who instructs Jem and Jean Louise, the white children, in the ways of the black community. Calpurnia takes them to church with her, and here they see something of her role as a "handkerchief head" who is resented by at least one black for her alliance with whites. They glimpse not only a different meaning to Calpurnia's employment in their home but also something of the masks worn by blacks in dealing with whites. Being with Calpurnia in the black community, the children ask questions about her personal life. They learn for the first time of her background—of her youth on the plantation of their mother's family. They learn that she speaks differently with black people than she does with white people and why she does so. They learn that many black people do not have the opportunity to go to school or to learn to read. In their visit to the black church, the children first realize also the separation between themselves and Calpurnia. The girl child, Jean Louise, in particular, begins to consider the implications of being black or white.[1]

Like Jem and Jean Louise, white children in real life accompanied black domestics to church, visited in black homes, and witnessed discrimination toward blacks on bus rides and on ventures into the city. In so doing, white children heard the talk among blacks and thus heard something of the way blacks spoke of their own lives. Many of the white interviewees spoke of such memories, revealing some sensitivity toward, and understanding of, black life as it had been known to them as children.

And yet, white children could only *begin* to learn of black life through black domestics. After a certain age, usually around eleven, the white child was denied the opportunity to visit with black domestics. At a certain age, the white child was instructed to turn away from his or her nurse, not only because of age but also because of whites' assumption of their own superiority. White children were taught that this black woman, as well as all black people, were forever children and that their ways were thus not really worthy of consideration.[2]

So whites, as they grew older, knew less and less of black life. But black domestics, as their years of service with white families increased, knew more and more about whites. Thus, the relationship between servant and employer became more and more one-dimensional. Black domestics were witnesses to the most intimate details of white life. As one white woman stated: "We will tell these maids things we wouldn't even tell our best friend." Whites, on the other hand, knew only what the domestic chose to tell about her life. The memories from childhood, then, remained central to most interpretations of black life by white adults. "We know them and we don't know them," said another white woman. "We see them almost every day, but we don't see them every day as they really are."

Walker Percy noted this dichotomy of knowing and not knowing in an episode in *The Last Gentleman*. The reader is told much about the relationship between the Vaught servants and Will by one simple statement: "The engineer was the only white man in the entire South who did not

1. Harper Lee, *To Kill a Mockingbird* (Philadelphia, 1960), 127–36.
2. The turning away from the black nurse by white children is discussed notably by Lillian Smith, *Killers of the Dream* (Rev. ed.; New York, 1961); Adrienne Rich, *Of Woman Born: Motherhood as Experience and Institution* (New York, 1976); and Robert Coles, *Farewell to the South* (Boston, 1972).

know all there was to know about Negroes." As Percy implied, most white southerners feel that they know blacks. They feel this way because they know black servants: "A Southerner looks at a Negro twice: once when he is a child and sees his nurse for the first time; second, when he is dying and there is a Negro with him to change his bedclothes. But he does not look at him during the sixty years in between. And so he knows as little about Negroes as he knows about Martians, less, because he knows that he does not know about Martians."[3]

Like Percy's southerners, most of the white interviewees felt that they had some intimate knowledge of black life through knowing black maids. I did, however, find some variations on Percy's observation. Perhaps because I was *asking* white southerners to discuss their memories of black domestics and therefore asking them to look at blacks, I found that many had pondered the relationships between blacks and whites long and hard, particularly such relationships since the 1960s. It may be that my observations differ from his because of changes in southern race relations in the last quarter century. Perhaps, too, my observations are different because I spoke with white women, who had more occasion to "look" at the blacks who worked in their homes, to know something of their problems, and to feel, though usually in retrospect, shared problems.

The white interviewees who thought about and observed black women most intensely seem to have done so in response to the civil rights movement, to personal crisis, or to the interview itself. The civil rights movement frequently brought the first opportunity for white women to hear the views of blacks expressed openly, to read the works of black authors, and to see films about black life. Only then did most of the white interviewees begin to ponder the lives of blacks.

White women who were going through changes in their personal lives also remembered the example of black domestics. Younger white women, especially, remembered the lives of black mothers who worked as domestics. These white women often recalled how black domestics coped with child care problems, marital problems, and financial worries. These white women—who frequently were entering the work force, becoming divorced parents, or acknowledging violence in the white family—drew upon what they knew of the coping mechanisms of black domestics.

3. Walker Percy, *The Last Gentleman* (New York, 1966), 194, 195.

Finally, the interview itself often seemed to serve as an impetus for white women to look at the lives of blacks in general, as well as of domestic workers in particular. In follow-up interviews most of the white women declared that the initial interview had made them realize how little they knew of black life. They frequently acknowledged some confusion about the differences between white and black life.

They also spoke of past feelings of sadness that were re-created in the interview. They remembered that as children they had felt sad about the vast material contrasts between their own lives and those of the domestics. They recalled that their sadness had been explained away by white adults, who pointed to the poverty whites had known after the Civil War or who said that blacks were people from a primitive culture who were only beginning a long journey toward civilization and education, let alone material wealth. Many of these white women remembered being told that the family's domestic was an exception—a "good black," unlike most. They remembered that she was frequently contrasted with her "childlike" husband. Her perseverance under adverse economic conditions represented not the unfairness of a segregated society but her own strength, her innate ability to care for others. Singling the domestic out as an exception was also a convenient means to blame black men for the economic conditions under which blacks lived. She was a person pointed out to white children as deserving of her position within the white community, as someone other blacks should emulate. If only they would do so, it was said, the conditions under which blacks lived would change.

Many of the interviews re-created, too, much of the confusion that white women felt about the black domestic whom they had loved in childhood. The memory of her affection, juxtaposed with an awareness of past inequalities and present tensions between whites and blacks, seemed to linger as an unanswerable question—a riddle of how it was possible to be so close to someone without really knowing her, indeed of "how well we can ever know other people," as one woman put it. The white interviewees' childhood memories of domestics thus seemed to be a symbol of a failure in the past with repercussions today.

For almost all the white women I spoke with, even those born in the 1950s and 1960s, their childhood exposure to black domestic workers remained their most extensive contact with black people. It is not difficult to see how the memories persisted and became exaggerated. It was mainly through black domestics that whites came to know, in Percy's words, "all there was to know about Negroes." In the interviews of the white women, black domestics remained as symbols of a time when a degree of understanding of the lives of blacks was at least possible.

These symbols remained, perhaps, because they were central to the practice and interpretation of race relations within the South. Whites, after all, lived in some fear of blacks. Although legal, economic, and social measures had clearly established whites as the dominant group, whites also believed that blacks had an underlying tendency toward violence. To live in communities that were almost equally divided between black and white, whites had to feel that not all black people, given a choice, would kill them. By remembering the time when they knew black domestics and the families of black domestics, whites could continue to locate "good blacks" within the black community.

Some of the interviews with white women suggested that they unconsciously reduced their fears of blacks by "knowing" a few key persons whom they designated "good blacks"—the exceptionally clever cook, the hardworking yardman, the forgiving black nurse.[4] They often discussed these persons immediately before or after defending segregation on the grounds that blacks in general could be considered lazy, immoral, ignorant, and at times violent. The contrast between "good blacks" and "bad blacks" seemed very important to them in their defense of segregation. They would then go on to identify blacks who were "happy with things as they were," and they might recall slaves who remained faithful after the Civil War and servants who professed disdain for the civil rights movement.

Domestics, for their part, played back to whites an affirmation of the whites' belief in domestics as exceptional. In so doing, these black women solidified their position and gained greater balance in their economic and psychological existence. But in so doing, they also sometimes spoke of other blacks as inferior to themselves.

David Katzman has noted that employers often found negative characteristics in a domestic and then applied these characteristics in sweeping generalizations to the entire ethnic group that she represented.[5] But in the interviews we did, I found that the employers typically were con-

4. This way of balancing one's fears of a group against "good" persons who belong to the group needs further study. Some social psychology theories on assimilation and contrast might be relevant. And for the relevance of this balancing technique to conservative southern politics after the Civil War see C. Vann Woodward, *The Strange Career of Jim Crow* (2nd rev. ed.; New York, 1966), 50–51.

5. David M. Katzman, *Seven Days a Week: Women and Domestic Service in Industrializing America* (New York, 1978), 222.

vinced of the exceptional characteristics of their black domestics but then had to make sure such characteristics were understood to be lacking in the rest of the black race.

The white interviewees also identified the exceptional domestics as black persons with whom they were friends and with whom they could work in a system of mutual obligations. This idea was sometimes expressed as a longing for a return to a *Gone with the Wind* version of the South. However, it was also expressed in statements such as "We were all connected to one another," "We were easygoing with each other," and "We had to get along one way or another." These statements suggested to me that in feeling that they knew black life through black domestics, white women convinced themselves of the wholeness of their world. Thus, many white women clung to the illusion that the segregated South, as represented by the black domestic worker and her status as "part of the family," was a viable and just social system.

For some whites, a belief in their knowledge of black life was necessary for another reason as well. Only through believing they possessed such knowledge could whites confidently proclaim themselves securely in control of the blacks. Surely, it was for this reason that many white politicians told stories of their old mammies. And the average white person, with less devious intent, discerned the popularity of such stories and repeated them. These stories were popular with whites because they spoke of the Old South and of the continuing superior position and beneficence of the dominant race. Whites of all social classes, then, came to discuss, as well as exaggerate, their only real personal contact with blacks—their contact with black domestics.

For every bit of information whites knew of black life, blacks knew ten times as much about white life, also through black domestics. This process began for blacks, as it did for whites, in childhood. Black children, for example, often accompanied their mothers to work in the homes of whites. Sometimes they went literally to work—polishing silver, dusting furniture, standing on milk cartons to wash dishes, baby-sitting for white children who were just a year or two younger than they were. Here they learned of the relative wealth of the whites' lives. They saw the many bedrooms and bathrooms, the toys, and the sparkling floors of the whites' homes. Here, too, they might be told that black people must stay in the kitchen, that they must use a certain toilet and eat out of certain dishes, and that they must let white people go first.

More often, black children saw their mothers leave home for work. Or from the child's perspective, they saw themselves left by their mothers, who went to care for white children. Black children, then, felt that the white children usurped their rightful position in relation to their mothers. In addition, the white children seemed disrespectful, since they called the black mother by her first name. Black children also often heard—directly and indirectly—the stories their mothers told of white people. Their mothers spoke of many whites as people who could not cope with the good luck they had and as a messy, lazy, and inconsiderate people. Many black writers and black civil rights workers have described the process by which they learned about whites through their mothers' work in white households.

For example, Alice Walker, in one episode in *Meridian,* portrays a young black woman recalling her knowledge of whites.

> Her mother, though not a maid, had often worked for white families near Christmas time in order to earn extra money, and she told her family—in hushed, carefully controlled language . . . about the lusty young sons home from school for the holidays, calling her by her first name, of course, and begging and pleading and even (and her mother scoffed) getting all blubbery the way white men get. . . .
>
> Yes, it was understood about white men. . . . And when she described white men it was with weary religion-restrained hatred. . . . She spoke of their faces as if they were faces of moose. . . . Besides, she said, they were manipulated by their wives, which did not encourage respect.
>
> But what had her mother said about white women? She could actually remember very little, but her impression had been that they were frivolous, helpless creatures, lazy and without ingenuity. . . . Her grandmother—an erect former maid . . . held strong opinions which she expressed this way: 1. She had never known a white woman she liked after the age of twelve. 2. White women were useless except as baby machines which would continue to produce little white people who would grow up to oppress her. 3. Without servants all of them would live in pigsties.[6]

Other black writers have described the feelings of resentment that rose in them because of their absent mothers. John A. Williams, in "Son in the Afternoon," presents a grown black man, Wendell, who remembers and still resents the fact that his mother left him to care for white children: "But somehow when the six of us, her own children, were growing up, we never had her. She was gone, out scuffling to get those crumbs to put into

6. Alice Walker, *Meridian* (New York, 1976), 103–105.

our mouths and shoes for our feet and praying for something to happen so that all the space in between would be taken care of."[7]

Black domestics remembered being taught as children that the few whites who were worthy of some of their good fortune were exceptions. As with the whites, this choosing of exceptions worked to alleviate some of the fear of the other race. Blacks, after all, were also taught to fear whites. And more important, they had everyday examples upon which to base such fears. Every day black children saw their parents cast as second-class citizens in the eyes of whites. Black children were taught that white people had the power to destroy black life—economically, as well as through force, if it came to that. As one black mother told Robert Coles during his interviews about school integration:

> Just the other day my Laura started getting sassy about white children on television. My husband told her to hold her tongue and do it fast. It's like with cars and knives, you have to teach your children to know what's dangerous and how to stay away from it, or else they sure won't live long. White people are a real danger to us until we learn how to live with them. So if you want your kids to live long, they have to grow up scared of whites. . . . So I make them store it in the bones, way inside, and then no one sees it. Maybe in a joke we'll have once in a while, or something like that, you can see what we feel inside but mostly it's buried. But to answer your question, I don't think it's only from you it gets buried. The colored man, I think he has to hide what he really feels from himself.[8]

To hide what they really felt, black southerners, then, had to find some way to balance their fear. They often found it, as whites did, by locating "good" people among the other race, and they often did this, as the whites did, through domestic workers. The reason why they did it was probably so they could tell their children that the life given them was not all bad, that there was hope for their future, just as there was for that of the white children. The black mother told Coles, "We have to live with one another, black with white I mean."[9]

The system blacks worked out to live with whites involved maneuvering economic as well as social forces to control as much of their own destinies as possible. One of these maneuvers involved using the knowledge of whites—gained mainly through domestics employed in white homes—to the best advantage. Once they found "good whites," black

7. John A. Williams, "Son in the Afternoon," in Langston Hughes (ed.), *The Best Short Stories by Negro Writers* (Boston, 1967), 291.

8. Robert Coles, *Children of Crisis: A Study of Courage and Fear* (Boston, 1964), 66–67.

9. *Ibid.*, 66.

women then worked to achieve some psychological balance. To ward off the problem of accepting the perceptions whites had of blacks as inferior, black domestics used their knowledge of whites to create their own self-images. In so doing, they compared themselves favorably with their white women employers. They did so with confidence because they knew the lives of white women as well as they knew their own. Their knowledge of whites also helped them to fool whites—to play the part expected of them. Their knowledge of whites also allowed them a sense of victory: they felt that they knew which white people would and would not "find their way to heaven."

Black domestics, through their knowledge of whites, could also establish some leverage for other blacks in the workings of segregation. Many of the black women who were referred to Mary Yelling and myself were described in terms of their longtime association with white families, and indeed they were referred because of what this longtime association meant. A domestic who worked for a white doctor, for example, was remembered because she always helped her neighbors get proper medical care. A domestic who worked as a washwoman for many families would point out those families that behaved decently or indecently toward black females.

Thus, in the memories of both whites and blacks the domestic appears as a key person in the formation of their perceptions of race and of the working of the community as a whole. The narratives of Part V speak of this key role of the domestic. Like the narratives throughout the book, they speak also of individual bonds that joined the two groups of people together. The black domestic as interpreter of the two races made the reconciliation of the two seem possible—if only for some moments, for scattered individuals—and made the ways of each group known to the other, to some extent at least.

Clelia Daly

As generation after generation of black women entered domestic work, a body of knowledge about how to deal with white employers was formed. Black domestics repeatedly spoke of advice given them by their mothers, aunts, older sisters, and friends. I heard such advice repeated so often that I feel that stories about it should be considered a standard part of how domestics coped in the world in which they lived.

For example, a number of black women stated that older women told them, "Never marry yourself to a job." Three domestics spoke of learning from their mothers that in order to preserve their independence, domestics should not borrow money from whites. Three other domestics stated that it was considered best not to tell the truth to whites concerning one's hopes and aspirations. Said one black great-grandmother, "We've known since slavery not to let them know we want education for our children." Thus, though young black women entered the homes of employers alone, without the support of co-workers, they took with them generations of advice.

A warning to black women just starting out as domestics appears in Aletha Vaughn's narrative. She noted that whites "treated animals better than they treated black servants." Three other black women echoed this observation. One black domestic, for example, noted that the cats in the employer's household were fed in bowls from the family china—"all the pretty flowered china that she worried so that I might somehow serve myself from!" One white woman also described a domestic worker who resented the fact that the dogs were fed ground meat. The domestic, she recalled, "got so mad at me for asking her to fix the dogs' Christmas breakfast that she put her head in the oven one Christmas morning." The domestic did not die, I was told. "We caught her in time. We just sent her home."

In her narrative Clelia Daly (b. 1913) recalled a story that her mother told her when she was young. It was essentially a warning to her that whites, though they might profess affection for black domestics, really considered them as interchangeable among one another and easily replaced. This is advice she has not forgotten.

Daly's voice was tired and bitter. At first she was slow to speak of the pain behind this bitterness. As the interview proceeded, however, her voice became stronger and she spoke more quickly—more like, I suspect, the woman known in her neighborhood for her refusal to let whites "get her down." In her career as a domestic she had both taken her mother's advice and worked with the understanding that her white employer would act as an intermediary in dealing with the white-dominated legal system. The first means of coping worked for her; the second did not.

Her front yard is striking. On the day of the interview sunflowers ran along the narrow wooden porch. In rows beneath the sunflowers were purple and pink phlox, snapdragons, periwinkles, asters, and impatience. Her neighbors said that she has a garden for every season and that some summers she plants only one color of flower.

I was born here in Mobile and went to school here and graduated from school here—and come out of school and didn't want to go to no other school. My mother wanted me to be a nurse, but I didn't have enough initiative to want to be nothing, I guess. I just went working around houses.

My mother she washed and ironed in those days—at home. She worked for a very rich family. She did their washing for about twenty years. She'd go get the clothes on a Monday and carry 'em back on a Friday. She done the washing out in the yard in washtubs, boiling the clothes in those old black iron pots, and then ironed them with those old smoothing irons—coal irons.

My first job I had when I was in school. I helped a lady wash, like I had helped my mother. And then when I got out of school, the lady that this lady washed for wanted somebody to clean up. So she gave me the job there. I worked there every day about two or three hours a day. I just vacuumed and housecleaned and washed woodwork and windows. Made three dollars a week.

And then I got married. I was seventeen, and I stopped work with the children. And I didn't go back to work until my husband passed. He passed in '56, and then I started working with a friend of mine for the Parrs.

I didn't mind going back. If I had to do anything, it wasn't hard with me. I just accepted what I had to do and just done it willingly. I never complain because it's something that I have to do. And I just done it with a smile.

I worked there about five years. Then I took care of my grandchildren for eight years. During that time I remarried, but it didn't work out. It was just horrible with him. I couldn't go nowhere. I was just like a prisoner.

And to pay for me a divorce, I went back to work again. A friend of mine lived around the corner, and I told her I wanted a job. She told this judge she had worked for about me. So he called me and asked me if I was ready to go to work for 'em—Judge Sayers. I told him yes, so I worked there to pay for me a divorce. I worked until retirement out there. She begged me not to stop, but I told her, "No, I had enough." I told the Lord if I didn't get nothing but a dollar a week, if he'd help me stretch that dollar, I would stay home.

See, I worked because I had to work. I never liked to work, 'cause I can find plenty to do right here. I'll get out there with my flowers and my yard and look at stories [*i.e.,* watch soap operas], and I'll have a full day. But I'll go back willingly to work in houses if I have to. Never even give it a thought to have another type of job. You know you have to have initiative to do things, and like I said, I don't have initiative.

But I also thought I was good as anybody now. I always thought I was just as good as white people. I came just like them. All of us come in and have to be washed and bathed. But I just say they're a lot of your own people you don't want to come in contact with because of the way they carry on. And I don't blame white people for not wanting to associate with some people.

But I mean I didn't love the white people the way some people say they do. I never been like that about white people. Like Mrs. Sayers—she was nice to me, and I was nice to her when I was working. But I never call 'em after I left, or go visit them.

I wouldn't go visit the Sayers. And I tell you really what made me leave from out there sooner than I would have—I went out there one day and I asked Judge Sayers if he could help me with one of my grandsons. And he told me, Judge Sayers did, that if it was money, he could help me. I didn't need his money, and I told him. I thought if he cared for me like he said, you know, he would have got in contact with some higher-up some way or other and tried to help my boy. Wouldn't he? I explained that my boy needed to be in a hospital. He done wrong, but he was very sick. Judge Sayers said, "I don't know, but I think if it was my son, I think it would be best to let him go to jail." And he went on with all that.

So I thanked him very much, and I left from out there. He wasn't really being truthful. Onliest thing I wanted him to do was to help me get the boy in the hospital. He eventually got in the hospital, so I was right. He'd been in Vietnam.

But I'm out there wasting up my health and strength and all that. And if you can't have somebody to help you when you're in trouble, you don't need to be around them, do you?

His wife she told me when I first went out there that she was as close as the telephone and that she did have a bank account of her own and if I ever needed anything, she could always let me have it. But I don't care where I work, I ain't going to get no money from them white folks. See, a lot of people just be in so much debt with them that they really have to love 'em. They have to come when they say come. No, I'd do without till I could get the money myself.

I always had a feeling that people they like you as long as you're able to do their work. My mother told me that. I told you she worked for a very rich family, and she was up in their house one day helping out with the old grandmother. And this old black man who had worked for them since he was a boy, he passed up there in the house with them. So my mother said, "Oh, I know they're going to miss him." And the old lady said, laughing: "I don't know, Margaret. You can always get another darky, just as good or better."

So I told Mrs. Sayers that when I was leaving. She said, "Oh, I don't know what I'm going to do without you." I said, "Well, I'll tell you the little tale my mother told me about the old man." I told her the tale. "You can always get another darky just as good or better." She turned red! She went back up in that room and locked the door. "Oh, you know I wouldn't think of anything like that, Clelia," she said.

I know a lot of people, they just dearly loved those white people. But I think those white people now, they think like that old lady that told my mother, "You can always get another darky."

From an interview with Mary Yelling

Zelda Greene

In comparing their own lives with the lives of white women, black domestics had much information to draw upon. The very nature of domestic work made the servant privy to almost all happenings in the household. The very nature of southern white and black interaction, especially the fact that whites considered themselves inherently superior, made for a situation in which whites often unthinkingly displayed temper, passion, and other private feelings in front of black servants. Black domestics, therefore, knew almost everything of the personalities of the white women for whom they labored, and they knew much about the conditions under which white women lived.

Black domestics were aware, then, that passivity and idleness caused emotional problems in some white women. As black women witnessed such problems and told of such problems, they became experts on white behavior and were sought out for advice by other blacks. Zelda Greene (b. 1915) is a domestic who was referred to Mary Yelling as such an expert. She seemed to enjoy this position, and she spoke with humor as she explained the behavior of whites.

She wears shifts of different floral prints and slippers when at home. She offers lemonade to guests and invites them to sit on a gold couch covered with clear plastic. In winter her house is kept warm by a floor furnace; in summer it is cooled by window units. The walls of all the rooms have gray paneling. On the living-room wall are photographs in plastic frames and taped Hallmark cards.

I'm Zelda Greene. My date of birth is November 19, 1915. Mary Washington was my mother; Victor Washington was my father. She did domestic work all her life; she worked for two or three different families. My father did yard work.

I was first employed when I was very young, for the Rendons. I worked for them . . . Like you would, on the way to school, go by and wash dishes in the morning and come back in the afternoons and work, and work on Saturdays. I worked like that for her for about ten years. By that time, I imagine, I was about seventeen, because then I started working full-time. I worked for some of them five years, some fourteen years.

And the lady I'm working for now—me and her cook were good friends. Her cook was getting married, and the people I was working for was leaving town. So I decided, I just told Miz Holland, "I'll come over there and work for you, since Callie is leaving town." I started working for

Mrs. Holland, and that's been twenty-eight years ago. She pays pretty good—the minimum wage.

In the early times the people weren't like the people now. The older white people—if they didn't like you, they pretended that they did. They were good pretenders. But most of the time these younger people, if they don't like you, they'll let you know it. The older people would do you all kinds of favors and everything like that. Now these young people won't do as many favors. Now the lady where I work, she's always been real nice. No, I don't think it has to do with the minimum wage. I think it has to do with people nowadays being different.

But white people they have a way of letting you know through their children. I used to see that. Like I used to take the Dawson children out walking and they'd ask the *children,* "Where have you been?" And I was standing right there!

A lot of things black people had to put up with, but they went on and smiled and put up with it. People had to take and swallow a lot because they thought that they would lose their job.

But I always had good people to work for. I was fortunate. After I stopped that ironing and stuff, I always was in the kitchen. They'd always tell me if the cook don't add enough to the pot for herself, she don't think much of herself if she leave herself out. The cook always got the top best. Most of the rich folks give you the privilege of being over the kitchen. And most of the people that would be at the place where I worked—like the sister would come in from out of town—they'd get somebody extra to do the ironing.

I always got along good. I'd do my work and let them do theirs. We'd get along fine. Some people, the cooks especially, begin to think they own the house. That's what makes the trouble. My mother used to always tell us, "Never marry yourself to a job." You go out there; you're hired on a job; you do your part what you supposed to do. You know how a lot of people think they own the people's houses and stuff like that. No, when I come home, *that's* my home.

And I always worked, too. I wanted to be independent. When I'm making money, I can spend it just like I want to.

So I think I had a real good life. My daughter, before she went to college, she did baby-sitting and working like on Saturday jobs—the extra money to have to spend. I always taught her to try to make an honest living—always have your own money.

Now Miz Holland she was for my daughter going to college. A lot of people told me they were scared to let the white people know they were sending their children to college. But I wanted them to know mine was going, because most of the time . . . I'll tell you the way white people used to be long time ago. They would say, "Well, if your mother used to work for me, you grow up, and then after she got too old, the children will work for me." They would just keep it coming on down from generation to generation. I say, it's going to stop right there! My daughter she won't need to think she need to do that days work for a living.

But I always liked domestic work. I tell you, it's not so much the work—it's the people you're working for. That's what makes the difference. I never had anybody who tried to demand so much out of you in the run of the day. Most people I ever worked for had their work planned. Something like an assembly line—what you got to do Tuesday and what you got to do Wednesday, like that.

Matter of fact, the lady where I work now, she's got it *all* planned. Just like you go to work every day and not all of a sudden something spring up. Like she plan company, she plans ahead of time. She don't wait till that day when I get there and say, "Oh, we going to have company, Zelda." She don't do that the whole twenty-eight years. I never known her to plan company the same day she was going to have it.

Like she had planned yesterday morning for the Junior League sustaining members. They came and had coffee and discussed business—like, you know, saving energy and stuff like that. I say stuff, because, you know, where we would think, it would be nothing. Wouldn't give it a thought about it, because it don't be nothing. Like this white lady say, every time she go out the room, she turn the light out; she go back in, she turn the light on. I say to myself, Now what is that to talk about over coffee? It didn't sound interesting to me.

Otherwise it was socializing. They get together, and it's women of her age. They get together and discuss different plans about energy, who's going on a diet. Lord, you wouldn't believe what they be talking about—whether they going to get a permanent, what beauty parlor they go to, whether she any good or not. Lord! But you know, when they have their meeting they stay one hour. They come in there at ten o'clock, and they have that meeting, drank that coffee and eat them Danish rolls, and eleven, they getting ready to go. They don't stay over.

Most everything they do is planned. And the sustaining members they all take their clothes down to the Junior League shop. They have to clean out their closets before their husbands let them get anything else. Miz Holland's husband's dead, and she buys whatever she wants to buy. They buy seasonal clothes. They don't go buy just to be buying. Everything is planned. They don't just say: "Well, I saw a pretty dress. I think I'll just buy that dress." It's got to be for a purpose. It's planned for the winter, spring, summer. They *live* planned lives.

Now she have winter clothes. She just begun to wear wool. She say, "I'm so glad it's cold so I can wear these wool dresses." She got jersey dresses. When it's not so cool, she wears them. Now what you call Indian summer, she got these dark cotton—she wears them at that time. Then come spring, she got spring clothes.

It's closets—just a whole walk-in closet—closet about that long, the whole length of my room. Here over this end, cotton things; over here, the wool things; over here, the robes, and so on. Those condominiums have lovely closets. I'd like to have a closet like that so your clothes won't be jammed. They can just hang anything up there. Its almost like a department store. And they have closets of gloves and evening dresses. I'm telling you, their lives and our lives is like night and day!

From an interview with Mary Yelling

Aletha Vaughn

Among the black interviewees, Althea Vaughn (b. 1930) was the angriest woman to whom we spoke. After I first listened to the interview on tape, I phoned Mary Yelling, and we talked about this anger. I expressed surprise that we had not heard more anger in the interviews with black women. Mary, in turn, spoke of the prohibition against feeling anger toward whites. Southern black children, she reminded me, are taught to suppress anger, since it would be foolhardy to act with anger toward whites in a white-dominated society. Moreover, she said, Vaughn does truly like whites. She lives near whites, and she knows good things about whites.

From the black perspective there is also sometimes a duality of love and hate for the other race. Whites and blacks in the South have been neighbors. They have borrowed sugar from each other. Especially in the days before air-conditioning, they could hear each other's voices between houses, voices that expressed life's most private emotions. They have gone to each other for help in times of birth, sickness, and death. Thus, they know each other as individuals and, at the same time, as representatives of their respective races. As a black neighbor once told me: "Some days I see you as a white; some days I see you as the person down the street. It depends on what has gone on that day."

Within the domestic worker–employer relationship, there was less chance, however, to see each other as simply human beings living on the same street. By going into whites' homes, black women were reminded daily of the relative material wealth of whites. When black domestics labored for working-class whites, they were reminded that whites could get jobs not open to blacks with the same education and training. In the deference they gave white women, black women were also reminded every day that they were seen as inferior. And they were reminded almost daily that they had little recourse to change conditions even within their workplace.

One way black domestics dealt with such feelings of powerlessness was by tricking whites—by manipulating the situations in which they were perceived as childlike, lazy, or inferior. Black women, as Aletha Vaughn said, would not work as hard for white women who had commented on the laziness of blacks. Or they might decide not to come to work on days when they knew company was expected. This latter action might be in response to having overheard white employers express disbelief in reasons given for previously missing work, reasons given in advance. As Trudier Harris has noted, domestics might "use quiet indirection to sabotage the mistress's work schedule and to appropriate what they can for their families." Harris cites Verta Mae Grosnover's account of a laundress who worked out a system whereby her child could wear, without the knowledge of whites, the clothes of white children on a regular, rotating basis.* Domestics,

*Trudier Harris, *From Mammies to Militants: Domestics in Black American Literature* (Philadelphia, 1982), 30.

operating in ways that took advantage of the stereotype, might also purposefully ruin the food of whites in order to be told to take the other casserole (which had been fixed according to the correct recipe) home.

Such measures, of course, did not alleviate the long-term bitterness and anger many black domestics felt and could not express outwardly.* Like Aletha Vaughn, many former domestics decided that only by stopping their work for whites could such bitterness be decreased.

Vaughn is well known to both whites and blacks in the little town where she lives. She is thought of as a neutral person who speaks out at city meetings for both whites and blacks. She likes to talk.

She lives on an unpaved, clay-dirt road lined with the houses of whites and blacks who have lived there for generations. The houses look much the same. They have small, open front porches, and small windows on the front. There are just a few new brick houses and also some trailers belonging to younger family members.

I myself, I always worked. I always worked all the time. Even when I was real little, I did a lot of work at home because I was the oldest of nine.

When I was eleven years old, I went to working out. My mother was working for some people, and she got sick, and I had to go in her place. I was eleven years old. And I've worked ever since. But I've had enough domestic work. The bad point is when you resent the person you're working for, for being, I guess you would call it, prejudiced and cruel and wanting to be superior to you. Just because you're working for 'em as an individual, they don't see that they're not any more than you are. They treat you like some type of animal instead of a person.

In fact, the animals get treated better than the servants. Plenty of 'em let the cat sleep in the bed with 'em! And then they'd be afraid you'd sit on the cat. And then they were afraid of you! Me I was told if you lie down with dogs, you get up with fleas. Not them.

But you could prepare their foods for 'em, and they trusted you. I could have felt the same way they felt, but I wasn't raised to be evil, so I'd just go on and do my work. A lot of time I felt like spitting in their food, but I didn't. I would just go on and say: "Well, they'll get theirs. This is their heaven, I suppose."

'Cause I don't see how anybody could see the Lord, the way they act. It's true! They even had separate bathrooms! Oh no, you didn't go in the

*The long-standing, often unexpressed anger and bitterness of domestics toward whites is discussed by Judith Rollins, *Between Women: Domestics and Their Employers* (Philadelphia, 1985), 225–32.

bathrooms they went in. They had separate bathrooms and everything for you—everywhere, in those days. They would build a outhouse and put a bathroom outside before you could use the bathroom that you cleaned inside. They didn't want any stains in their bathrooms! It's just been in recent years, they've started letting people go in their bathrooms. And they had certain dishes you could eat out of. You ate out of certain dishes, and your particular plate and fork and spoon went in a certain place.

I don't know. I just don't understand the whites' superiority to start with. That's why there is so much turmoil now, because everybody's suppose to have equal rights and just the white folks can't take that.

See, white people they don't have any interest in nothing but your work. They will butter you up, work fire out of you, and work you to death if you listen to the junk they say. They'll tell you they love you and be so nice and bribe you.

And with all white folks, the servant ate in the kitchen, and you had to wait until they got through eating, and what's left, you got some of it. That's the way that works.

And I've seen people of today like that. You get something that's left, or they'll serve themselves certain things and tell you to get a bologna sandwich. You done worked all day, and now they get the hot meal. "It's plenty of iced tea and bologna and a little ice cream," they'll tell you. And I wouldn't eat. I'd go home and eat. And maybe that's why my health is bad, because someone could act funny about food and I wouldn't touch it.

I've had them tell me, "Now anything that's here you can have except the things I've marked." She'd mark an **X** on things she didn't want you to have. That would be the best food. The rest would be maybe peanut butter and jelly or maybe a wiener or a piece of bologna or something like that. The rest of it would be hot food—vegetables or a beef roast or baked chicken. You didn't eat that. You eat the cold stuff.

I've had one to tell me, "Oh, banana sandwiches are nice!" And I'd never heard of a banana sandwich—mayonnaise and bananas. She just raked it on in the garbage when I didn't want it.

And you'd work all day, and they ain't doing nothing but on the beach swimming or laying around thinking up something to work your brains out with. I had one lady we worked for—oh, me and my cousin worked for—one summer. And with this lady was three daughters-in-law. They used to come from the city, and it was their summer home. Two of the daughters-in-law were just as nice as they could be. They didn't act prejudiced at all. But one was a hellcat. She was a devil. She was a hellcat, and no good luck never did follow her.

She divorced her husband, and her son was killed, but those other ones are still living in the house. They were rich people, but that girl— oh—but I lived to see her get everything that she put out. She's been pushing up daisies about seven or eight years, and I'm still here.

I couldn't stand her for nothing in the world. She [was an] old redneck hoo'ger, those kinds that weren't used to nothing.* And when she got in a family that was used to something, she just wanted to throw her authority around. She'd do anything. Misplace things, something of hers, and pretend you're stealing—she did that. And I quit there on account of it.

I was real young then, sure was. And I just think about people along that you work for and the differences in some. But they all got that same thing: You're a black person. Deep down, it'll come out if you push 'em.

Now they'll "Yes ma'am" you and everything else. They're trying to get more money like that, pay you less. But it used to be a time that—oh—no white woman would say "Yes ma'am" to you. I don't care if you have five children older than they is. If they was fifteen years old and you were working for 'em, she was Miz So-and-so and you was old Sue or Sally or whatever. If you were ninety years old, that's old Sally.

They never respected or put a handle to an old black person.† And right now, some of 'em will come up to you and ask you, "Do you know where Marie is?" Marie is my neighbor, and she's seventy-four years old. "Could you tell me where Marie live?" I tell 'em, "Mrs. Rivers live next door." That's to let you know that she's not Marie to you.

Once I had a lady come in, complaining about my work. She said something about "you niggers," and I told her to take her mop and mop her own damn kitchen. But if I had the opportunity now, instead of just walking off and leaving the mop in the bucket, I'd take the mop and whup the woman's behind with it—period. I couldn't take it. In fact, I wouldn't be saying "Yes ma'am" and "No ma'am" like I used to.

And old white people will call you Aunt This and Aunt That. I had a next-door neighbor, Miz Alice Smith. White people come out there and ask her, call her Aunt Alice. She said: "I ain't none of your damn auntie. I

Hoo'ger is a slang term that blacks use to refer to a common white, usually a common white woman.

†*To put a handle to* means to call a person Miss, Mrs. (Miz), or Mr. rather than their given name alone.

ain't no kin to you. My name is Alice Caldwell Smith, and nothing that white is in my family. You see how black I am. I am not your aunt. Don't call me aunt."

That's right. There's no justice until God comes through here. And it's going to take God to straighten some of this out. He's been through here with Hurricane Frederick, but next time people going to be laying down instead of trees. Everybody was without water when Frederick come along. Everybody was out of gas, from the rich house to the poor house. When the Lord get into something, he's even.

We know how to stand in line. We've been in lines before. They ain't going to know what to do. They going to be confused, but we really know how to survive, because we've had to try to survive all our lives. We're still trying.

I've lived to see things that my grandmother told me was going to happen. So I know more coming, too. It ain't going to be no more slavery time. You can just put your foot on that, because I ain't going to take what my grandmother took.

But well, if they'd treat people better, really I don't mind domestic work. Work is just work, but just how you be treated and then how you be paid. They were unfair with the pay, and they probably would hire a white girl now and pay her $3.00 or $4.00 per hour just to baby-sit and want to pay you $1.75.

I know I've resented a lot of things they've done. But I had to work, so I did the work. But now I wouldn't do it no more if I had to eat lizards for a meal. I've learned better. It don't take all that to survive. Oh, the white man really had the black folks fooled. They had 'em fooled a long time. Some of 'em still fooled. And those old people, I try to explain to 'em so they will know better.

Explain that they don't have to call that young lady Miz So-and-so to eat, 'cause the same hand feeds her feeds you. And until we realize that, we're forever be taking some kind of old fare from these white folks.

From an interview with Mary Yelling

Eva James

A few of the black interviewees spoke of how they "handled whites," how they presented themselves to whites, and what they would and would not "put up with." Black domestics exerted the one prerogative they had in the labor force: they did not stay with employers who acted in ways that fell outside certain standards. Such standards of behavior dictated what was considered fair. Employers, for example, seemed to be expected to pay on time, give gifts at Christmas, provide decent meals on the job, talk with politeness and not order domestics about, and act with respect toward religion. White children also were expected to understand that when their mothers were not at home, they must obey black domestics. White children also were expected not to talk with disrespect to domestics. In particular, they were not to call any blacks "niggers."

If any of these standards were not met, black domestics typically did not continue to work at the offending household. They did not, it seems, directly confront the employer or even formally resign. They generally seemed to speak to their employer of quitting only at the last minute—on the way to their car, for example. They wanted to be sure they would be paid, and they knew that confrontation would get them nowhere. Indeed, it might hurt their chances of finding another job. In some cases they would "just be sick and not come back" or "not show up." Or as a number of women told me: "Something happened. I don't remember, but I didn't go back." Their manner of speaking suggested to me that they left pretending that they would come back.

Regardless of the method of quitting, domestics did not feel financially bound to employers who were blatantly unfair. As Eva James (b. 1935) said, "A private home job, you can get anytime." White women, it seems, knew that certain kinds of behavior might even get them reputations such that no black domestic would work for them. A certain line was drawn—call it a line of decent behavior—that, if crossed by white women, meant they were not acceptable as employers. As Jacqueline Jones noted, "Black communities frequently demonstrated their own 'code of color ethics,' which stipulated that a person should not work for a white woman who was a well-known unscrupulous employer, or one who was particularly ' "finicky" or hard to please.' " Jones also observed that "mutual support and cooperation among blacks gave the appearance of an 'organization' " that kept tabs on the behavior of employers, an idea that many white women feared.*

Eva James and her friends gave one another such mutual support. In the interview she spoke of domestic work and the knowledge of whites that it required. By then she had left domestic work. It provided a steady income when her children were in school, but once her child-rearing ended, she fulfilled a lifelong

---

*Jacqueline Jones, *Labor of Love, Labor of Sorrow: Black Women, Work and the Family from Slavery to the Present* (New York, 1985), 133.

dream to become a beautician. Today she has a beauty shop set up in her home. The first two rooms smelled like perfume. She swept the linoleum, laid especially for the shop, as she began to talk.

I was first employed when I was eighteen. My husband was then making about thirty dollars a week, bringing home about twenty-five dollars, so I took a job in a private home. And I worked on and off in private homes for about fifteen years.

The first family I worked for was the Fitzgeralds. At that time they had two daughters, and the only job I did there was basically cleaning and washing and ironing. They were very considerate. They never—like some people would say, "Fix your lunch and eat in the kitchen"—the Fitzgeralds, when they came in for lunch, they fixed my plate right along with theirs. I can say *that* for them, and that was back in '53 or '54. That's something that very few whites did at that time.

Next I went to the Eastburns. Now that was a family! She asked me could I read and write, and that was when Kennedy was running for office. Then she wanted to know if I was a Republican or Democrat. I told her I was a Democrat. She said, "Everybody that works for us have to be a Republican, because Kennedy can't be elected president." That made me mad, but I was real quiet then. I didn't have much to say to nobody.

So I worked for her about three weeks. At that time I would drive the days that my husband wasn't working. That Saturday when she got ready to pay me for the week that I drove the car, she left my money on the counter top, and she didn't include busfare. And I thought about how she asked me could I read and write. I decided then I really didn't like working for them anyway. So I decided to write a nice little note and tell her, "No, I cannot read or write, nor can I count money."

Well, you know, that's when I started working for the Morans. A friend of mine recommended me to them. They had three children. My job was nursemaid to them, cleaning up, and fixing lunch. They were nice and middle class. They both worked, and her mother was living with them. But like any of them, every so often you have to let them know that you not as dumb as they would like to think you are.

One time she called me a liar, and that hurt my feelings. It happened because I had two children with asthma, and one night they both had bad attacks. The next morning I knew she had planned to take her mother to the doctor. But I called her and told her, "My husband will be wanting to go to work at two o'clock." She had an appointment at ten with the doctor. "If you want me to"—I told her about the babies being sick—"I will run out there and stay long enough for you to take your mother to the doctor." She agreed to that, and I went around there and worked till she got back.

About twelve she got back. And at that time I had a neighbor that worked right around the corner from the Morans. This lady had asked me about doing her hair. And I did her hair every two weeks. This was the day I was going to do her hair, and since she got off anyway at twelve, I told her I could take her home with me, if she didn't mind me seeing to the kids in between. And so she told the lady that she worked for that I was doing her hair and that she was riding home with me.

The next day, when I went to work, she didn't speak, and I went on and started doing my work. All that week she didn't speak to me, but I felt like maybe her and her husband had then had it and she was in one of her moods. But Friday, when she got ready to pay me off, she says, "I was going to pay you for a full day until I found out you lied."

She and the lady my neighbor worked for decided that my kids weren't sick and that we just wanted to leave early. And boy! I will not repeat exactly what I told her, but I did tell her that *that* job was hers, mine was at home with my family, and that when the day come that I had to lie about one of my children being sick to hold a job . . . We'd had it.

It was Good Friday that day, too. And she always fixed a great big basket for my children. She had bought the basket way ahead of time and decorated it. When I told her I didn't need the money, she said, "Well, don't forget the children's basket." I told her they didn't need it either, that I could buy them all the candy and junk they wanted to eat. I didn't have but that little money I had just made. Wasn't no way that I could have bought no candy. But I left it sitting right there, and I stopped working for her for about six months.

They called every day. All the neighbors called, too, because really they couldn't control the two children they had. And the children they would call two and three time a day, crying. So I finally let them talk me into coming back. She raised my salary, too, and helped me to buy a car. I mean she financed it, and I paid her back so much a week. At the time, in order to get to work at eight, I would have to leave home at six-thirty. I had to catch one bus and transfer to another. That means that I had to get up in time to get my kids dressed for school and take the ones that were little to the baby-sitter. And half the time we had to stand up all the way to work, and it was plenty of seats up front. That was before Martin Luther King broke it all down where you could sit anywhere you wanted. So with the car everything was much easier.

With white people, it ain't hard to keep them in line. If you're fair and you know how much you can put up with, how much you will put up with. Because, look, a private home job, you can get anytime. You didn't go there to fall in love with the people. And the job is not hard if you get a good understanding with them. Look them dead in the eye. You definitely got to look them in the eye, because if you drop your head, they felt like, "Oh, well, I got a good thing here."

From an interview with Mary Yelling

Voncille Sherard

In her interview Voncille Sherard (b. 1942) told of being propositioned by her white male employer and of his friend exposing himself to her. Black domestics in white homes were not always in safe environments. Although the black women to whom we spoke were only a small sample of domestic workers, they agreed that sexual harassment of black women by their white male employers was a clear possibility.

It was a possibility denied by white women, and as Sherard suggested, it was not always discussed among black women. Both Mary Yelling and I got the impression that the black interviewees were reluctant to discuss rape. This reluctance may be accounted for in two ways. First, as in other areas involving race, black women were taught the necessity of silence. Sherard, for example, recognized in the reactions of her mother and her grandmother that, above all, she was not to tell her father of an incident that had nearly been a sexual assault. This instruction parallels the comment of Priscilla Butler on the helplessness blacks felt when rape occurred: black men could be killed for protesting the rape of black women.

Their silence also reflects the fact that most women tend to deny rape. Women are taught to believe that rape will happen only to those women who "ask for it." There is some psychological protection in believing this idea. Black women sometimes had no other choice, given the socioeconomic structure of the South, but to send their daughters into white homes. The silence of some of these mothers suggests that they may have hidden their worries and fears for their daughters. Such silence may have mitigated daily fears.

Voncille Sherard is very glad she does not live in the South of the past, where her daughters might have had to work in white homes. She is glad she will not have to warn them about what she learned of whites in their homes.

She talked quickly, in a forceful voice, racing through such topics. The mother of a large family, a full-time professional, and an activist in the community, she has a busy schedule. The interview was conducted in stages at various places, amidst many other activities. At the time she had a new four-bedroom house and employed a full-time domestic worker.

I was first employed at eight years old as a sort of companion to a very old man who always tried to run away. His daughters hired me for a couple of dollars a week. They were white and lived down the street. They both worked, and their mother was dead, and their father was half out of his mind and senile. That's why they decided to pay me to look after him. They were two sisters and one, Miz Radford, looked after me like I was her own child. She would have to go to work at one, and I stayed with him after school.

And then the white man that she worked for got me to work for a black lady, his mistress. He offered me more money, maybe three dollars a week, to help around the house, clean, wash the clothes, plant her garden, or anything she wanted me to do.

She lived on the same street, too, so I could work both jobs. I didn't have to stay at this black lady's long because she was basically clean about her house herself. I think it was just a thing where she was this man's woman and she wanted someone. I'd just go down there every day and see what she wanted. And then I'd go down to Miz Radford's and work for her.

I'd do anything for Miz Radford. And she was good for me in that she used to take me places. I remember one time we were at the A & P—we'd make groceries together. She would make a big deal out of having me with her, hugging me and calling me baby and all this. This man filled the bag full of groceries and reached out and handed me this real heavy bag. She just cussed him out: "You don't give that baby that bag . . ." and went on and on.

And like when we got on the bus, she'd sit in the front and sit me right by her or sit me on her lap. That was when blacks sat in the back. And she would go on vacations and she'd send me these cards of Little Black Sambos. She would also buy me things, like flip-flops and little chains and bracelets. I spent most of my time with her, really, for years. I just hung around her. I'd even go and help her at work sometimes.

When I started high school, I started working for a lawyer and his wife, very rich people. I was a companion for their daughter. It was agreed that I would work each weekend for six dollars a day, spending Friday night, Saturday night, and Sunday night. I would get there about four on Friday and wouldn't get back until she'd bring me to school on Monday morning. I was only supposed to work in the afternoons and until the little girl went to sleep, but I would end up working the whole weekend. And she always said she would pay me extra but that she was saving my extra money back for me because she knew I wanted to go to college. But when the time came to go to college, the only extra I got was two skirts from the Spiegel catalog.

So I went off to school and stayed a year and a half and had to stop out the first semester of my second year. I went then to New York and worked days work. I had a sister there. And then at Christmastime, Daddy came up and got me, and I came back and got a domestic job keeping a little baby about six months old.

On that job the mother was the one that hired me, and she was very nice, very young, and very eager to go to work herself for the first time. They lived in a small two-bedroom apartment—two bedrooms and a bath upstairs and a living room and kitchenette downstairs. I wasn't to clean up or anything like that. I was just suppose to watch the baby, but the apartment was so small I would clean up to make my day go by. I had to be there at eleven. The husband got off at five or six, and he would take me home, because she worked from two to nine.

Anyway she was never there in the afternoon. It was just him, and he would sometimes bring a friend home. The friend was a Canadian-American.

One day the husband came home alone at about one or two. I was upstairs making the beds, and he came upstairs and tried to force me in the bed. He asked me how much his wife was paying me. I told him thirteen dollars a week, and he started to tell me how much more I could make if I would go to bed with him. I just started hollering. Well, with my screaming, the husband left. Later on that evening he came back and apologized and promised me he wasn't going to bother me anymore and asked me please not to tell his wife.

I didn't tell my parents, because he really hadn't done anything to me. But then I told the wife she was going to have to make some other arrangements about getting me home. It just kind of drifted along for a week, and the only arrangement that was made was that the husband *and* his Canadian friend would take me home.

Now the friend—the reason I brought him up was because I felt comfortable when he was with the husband. The husband was a typical redneck-looking person. The friend was of a more slender build, and he was very nice and very polite. And he would always talk to me about my ambition to become a CPA, how he felt like I would make it.

But then one day about a week later, I'd finished my cleaning and the baby had gone to sleep, and I had put me a chair at the end of the stairs where I could sit and watch and still listen for the baby. It was hot. It wasn't air-conditioned. Looking back on it, they weren't really rich people at all. I had the screen door locked, and I heard the Canadian knocking. He asked if he could come in. He said he was working in the neighborhood and wanted to use the rest room. Well, since I knew him, I told him, sure. So he went upstairs, and a few minutes later I heard him say, "Voncille."

I looked up the stairs, and he had taken off all his clothes. He just had on his undershirt. All of his bottom clothes were off. And I had never had the experience of seeing a naked man. It was the most frightening thing that I had ever seen in my life, and I just ran. I just grabbed my raincoat off the sofa and ran out the front door and left him and the baby there.

I was in a white neighborhood, and I didn't know anybody. So I ran until I saw a filling station. I saw a black man working at this station, so I ran and asked him if he would loan me a dime, because I did not have a penny. And I told him what happened. He wanted to go and try to do something about it. And I told him, "No sir, it's all right. I'll just call a cab, and my daddy will pay for it when I get home."

When I got home, my mama and grandmama was there. I can remember their faces and the way they said, "Please don't tell your daddy about this." Their faces—it was like they'd heard this before. And we called the mother and told her I'd left the baby there, and she was very upset. She cried and worried so about the whole thing and promised mother she would pay the money that she owed me. It was Friday, and she owed me for the whole week.

My mother never did get the money from her, but the good thing that came out of that story was it made me know I was not going to be a domestic for the rest of my life. That experience really forced me to make a way back in school. It was just a little job—she didn't even have a car. To tell the truth, that thirteen dollars probably didn't leave her a whole hell of a lot. But it changed my life. I finished school. We called the president of the college that day, and I was able to get grants and jobs on campus.

But it was just a way of life to Mama. And she always knew she could do it. And since I had to work, it was what I could do, too. But that day I knew I wouldn't do it again.

The other jobs were really almost as bad—the ones I had before that. Like when I was the companion to the little girl, I *did* everything. I didn't know any better. They used to have me on the top of the house. They had a three-story house and windows straight up to the top of the house with small balconies, and I would go out there and clean windows, get on ladders! I'd wipe venetian blinds, whatever!

Now the lady at that house always dangled a little charm before me. Always told me, like, "If you go up those ladders, I'll give you twenty dollars for that." But they never did pay me that extra. She was a pretty lady, though, and her husband just catered to her. He was ten years younger than she was, and he had been engaged to marry her cousin. This lady, my lady, had gone up in the Delta somewhere to help her cousin prepare for the wedding. And she took her cousin's husband. I mean, the marriage never took place. And the cousin was pregnant, and they made an arrangement, paid her, and took the child. So the child, Nancy, was actually her husband's child, but not hers.

These kind of soap opera things you learned. You got all this information from bits and pieces. Most of it I got from the next-door neighbors, because they had a fight with my boss lady and they'd talk.

And looking back on it, they would have something like orgies. On the bottom floor they had all these beds and a slot machine. And all these people came in there, and afterwards I'd have to go down there and clean up, and all the beds would be pushed together.

Now they also kept down there a big wooden box. It looked like a jewelry box with intricate work on it, but it had "PRIVATE" written on it in big letters. And *that* was just like telling me to wonder what the devil was in this box. Now I never stole from any of these people I worked for, never took anything. But I was so curious about that box. It was just the whole kinky way we lived in that house that made me so curious, I guess. And I don't know how long it was before I finally got the key to open that box. I tried every key I could find. And in that box were pictures, I'll never forget, of naked people—of my boss lady, and the lady next door and her husband, and all these people. And every time I'd go back to that box, there would be a new set of pictures. This went on for a long time, so I realized that was where it was—in this room on the bottom floor, something like orgies.

They used to like me to show them the dances. "Come on. Show us," they'd say. And they thought I could do the cha-cha real good. One day they called me downstairs to teach this man how to cha-cha, and the lady said something like, "What are your constituents over there in Mississippi going to believe were they to hear that you, the big district attorney from Somewhere, Mississippi, is down here hugging on this little black broad teaching you how to cha-cha-cha?" And he just grinned. That was an experience to those people.

They had a housekeeper and a cook and me. The cook and the housekeeper worked only five days. But in the summers I'd stay all the time and maybe just go to my sister's on Sunday. My sister Lillian lived nearby, and they'd take me there and pick me up.

I liked the man because I felt sorry for him. She would have me to do so many dirty things to him—lie to him about where she was and who she was with. I hated lying to him.

But I was like a child to them. I was comfortable with them. I fussed back at them and things like that. But I never felt good about lying to him for her.

And their life was so different than mine. I never saw them go to church. I was brought up to say my prayers before I went to bed, and I would do Nancy the same way. She was just a little bitty girl, and I taught her to say, "Now I lay me down to sleep . . ." She told her parents, and they told me not to teach her prayers. They said she was having nightmares about people dying in their sleep.

Now in the North, where I did days work, that was worse. I didn't have any really bad experiences, but that kind of work is cruel and pitiful, that days work. You didn't work for one person but once a week and maybe have unbelievable amounts of work to do in an eight-hour day—cleaning up the house, mopping, vacuuming, dusting, polishing furniture and silver, baskets of clothes to iron—constant, constant work.

All in all I'd say what I saw was worse in the North than in the South. Up North you had too much work to do, and you weren't people at all to them—you were a machine.

But I can't say that I didn't learn from all those jobs, in the North and in the South. I learned about valuable furniture, the importance of buying good furniture. In my house I wasn't around good things, and even in other black people's homes I didn't see quality things like I did in white people's homes.

And from one lady I got interested in reading novels. I would go to work for her in Mama's place. Mama had worked for her for years and years, and when I was home from college, I'd go for Mama when she was sick. I couldn't stand her, because Mama was so dedicated to her. She called Mama Emma and treated Mama so differently from the way Mama treated her.

One day I was dusting her books. She had a whole shelf of novels—not hardbacks, regular paperbacks. While I was dusting, I looked at the titles, and she noticed and asked me if I liked to read. I told her yes, even though at the time I didn't know I liked to read. She told me: "Well, read that one. See what you think about this one." She liked me to read and then come back and discuss them with her.

And working in people's homes, I saw a kind of life I would not have seen otherwise. It was like a living adventure, and people underestimate their servants' intelligence. They leave things around. They say things. I was unexposed to such things, and it seemed exciting and mysterious to see little notes around and know who was upstairs in a private section of the house when you were told to take the child on a walk and not come back for four hours.

It was overall a negative incentive—"This is what I don't want to be," [I would say to myself]. But it taught me the importance of incentive. I try to give my children incentive in other ways.

But I think it gave me a negative feeling towards white people. I think they all just categorized me—as a servant, as a black. I only remember one household in which I ate with the family. And they always opened the back door of the car for you so you'd know not to get in the front seat. I think the bad things that happened did so more because of the individuals involved and because you were a domestic than a black working for whites, but it is hard to separate them all out. The things that hurt the deepest were racially motivated—like the lady who the first day I got there took out a fork and a plate and told me that this was mine to always use. They gave me the impression that I wasn't clean enough.

But the richer the people were, the nicer they were. I learned that— that money gives people more exposure to life, and people with more exposure treated you better. And I'm trying to give my children that. I'm trying in ways that my parents couldn't. Like I said, it was a way of life then, and Mama just let me do it, sometimes not even knowing where I was. But I would never, under any circumstances, let my daughters work in a home.

From an interview with Mary Yelling

Helen Reed

In *Killers of the Dream* Lillian Smith recalls an incident in her early education about racial customs in which a young child with light skin was seen living in a black home. White community leaders removed the child from the home, and she came to live in the Smith home, side by side with Lillian and the other Smith children. But after a few days it was discovered that the child was not, after all, "white"—she was a mulatto with a black mother. She was, therefore, sent back to the black community.*

A number of white interviewees described less emotional but nevertheless significant memories of not being able to tell if a child was white or "colored." For example, a white woman born in the 1930s remembered that on one occasion a classmate who had been attending a white Catholic school since September was suddenly removed in December because it was found that her mother was actually "colored." Such occurrences, which revealed to children the arbitrary and unfair nature of segregation, were, it seems, common enough in southern society. Many southern white children, then, met with some early event that told them that something was amiss with the system, that skin color was not always the clear boundary about which they were instructed.

Whites reacted in different ways to such early confusing dilemmas. Women like Helen Reed (b. 1900) tended to deny the presence of many mulattoes in the community. Others, such as the ones who described the children whose race came in question, appear to have had a confused, more emotional response.

And yet, following their responses to the questions about race, white women almost always talked of a harmonious system based upon a sort of plantationlike interaction with inferior but happy blacks. Such speeches seemed more than a defense of the past or present. Perhaps they were rooted in the tensions between a publicly recognized democracy, a publicly recognized segregation, and hidden examples of a hollowness and injustice that belied both these ideals. Many, like Reed, spoke with what I would call a yearning that there was no hollowness. They wanted to be sure I understood that life then was "really all right." They wanted to believe the system had some just design, and they located this hope, as Reed unknowingly but aptly reminds us, in the domestic worker, through whom everyone could sing "a hymn where we all joined hands."

Because they so wanted to believe in the fairness of the segregated community, Reed and others like her did not see beneath the masks worn by black servants. Thus, we have no way of knowing if the servant who is described as calling civil rights activists "irrigation workers" was merely protecting her job or was actually uninformed. Reed preferred to accept the latter explanation, as did many other whites who said, without any doubt in their voices, that black servants had been

*Lillian Smith, *Killers of the Dream* (Rev. ed.; New York, 1961), 34–39.

uncomfortable with the civil rights movement, that they had been happy with the situation as it was.

These masks, of course, were worn almost uniformly, and certainly very convincingly. As Jacqueline Jones has pointed out, black women threatened with the possibility of losing their jobs often complied with "the time-honored 'deference ritual' perfected by their slave grandmothers. This strategy could at times enable a movement supporter to keep her job. . . . 'Anna Mae,' 'one of the best block captains and most militant civil rights workers in Greenwood,' sang freedom songs at night, but in the day, queried by a suspicious white housewife, she would profess ignorance of 'silver rights workers.'"*

Helen Reed wore a silk flower-print dress for the interview. She poured tea from a teapot with a colorful tobacco-leaf pattern. We sat in her sunroom on a hard green velvet love seat. A maid in a starched white uniform had carried the tea in on a polished silver tray.

You want me to talk about my life and my connections with the blacks? Well, I suppose I could. I do always think of how much of our lives here revolve around them. If they're not working out just wonderfully, they're somehow causing one's life to be rather hectic. I mean, we depend on them so.

Well, there is a great deal of continuity about life in out-of-the-way spots like this, for both colored and white. We've known each other for generations. I've known a good many here in Monroe County, because I was born here in this little town that was founded by my great-grandfather. He was an Indian agent, and he settled here and befriended many of the Choctaw Indians. A lot of the Indians and colored people around here are named for him—the colored because they intermarried with the Indians or because they always asked for help in naming.

They were uneducated, you see. They still are, really. They can't even pronounce things they believe in—like one girl who worked for me said "the irrigation workers." She meant "the integration workers." But I'd known her mother. Her mother worked for a friend of mine. Like I said, there is a great deal of continuity about life here. And in our family we had four generations of help from the same colored family. Uncle Isaac, Aunt Mary, Abigail, Lucretia—they were all from the same family.

My grandfather had Uncle Isaac. Uncle Isaac had gone to war with him

---

*Jacqueline Jones, *Labor of Love, Labor of Sorrow: Black Women, Work and the Family from Slavery to the Present* (New York, 1985), 288.

and saved his life. They'd given Grandfather up for dead, and the Yankee troops were coming around to chop off his finger, to get his ring off. They came to Grandfather, and Uncle Isaac said, "No, he's not dead." They insisted he was and called Uncle Isaac an old nigger and a fool, too. But "No," Uncle Isaac said, "let me just carry his body off." So he carried him away and set him under a tree and watched the Yankees ride off. Grandfather would have been trampled to death by their horses. But Uncle Isaac saved his life and brought him on back home.

And Uncle Isaac lived behind our house until he died in, I believe, about 1890. Well, then the house was vacant. They were saving it for his daughter Mary. She only worked for my family in the winter. She loved field work, and from spring to fall she'd go all over the state, working on different plantations.

Well, in the fall of 1891 she was gone, and that's when Julia came. Julia was Mammy. And she came and begged Mama and Papa to hire her. She told them her husband was going to kill her. Julia had lived there in the neighborhood, and everyone knew her husband beat her and ran around with other women. So Papa went and spoke to him, and Julia came and stayed.

Joseph was her husband's name, and he was always very meek around the white folks, Papa said. But now the white families often had to intervene for their help. The colored men were not advanced enough to act civilized. Joseph got killed, in fact, not long after that, at another woman's house. Her brother or her husband or somebody shot him.

This was before I was born. But Julia she became Mammy, and she was there for all our births. I was the middle child of seven, and she gave us all nicknames.

And she loved us all, and she loved her little house. (They had to build another house for Aunt Mary, Uncle Isaac's daughter, so that when she came home, she could help us out, too.) We called it Mammy's house, and it was a two-room affair with a big fireplace and a porch. And she had a pipe organ. My father helped her to order it, and she had a gentleman friend who called on her, and he played the organ so beautifully. I thought I'd rather listen to him than go hear a symphony orchestra.

She loved that house, and she never even wanted to go on vacation. Mother would have to make her go. Mother was so concerned about her that she even loaned her the buggy so Mammy could go to church in style. But half the time she wouldn't go. We'd come home from our church, and

Mammy would have been in the kitchen the whole time. She'd baked a cake!

Once she went as far as Chattanooga on the train. We asked her if she'd had a nice time, and she said, "Yes, everyone treated me just like I was white." She was surprised, I guess, at how pleasant everyone was. She was a very dark-skinned colored woman though. You didn't see many light-skinned ones that weren't part Indian in Monroe County. I know people say there was some, but I didn't know of any. I don't remember Mammy speaking of any.

Mammy wore gingham dresses and an apron. I have a picture of me with her, and I wouldn't take anything for that picture. The traveling photographer came through town, and she asked Mother could she have her photo taken. She chose me to go with her, and I was so proud.

And she wore her hair in corn rows. She had a woman come and fix her hair. I used to love to watch that being done. They'd pull so hard, but it was wonderful to watch how quickly they worked.

In 1924 she got very sick. She had some sort of cancer, and Mama got Abigail to come take care of her. Abigail was the daughter of Aunt Mary. Abigail came and worked taking care of Mammy.

But Mammy died in 1925. She was buried in Mount Rose Cemetery. When they buried her, all the colored people from that little church and my family were there. They sang a hymn where we all joined hands and swayed. I can't remember what the song was. They said how Mammy was very respected, and they asked my father to speak of her, and he said what a loyal person she was and how we all loved her.

She left all her money to me, my mother, and two other sisters. Of course, it wasn't much. I believe it came to around five hundred dollars. We donated it to a nursing home for colored women.

Then Abigail stayed on in Mammy's place. She stayed until she died in 1942. And then she had a daughter named Lucretia. Lucretia was an illegitimate child, I believe. I can't remember who Lucretia's father was. Of course, many of them had illegitimate children. They didn't know any better. They still don't. But the families always took them in and raised them. They were no burden on society. You didn't have welfare just for having them then.

Lucretia lived until just a few years ago, and she worked for my sister and then for my niece. So that made four generations of Uncle Isaac's family working for us. Lucretia was very proud of that. She was proud of our family and we of hers. And when my nephew married a girl from a nice family in Mobile, Lucretia went down to the wedding. At the reception she met this girl's maid, who'd been with their family so long. And the maid said to Lucretia, "I hope you know that your Edward is marrying the cream of Mobile." "Well," Lucretia said, "Mr. Edward, he ain't no skim milk himself!"

So Lucretia was very devoted, and such a wonderful worker and just as smart as she could be. She always knew all the phases of the moon and was very interested in the weather. And she could tell you about all the different flowers and plants. But she never did learn to read or write. I don't know if she went to school. The schools for the colored weren't so good in those days. I don't know why. Money, I suspect. Because the ones who had the colored as slaves, they treated them well. But when the plantation system was gone, there was no one to take care of them. They weren't yet educated or advanced enough for freedom. Of course, slavery was a barbarous institution, but not as barbarous as the Yankees will still have you believe. The slaves weren't beaten. Now why would you beat someone who worked for you, who you needed in good health?

Lucretia was one who was in this gap—not educated because she was colored and yet not taken care of because she was free colored. Now they have schools. The government takes care of them now. The government is master, and not such a good one.

But anyway Lucretia had a smart mind, but she didn't reason things out about modern life. She decided one day to take up smoking cigars. And no one else in my niece's house smoked, so she only smoked when they were out. Well, the first night, Connie came home and smelled smoke. She didn't know what it was, so they looked around. Well, they didn't find anything. Then Lucretia said, "I remember there was a man on TV, and he was smoking a cigar." So that man he always smoked when my niece was gone. On TV!

But the young ones! I wouldn't dare try to have them work for me. I won't even discuss them. I hate to talk about race, and I only wish they weren't so touchy. It is too difficult to explain. They're just so touchy, and you don't want to hurt their feelings.

From an interview with Susan Tucker

Eileen McLean

Almost every white woman we interviewed singled out black domestics as different from most other blacks. The remarks of Eileen McLean (b. 1909) further illustrate this process of seeing the domestic as an "exceptional" black. Sometimes white women chose exceptions in order to explain that they did not pretend to know all blacks, merely one person who happened to be black. Less frequently, they seemed to explain the exceptional qualities of the black domestics with the reverse reasoning: These white women felt they did know blacks or knew enough about blacks to proclaim them a generally lazy, childlike, inferior, and sometimes violent people. And they were surprised that the ones known to them as domestics were "not like other blacks."

McLean singles out black women domestics for this latter reason. She unabashedly and unapologetically finds blacks inferior. Because of her openness, she is easy to interview. She is not confused by the South, where she grew up, nor by any guilt. She does not hide any early ideas she was taught. She has no fear of saying the "wrong thing."

In her narrative one glimpses just how hard it has proven for working-class whites to align themselves with working-class blacks. Many working-class whites learn early to feel superior as whites. They are thus sometimes forever unable to see blacks and whites as equal.

McLean's comments also show how white women associated the presence of mulattoes in the population with the "different morals" of black women. By labeling black women as sexually uninhibited, different from white women, and "easygoing," white women may have in part been denying the existence of rape and certainly were rationalizing the existence of black women who had white male lovers.

Eileen McLean enjoyed discussing her ideas on these subjects, though she found my inquiries slightly humorous. "Maids? Well, of all the odd things," she said to me. She is a woman who speaks like a character out of a Flannery O'Connor short story. She is very plainspoken and has a strong southern accent. She lives in a two-bedroom house built in the 1920s and painted every four years. She has a porch swing. She offered me a drink made with bourbon that she called a Boxcar Special.

My mother kept house when I was growing up, and my father was what I would suppose you would call a clerk. I really don't know what he did—I mean the different jobs he had—but I remember he worked at a clothing store. And well, he did work for a while at a grocery store, and then he was a water-meter reader for the city once.

My mother never had any help. She did her own wash with her scrub-board. About 1916 or 1917 is the earliest I remember seeing a domestic servant. She was a washwoman and a maid, and I think she worked for my aunt and grandmother, and then when I got married, she worked for me for a dollar a day. Her name was Sarah. And she worked for another lady in whose house Sarah dropped dead one day.

The next one was Deidre Miles. She was about my age. She, too, worked for a dollar a day once a week. She worked for me it must have been twenty-five years, and I was paying her a dollar a day when she left, too. She was a big, heavyset woman, and the cat I had then was scared to death of her. She kind of stomped around the house. She had a hip replacement, and she had to quit work. She went back to work for some people, but she never did come back to work for me.

I'd already found another one. But now Deidre always liked me. She had three children by her second husband. The first boy she named Michael, Jr., and the next one, a girl, she named Suzanne, and the next one she named Henry Herbert, after my husband. She told me, "I was going to name it after you if it was a girl."

And I said to my husband: "Herbert, you were just unlucky. It was a boy!" That boy is *no good.* He's been put in jail. I think he robbed one of these savings and loan places. And he tried to kill her one time. And then one time, he tried to—when he was a little boy, about six, seven, or eight years old—he tried to set fire to their house. So she said that she had tied him up and put him out in the yard and she had built a fire around him! My husband told me the other day, "It's too bad she didn't let him burn up!" It really is.

She used to bring those children to work, and Henry Herbert used to play with that little boy that lived there on the corner. She brought the daughter, too, but she made the daughter help her. And now when the daughter was a senior in high school, she had an illegitimate child, and Deidre used to bring that baby with her, too. We knew them all.

Deidre used to be a schoolteacher, but she could not write very well, and I can't remember the words she mispronounced—like *miracle* with a long *i.* And she'd say she didn't know "what in the junesproon was going on." She meant what in the name of "jurisprudence." And she called spinal meningitis the "smiling mighty Jesus."

After she left, I had Melinda-That-Got-Drunk. She was here off and on until this year. If she got drunk, she got drunk at home over the weekends mostly. And when the weekends were over, Melinda was still drunk, and she'd sometimes not come to work for three days. She said she was sick. Well, I found out what was wrong with her.

But she would call up no matter what condition she was in to tell me that she couldn't come. And during that time—let's see, she has three daughters and two sons—one got killed in an automobile accident, the other one is in a mental institution, and all three daughters have had illegitimate children. Two of them are living at home with their children. And her husband gets drunk. In between times he does work. He has a truck, and he does hauling.

They live right over here near us, and the police go to her street nearly every night. It's two blocks long and trouble. But she's always lived over there, and she owns her house and another house on another street.

And she is honest and very intelligent. She had very little education, but she could write a beautiful hand. But she didn't like to write with a red pen. I had one up there to write the messages with, and she said, "When we see anything addressed in red, we know something's wrong with it." I think what she was talking about was voodoo—not exactly that, but something like that.

Now I got Lula. The one I have now is named Lula. Finally Melinda just didn't come to work so much till I called up a friend. She told me about Lula.

Lula came down the next day to see if I would suit her—she came *in* the house—because I heard of another lady who wanted her to work, and she wouldn't do it, because it was a big house. She wanted to be able to clean it up to where you could tell it had been cleaned up, I guess. Didn't want to . . . Well, she works all the time. She's slow, but she hates dirt worse than anybody I ever saw.

Anyway she came, and I seemed to pass the test. So I just turn her loose—whatever she wants to do. Herbert says we're going to have to have the inside of the house painted! She's going to get all the paint off of it! She cleans all these little cross pieces, all the stuff on the doors, under the beds, takes all the books out, everything. And she irons—she irons real well. Apparently, she's been doing this her whole life. And she is proper! I'm almost afraid of her!

Well, so I have only known the good black people, so they are good as far as I know. Now I do not like Nigras in general. Just . . . I really don't like them. But in particular, I do. The ones that we've had working for us were real good. They were honest, and you could depend on 'em, even if— Even Melinda-Who-Got-Drunk, well, she would call up and say if she wasn't coming. I let her pick out the day, and sometimes she didn't pick out a day for about three weeks. Well, after so long a time, you get tired of that.

But now Melinda's children, and Deidre's, too, for that matter, are no good. They work, the ones that aren't mentally off, but they're no good. The girls—all they do in between jobs is have illegitimate children.

The Nigras all do that. That is just the way. They don't have the morals we do. Well, now, one of Deidre's children, the girl, finally after three tries passed the state examination to be a practical nurse. And she has one child, the baby Deidre used to bring to work. But she must be about, oh, I guess she's about sixteen by now. She might have an illegitimate child by now for all I know. I've got to call up Deidre.

She lives up there in the middle of the oil country, and she owns five acres of land, and she told me a long time ago they were trying to give her five thousand dollars for that. Of course, all black people have lawyers. She's always had a lawyer, and he told her not to sell it. She's always had a lawyer, and when she was getting a divorce, she had one. And he was so busy getting the husband the benefit of the divorce till I went down to see him one day and gave him a piece of my mind. When Deidre came to work, she said, "My goodness alive!" Said, "That man told me, 'Don't ever send Miz McLean down here again!'"

I don't know if that lawyer did better by her or not after that. I think he was a sorry lawyer. There are a lot of bad lawyers. But 'course, there are a lot of good lawyers, just like there are some good Nigras. There are a lot more good ones than there are bad ones, fortunately for us, because if there were more bad ones, we would be in a fix, I think. About a third of the population is black, and goodness knows they increase terribly!

From an interview with Susan Tucker

Elinor Birney

❦❦❦

The narrative of Elinor Birney (b. 1917) is based upon an interview characterized by long pauses and careful attention to what was being said. She hesitated to speak of race, in observance of the childhood instruction to middle-class whites that to do so would only hurt the feelings of blacks. Her hesitancy to speak also centered around a post–civil rights era fear of saying "the wrong thing." Many educated southern white women now tread carefully through discussions of race. They feel the ideas of their mothers and themselves have been misinterpreted. They feel blamed for conditions over which they had little power.

Birney's hesitancy, as well as her discussion of change, reflects an altered consciousness on the part of some southern white women about blacks within their communities. White women like Birney—relatively liberal, well-educated, and well-informed—do see that certain formulaic stories of the past are now thought to be not quite what they once appeared to be.

Birney's comments also reveal something of the discomfort felt by at least some southern white women in employing black domestics. Most studies of domestic work maintain that the prime motivation for hiring a servant is the enhancement of the employer's image as a superior being. Yet, many women certainly must feel some discomfort, even when paying a decent wage, about the possibility of such a motivation, about the effects such work has on the domestic, and about the presence of a nonfamily member within the privacy of the household. There are many conflicting principles and traditions surrounding the employment of a socially and economically disadvantaged woman who goes daily into a wealthy home. One might feel discomfort if one were aware of any number of different types of ideas—feminist, egalitarian, religious. Something about the overall setup runs counter to the perception of American society as a democratic one. And I suspect that people who question the relationship between worker and employer, even in cases in which one has the historical and family traditions of employing servants, are those who choose not to employ domestics. Or they are the ones who, like Elinor Birney, breathe a sigh of relief when the need for servants seems to pass as children leave home.

Little has been written of other choices working women and men might have if they wish to maintain children at home and have housework done. As Birney points out, it is very difficult to have small children and remain active outside the home without help.

Birney lives in a large three-story brick house. We sat in the library, where a fire burned in the fireplace. Her husband served cocktails at five o'clock.

❦❦❦

I was born in New Orleans and I was one of two children. We were . . . a middle-class family, so that we always had *a* servant. I mean, we had just one.

I was not raised by a servant at all. My mother was always there in the home. She did some church work after I went to school and that kind of thing, but she was always home when I returned. The servant did the work at my house, but mother was there, and I was *raised* by my mother and father.

I don't remember any of those who worked, in particular. They would come and go. We had some for a long time and some not so long. But then, I can remember as a child . . . since I was a little bitty thing . . . a woman Mother had known all her life practically, who really was more a nurse than a maid.

Garrison, that was her last name. We called her Garrison and she rented from us. She lived in a house that my grandmother owned. They had owned the house forever and she lived in that house, and when we were born, my brother and I, she used to come up and sit with us.

Then when I was older, we'd always see her because we used to go collect the rent. In those days, you collected the rent. I would always go in and see her. And I can remember her being very sick and being in bed and not remembering me very well, not knowing me very well. And I can remember that we had the impression that her daughter was very mean to her. That kind of thing I remember, because she was a dear person to us.

She had been with my mother when her mother was ill. She took care of her. So she was just an old family "person."

And I can remember being very sad when she died, although she was very old and had been sick a long time. She was in her seventies or eighties, and I was in my early twenties then.

We had a servant in the country—Pauline. I was very close to her, too. Pauline was different than the others who worked for us in that she always wore a white uniform. This was her choice. She did the cooking and the cleaning. It was a weekend house, but my parents moved over there and lived there right after I married.

Now, with Garrison, there was a sense of taking care of her. But with the others, there wasn't. I know that when my parents moved to the country, they really did not do anything more about the city help. They were not on a pension or anything like that. In many families, they were. But in ours, they weren't. I think it might have been financial.

I don't even think my mother at times had help more than three days a week. Now my husband's family had a completely different set of circumstances. They had many servants. And their two maids were white and their cook was black, and the washwoman was black and the butler was black.

You would see the servants on the streets coming and going. Most of the servants walked or rode the streetcar to work. Because New Orleans is peculiar in that sense. In old New Orleans—I'm not talking about the suburbs, I'm talking about uptown and in the Garden District—blacks lived within a couple of blocks of any white neighborhood. Because they moved in as the whites moved up from the French Quarter, the servants moved up, too, and the blacks established neighborhoods. We always had blacks living within two blocks of us. But . . . I went to public schools, and of course, there were not blacks. So, through the servants, it was really the only way people of my generation as children knew of black people.

I didn't know them any other way until I started work. I'm a social worker, and I started in 1939 for the welfare agency, and of course, the agency was totally integrated. There was no separation at all, so that my outlook, since then, was completely different from many people.

Most people still only knew blacks as servants. No, I don't think the civil rights movement made them look at this relationship. I don't think they associated the civil rights movement with the domestics they knew. With the civil rights movement, I think many of them just thought that Negroes were inferior and they were to do menial jobs.

You know, my husband spent nine years in school in the East, and he always says that he took a lot of ribbing from easterners who really knew nothing about blacks and white southerners except with slavery and picking cotton and that kind of image. He says there was no concept of a person's association with an individual black who might be devoted to you.

So, people in the South loved the blacks as individuals, but not as a group. They associated the civil rights movement with the group, not the individuals they knew. And people in the North loved them as a group, but would have no part of them as individuals.

I would imagine that the blacks in the South felt the same way—that they feared whites as a group but loved them as individuals. I think this is true still, that there are many blacks who have good relations with individual whites but don't with a group.

After we married, we had . . . we've always had help. And we had a maid full-time, and then when we had the children, we'd have students to live on the premises, for baby-sitting. And they'd get room and board plus a certain number of dollars per week. We had an Xavier University girl. The first one we had was a wonderful person, and it worked out very well. Then we had another one that worked out even better. We had them each for two or three years. It was good for them and good for us. They enjoyed it and they had a nice place.

Then it began to be that the students didn't want to do that. Some of them had to because it was one of the ways they could get through college. So we had a couple of bad experiences. I mean, they were not happy with us and we were not happy with them. It happened at the time that so much of the civil rights stuff was going on, and I can understand where they were coming from, but still in all, it wasn't helping us to have them in the house. They were not interested in the children, so we gave that up.

I didn't work then. But still, if you're going to involve yourself in other things, you have to have some help. I was very happy not to work, and I didn't always have to stay home, because I had someone who could help out. I liked to be there, though, when they came home from school when they were little. And when they were teenagers, I went back to work part-time.

But, like I said, we always had a maid full-time, except when our children were all gone, and now we don't. We have somebody one day a week, which is very nice 'cause you get used to not having people around you. We felt we'd been liberated when our children got old enough that we really didn't have to have somebody in the house all the time.

I don't know how you can do much, though, if you have small children and no help. Our daughters don't live in New Orleans, and they don't have any help. And one of our daughters has a child, and she doesn't have five minutes of help.

I suppose it is a southern way to have help. I wanted my daughter to get a baby nurse when her son was born—just for a few weeks—and she said people didn't do that in other parts of the country.

I know in our neighborhood, the young people all have help. The thing that is interesting is some call each other by their first names. The servant calls the woman Mary and Mary calls the servant by her name. Now, I think your employer-employee relationship sometimes could get very sticky if you don't have some separation. But that is a change in New Orleans. I know many people who will not address a black as Mr., Miss, or Mrs.—

never would—and they certainly wouldn't let a black servant call them by their first name.

My neighbor next door, her maid is always getting locked out, and she'll say, "Anita forgot to leave the key." And it's just a whole different ballgame!

Now, other friends have a woman who works for them—Harriet—who must be near seventy. And she reared the man of the household. She worked for his parents, and his mother became ill when he was about four or five years old. She and the chauffeur would take him to the circus, they would take him to the park, they would take him to his friends, they would arrange things for him. She feels devoted to him.

She works for them a couple of days a week with his children, but not any more than she has to, because she says she's too old for another family! But the children adore her, and she is a marvelous woman, and intelligent, and acute and . . . is really good friends with us. She will complain that the little girl goes to this one school and she ought to be going to another private school with a better reputation for academic achievement. "She's bright enough," she'll say. Because you see, she knows all about the schools that these children go to.

Of course, she *certainly* calls everybody in that family by their first names. But I'm interested in the relationship of the younger domestics to younger employers. They shouldn't have to say Miz Susan or whatever. I think that part of it comes from the old plantation days. I really do. But I don't really know if calling each other by first names helps.

Some things have changed, and I guess this is just a sign of one change. I have a friend who is very liberal, and her daughter is very liberal. The daughter's child, just in kindergarten, brought a friend home one day who was a little black child. The mother of this little white girl was in the kitchen with the black maid. And this little black child says to her friend the white child, "Which one is the mother?" Which I thought was the most marvelous thing—Which one is the mother! So, I think it's getting filtered down, but I think it's gonna be a long time before there really is true equality.

You do see different sides of the race problem through the domestics. At least, you can. We had a very strange experience in Destin, Florida. This was in the mid-fifties. We had this Xavier girl, the first one we had, and we had a cottage down there on the beach. So Florence went with us. And the children were all little and Florence went swimming with them. She was a good-looking thing in a bathing suit, and so after about the first few days, the manager of the place said there had been some objection to her being on the beach in her bathing suit. She had to be in uniform.

I said: "That's the dumbest thing I ever heard. She's here to play with the children, how can she play with them in the water and be in a uniform?" I said, "I really would like to know who objected."

Turns out it was a woman from Washington State. From then on, every year when we got an advertisement about this place, it said that if you do bring your servant, they must be in uniform at all times. We were so mad! I was really so mad I was ready to die! You know, the ocean, the Gulf of Mexico. She couldn't be in the Gulf of Mexico!

I don't recall how we handled it. She didn't *have* any uniforms; she'd never worn uniforms. I just don't recall how we handled it. She probably had to stay out of the water. I think that was it. And I'm sure we had to talk with her about it, but I don't recall exactly what her reaction was. That was her last year with us, and she was leaving college to enter holy orders, so I know her reaction was not a violent one. And she was from a small town in Louisiana, and at that point in time, segregation was everywhere. I'm sure she was understanding about it. Probably more than I was.

Well, we did go back. It was our favorite place. But we never took another one of the Xavier girls again to watch the children. Once, we did go back with friends who brought an older domestic, and she always was in uniform anyway, so there was no problem.

From an interview with Susan Tucker

Sophie Stewart

Both Hegel and Fanon, writing of oppression, noted the "existential impasse" in which oppressors ultimately find themselves. The oppressed provide recognition and validation to the oppressor, to his or her superiority. But according to the whole reasoning of oppression—with one group of people said to be superior—this validation is ultimately worth little, since it comes from someone defined as inferior. Thus, the oppressor becomes weaker and lazy, feels no need to excel, and lacks the will and wish to change. Thus, said Hegel, the oppressed come to embody the future. The oppressed embody those people who, in response to material and psychological deprivation, "try harder."*

Sophie Stewart (b. 1940) spoke of the conditions under which she and others of her generation came of age. In the expectation that they, like their mothers, would be waited upon by black women, white women became handicapped themselves. Her comments on this turn of events made me think of the "existential impasse" described by Hegel and Fanon.

Stewart sees that the domestic worker–employer relationship worked to cripple both black and white women. She might never have realized this, however, if the law had not required that domestic workers be paid the minimum wage. She did not hide the fact that her changed awareness is linked to these increased wages.

As with many other southern white women, she gives only a hint that shared gender influenced the way white women may have acted toward black women. Shared gender seems most often to have been perceived by white women when they were teenagers and were beginning to think of themselves as women. Many white women remember their teenage comparisons between their mother and the black domestics known to them. As Sophie Stewart said, white teenagers then noted the difference in the way white and black women were treated in the external world. Nevertheless, these white girls, later white women, gradually did not seem to act on such observations.

Stewart lives in a raised wooden Creole cottage painted lavender. On the front porch were six large clay pots filled with pink flowers. We sat in a living room with antique furniture and old prints of southern cities in gold frames on the walls.

I'm a person you could talk to. I could tell you about Hattie. Hattie came to us in about 1944, and she stayed until the sixties. Her job then was to look after the house and me, and my life certainly would have been different without her!

*For a brief introduction to the theories of Hegel and Fanon see Hussein Abdilahi Bulhan, *Franz Fanon and the Psychology of Oppression* (New York, 1985).

We lived in a big house with my grandparents—my stepfather and mother and my two sisters, who were born later, and me. And Hattie came every day. She came at six in the morning—her husband brought her—and she left at six in the evening for two dollars a day. This was in 1948.

She used to say we were her children. She never did have children of her own. And she knew all the ins and outs of us. I think she realized she was a stabilizing influence on my life. When she walked in the door, things seemed to fall into place. And she had each person figured out. She would make fun of my grandmother's peculiarities. Hattie knew just how to joke with her. And she was perceptive about people. I think blacks are. And like my boyfriends would come to the house and she would say, "Now I want you to leave him alone," or "He's fine, but that other one, leave him alone." And she was usually right.

But she was also very superstitious. She would keep us at night sometimes and sleep at the foot of the bed on the floor with a hammer. She was protecting us, and we became her charges.

She was with us all the time, and she would travel with us to Atlanta each summer to see our aunt. This was the first time I thought of segregation. This was during the time blacks rode in the back of the bus. And Hattie couldn't eat with us, or we couldn't find a place for her to go to the bathroom. They had bathrooms that were "white only" then.

I always thought that was sad. I was about eleven when we started going there every summer. And I remember in Waycross, Georgia, they refused to serve her food. And I thought, she could live with us, look after us, and she couldn't eat with us. But this wasn't explained. It was just the way it was.

In Atlanta she would take me shopping. I would go everywhere with her, and then [there were] still a lot of places that I could go she couldn't. But I said, "Hattie, if you can't go in, I'm not going either."

And when I was about fifteen, she had to have a hysterectomy. And I remember going to visit her in the black ward, where they had the black patients, and how dirty it seemed—like it wouldn't be anything to walk down the hall and there would be a bloodstained cot. I knew it was different than how my mother was treated. And it took Hattie a long time to get well. She had a fibroid tumor. I think blacks have fibroid tumors a lot.

Then, when I went off to college, she began to get sick, crazy sick. She had a mental disorder with hallucinations and ideas that people were trying to get her. She would carry weapons in her sack, and about 1962 Mama decided to let her go. It was like she was disruptive, and of course, during that time the blacks wanted more money, and they should have had more money. They were hardly making enough money to eat.

And she's not in a very good condition now. She never did have any money. She still lives near where my mother lives, and I think I should do something for her, but I don't want to be involved with her. If I sent her money, she'd be on my doorstep, and I don't want that. It would just be too hard with her mental problems.

But she came to my wedding that last year she worked. Mama wanted her to wear a white uniform, but she came in her church clothes. She was very handsome when dressed up.

But she never lived well. Her house—I think once you've been in a black house, you never forget it—with all the little pictures around of her family, and she had little dresser scarfs on tables. You know, I was in the third or fourth grade when I went there, and I knew that was the only thing about Hattie I didn't feel at home with—her home. She had a dirty little kitchen, and they kept pigs in the backyard. I remember they cut the tail off of one pig to fatten him up. He would spray blood all around, you know, and they were going to kill this thing when it got big enough.

The two other maids I had, their houses affected me in the same way—little pictures, maybe lace curtains, crammed full of furniture. The other two maids I've known since I got older. I don't have anyone now. Those two, I hear from them still, but it got to be too expensive. It got where what they could produce for $3.39 an hour wasn't worth it. I just couldn't afford to have a black—I called them my black psychiatrists. They were "my black people who came," and we chatted and had a good time. I couldn't afford to pay them for that.

But those are the three black people I've known the best. No, I don't think I knew black people very well because I knew them. I mean, they came into our house, and there they adapted to the way we lived. And they talked about their religion, and they talked about what they did on their leisure time and how they treated their husbands and children, but we never were able to get in with them and experience what they were doing, not like they were experiencing what we were doing.

I think maybe we had a glimpse of their lives, but I don't think we really ever understood it. I do feel I know a little bit more about black people because I knew Hattie. Like I have a better understanding of black people's hair because one morning Hattie washed her hair and told us about it. She usually wore her hair back in a little bun, very close to her head and tight. But this morning she had washed her hair, and it was down to her shoulders, and she hadn't put any oil in it, and it was standing out like a bushel basket. We had a great time feeling her hair. She let us. It was like cotton. And they have no oil. She showed us that.

And then, too, I think she taught me to look at myself and laugh. She did that. And I think through all of those women, I had a glimpse of how they coped. I think with them they kept on trudging and they had faith. They really did have faith that if I keep on and keep on going, I'm going to make it, and they were happy with that. Even if they were poor, they had some sort of goal. It might be raising a child or buying a little house or paying a layaway off. And when the hard times came, I think they were a whole lot tougher and saw the situation with a whole lot more sense of humor than we did.

And when I think of Hattie, sometimes I see that today I can go up to a black woman of the new era—I'm talking about one that is not a maid—and I can relate to them as a person because I knew her. I know that black people are not foreigners or people that we can't understand. I always thought Hattie could have been included anywhere, and I never did quite understand why she couldn't.

But I think a lot of my generation have had trouble in their relationships with black servants. The blacks that were in their homes were a certain way, so when they meet one that isn't that way, they don't know what to think. And I didn't have any problem with blacks being outspoken or speaking up. I don't know why—maybe because Hattie was "uppity," too.

But for me there were other things that make me think the servant system as it existed worked to our detriment. We had this little black girl named Ernestine traveling with us one time. Ernestine would buy everybody in the car a treat when we would stop. She was Hattie's niece, and Hattie got her a job with us for the summer, when we'd go up to Atlanta. Her job was to baby-sit my sisters in my aunt's house. And on the way home she and I fought like cats and dogs. I remember I had black skin under my fingernails and she had white skin under hers. We scratched and fought, probably because we were the same age. And probably I should have been the one nursing those children. See, it was a detriment to have maids in a way, because a lot of us can't cope without them. It has taken us years to learn to cope with a house. So I think my generation, the transition going from being raised by them—having them, then a lot of us can't have them now—this transition has been hard.

From an interview with Susan Tucker

Cynthia Berg

The narrative of Cynthia Berg (b. 1947) includes a story of two white children being taken downtown by a black domestic, which reminded me of certain literary scenes treating black maids and white children in small southern towns. Through black domestics, white children were often able to see, for the first time, something of how race shaped the lives of southern people. As noted above, the children in *To Kill a Mockingbird* learn of race this way. Similarly, Berenice, the domestic in *The Member of the Wedding,* tells the young girl Frankie: "I'm caught worse than you. . . . Because I am black. . . . Everybody is caught one way or another. But they done drawn completely extra bounds around all colored people. . . . So we caught firstways I was telling you as all human beings is caught. And we caught as colored people also."[*]

For white girls who happened to be motherless, like Frankie and Jean Louise, the black domestic was often the main interpreter of race, gender, and a host of other human conditions. But for white children who were reared by their biological mothers, the lessons taught by the black domestics ran alongside lessons taught by the white mother. Which lessons they remembered, and which lessons they allowed themselves to question, depended largely upon the teachers. Ultimately, however, white girls knew they would grow up to be more like their white mothers than their black mother surrogates. Thus, they looked to their white mothers to explain the inconsistencies, the silences, and the other confusing conditions they witnessed in black life.

Many white mothers seem to have told their children that "things were just that way." Perhaps the overwhelming historical and social forces that shaped segregation seemed too difficult to explain. Other white women, like Cynthia Berg's mother, apparently explained their daughters' observations more thoughtfully. Berg has thus been able, at least, to put the two versions of black life—one seen in the lives of domestics and one explained by her mother—side by side in her memory. Having obtained no other stronger, more convincing explanations since, Berg explained black life to me based upon these two versions.

She spoke of the domestic Ruth's decision to better her life by leaving the South. The migration to points north often seemed, symbolically and literally, to be the only hope for southern blacks. As David Katzman said, "Although the mark of caste would follow them north, conditions there were different enough to promote a steady migration of young Southern black women northward between the Civil War and the Great Depression of the 1930s."[†] Ruth, though she departed somewhat later, was a part of this tradition. As Berg implied, whites often felt hostility toward such blacks for their desertion of the southern way of life and

---

*Carson McCullers, *The Member of the Wedding* (New York, 1946), 113–14.
†David M. Katzman, *Seven Days a Week: Women and Domestic Service in Industrializing America* (New York, 1978), 203–204.

particularly for desertion of the white household. But she took into consideration both what Ruth thought and what her mother explained. Berg was given at least a partial analysis that parallels historical facts: Ruth left because "that was what a lot of black people did," and she was motivated by something to do with "living standards" within the South. Berg also understood that Ruth's patterns of coping would change once she was in the North.

Cynthia Berg has an accent that is heard in small towns in northern Alabama, though she no longer lives there. At the interview she wore a fisherman's sweater and had her very long hair tied behind her neck. She lives in a small shotgun house that she and her husband renovated so that their two children would not have to walk through every room to go to the one bathroom at the back of the house. At the time of the interview she was working full-time and did not employ a domestic. Her children would leave with her every morning at seven-thirty and participate in the public school system's extended day program.

⤙⤜≽░≼⤚⤛

My mother was always very independent. Had her own business before I was born and was never confined to the home. So you know, I'm a good person to talk to, I guess.

Since my mother worked, it was Ruth that cooked supper before she went home every day. She was with us for twelve years, from the time I was about two. And in my mind it was like she was always there until my high school years.

Then she left and went to Cincinnati. You know, that was the thing, to go to Cincinnati. This was probably in the early sixties, and the thing was to go up North and make a lot of money. And Mother, I remember, Mother would explain things to me. There was no hostility about it. It was just Ruth was going up North because that was what a lot of black people did. Mother said—well, of course, she would say this, but I think she was probably right—she said, "It's not going to be like she thinks."

Oh, her living standards might have gone up somewhat. I'll admit jobs were very low-paying for domestics, but there were other benefits. And this is something I think I should tell you about, because it stands out so distinctly in my mind as a sort of benefit Ruth had with us.

Ruth had a boyfriend, John. I can't remember his last name. Anyway they would have a stormy relationship. One day someone, one of Ruth's neighbors or friends, called Mother and said, "Ruth has shot John So-and-so and she's run off and she's just wearing shorts." And I thought, "Gosh, she's topless!" You know how kids take things literally. And anyway I was very concerned!

So Mother and I got in the car and went over to Ruth's neighborhood and neighborhoods near there to find her, because we knew she was scared. She had *shot* him. And I was real concerned. Was he dead? And we rode around and around. See, my mother knew so many black people in the town. She had a loan company, and then she had a furniture store, and like she would be walking down the street, and all these black people would say hello. And she would know who lived in each house in the neighborhoods way far away from anything I knew. So somehow she tracked Ruth down, and I think she took me back by this time. But see, since Mother was a businesswoman, she knew the police chief, and she got Ruth and made her turn herself in. She said, "Look, turn yourself in." And Mother got her out immediately. But see, without Mother's help Ruth would have been in jail. I mean that was just a benefit of working for Mother. And Ruth got off, of course, as self-defense. I think John had to have his leg amputated. Well, they started dating after that again!

And at the time I didn't think a thing was wrong with such violence. It was just accepted, I guess, because Ruth was poor and black. It wasn't anything that she had done wrong, and certainly that she was not going to stop working for us because she shot her boyfriend. It was like, get her all the help you can get.

But I did wonder about other things. I think as a child I always wondered about the buses. We would take the bus downtown all the time, and Ruth had to sit in the back. We sat in the back with her. I remember being confused about it at one time. But no explanation was given, so it just became ingrained—the separation of the races—something you accepted.

Ruth loved to take us downtown, by the way. She would dress me up, wash and braid my very long hair. She always braided my hair. That's why I was so helpless growing up—because she always did my hair. Anyway she would always take us downtown, just spick-and-span, in these beautiful clothes. And I remember one day when she was off, Mother had just dragged us out of the yard [and taken us] downtown, and Ruth walked up to her and she said, "Miz Berg, I wouldn't bring these children down here looking like that!" We looked so bad, Ruth was embarrassed!

Anyway, I remember noticing things like that—differences. And I was always aware that black people had worse houses than I did. Like I said, I was in black homes probably more than your average young middle-class white child. Mother knew all sorts of people, and we would just be in different situations, in different homes. I remember feeling, you know, sad. I don't know that I felt it was an injustice. I don't know that I could have those concepts very young.

By, say, when I was eight or so, I knew there was a definite distinction between the races, though. And I knew my mother was my mother, and I never did think of Ruth as a parent figure. I was very distinct about that.

But we were kind of like companions. When I would come home from school, Ruth would be ironing, and there would be a movie that showed every afternoon at three. And we would watch the movie together. I enjoyed her company a lot of the time and didn't feel that she was bearing down upon me with any "Do this, do that." With her I felt a general freedom. I could do what I wanted to, whereas with my mother I couldn't always. Ruth was good in that I was so independent. I didn't like it when she didn't come, because then Mother was there, and I felt like—oh, I felt this way in other people's homes whose mothers didn't work—that it was kind of an impediment or a restriction. Your mother's there and kind of watching you more. I was much more on my own.

Ruth was sometimes like an adult friend, and then sometimes she would hardly speak to me. You knew that was just the way she was. She would always say, "I ain't studying you," when she didn't want to bother with us. So we would bow out some way or other. That's when she didn't want us to do something, or she didn't want to do a certain thing we would ask her, or we were bothering her. And she would just say she wasn't studying us. That was one of her famous expressions!

I think of Ruth a lot, though it's over sixteen years ago that I'm remembering. She was not your kindly one. She could be gruff and impatient with us, and I don't remember her imparting any knowledge or sayings. The biggest thing was I wanted to learn how to pop gum like Ruth! That was what I really did love. I thought she could pop gum wonderfully!

I wish my mother were here. She would be able to tell some things! Ruth still sends us Christmas cards, and Mother says over and over, through all the years, she says, "You know, if I had enough money, I would have Ruth come back and live with me if she wanted to."

Ruth's never married. She raised a child of someone else. She took— she had a son of her own, June Bug—and she raised a child that belonged to someone else. And they're both grown now.

Oh, yes, and I remember one thing that Ruth always used to do. It was a seasonal thing. When june bugs came, we would always have to catch one and tie its little leg to a string and then tie the string to the back screen door. I mean it was just like a ritual. You had to do that every year. Get a june bug and put it on a string. It was a ritual that she loved, which, I guess, is why she called her son June Bug!

Beyond the time that Ruth was with us, there were two other ladies. See, right now I can't remember their names. One of them was very young, and she would talk to me about all these children she had. And she wasn't married, and I was real surprised. I mentioned it to Mother. You know, I was maybe fifteen, and I said—well, I tried to act real calm and cool when she told me, but I said, "Gosh, Mother, she's not married."

And Mother said that she'd had some illegitimate children or something and that that was acceptable. Or something made me think that was acceptable in the black community. She was another one who had a stormy relationship with her boyfriend. He shot her in the back and killed her while she was working for us. And she was so very young and pretty. I'm sure she was very young—probably in her twenties. And I was so shocked. I remember when Mother told me about it, and I kept asking questions. I mean it was just like he walked up to her and shot her. I couldn't believe she was no longer alive.

So our next maid was an older lady, and I guess she worked for us a year, if not more. And she died of a heart attack. And my mother called me at school, I remember. She said: "Don't get upset. So-and-so has died of a heart attack."

And then when we were looking for someone else to work for us, Mother said, "*Do not* tell this lady that our last two maids are dead." She said: "Colored people are very superstitious, or can be," she said. I think anyone could be under those circumstances! But she said, "In no way tell about them." It was like this vow of silence about them!

I do wish you could talk to Mother, though. She would have more stories than me. And I guess a lot of them have stories. I'm sure many of them would have quite a few chuckles over us, because you can give so much responsibility to a person when they will take it. And they would take a lot of it.

From an interview with Susan Tucker

Epilogue:
Looking Backward, Looking Forward

In late 1979 I met a black woman named Tejan Muata, and our talk was one thing that encouraged me to continue research on this book. She and I are from the same town, and both of us, until 1977, had lived away from that town for many years. Upon meeting me, she immediately asked a question that I think many black and white southern women in similar circumstances would ask each other. She asked me if I was the daughter of a family for whom her mother had once worked. She remembered this daughter through all the long years between her childhood and adulthood, through those years of great change in the South. This little white girl, she said, looked like me. I was not the little girl Tejan remembered, but of course, I could have been.

I was glad she wondered about me, and about other whites she remembered from childhood. After all, I had wondered about her and about the other black children I had come in contact with. I had wondered about them in the years since I was a child and during the years I had lived outside the South.

I suppose I felt relief that she asked. In her asking, she broke what I have come to see as an unwritten code in our shared heritage by speaking directly of the separations and connections that centered around domestic workers.

Yet, Tejan's story and my reaction to it both suggest that we have not come very far in our efforts to change the society in which we live. We two—a black woman and a white woman—spoke of race to each other. But we did so in ways that still dramatized something of the old saying "All black [or white] people look alike."

Between white and black southern women there is a legacy of silence that we still observe. And after all the interviews, I found that southern women, both white and black, are still guessing about each other, still seeing each other in terms of one or another of the stereotypes of black and white women dating from the days of segregation or before. As one black woman told me: "Every white woman underneath, at one time or another, reminds me of this lady my grandmother worked for. I hated her for calling my grandmother by her first name—just that. That is all Grandmother let me see, but it was enough."

Throughout the interviews, I heard such memories and perceptions from the past again and again, still emotionally present in our thinking, still touching and wounding. The memories we have of our mothers and our childhoods still separate as well as connect us. And in many ways we do not have anything else but these memories to connect us. To a great extent, the South is still split along racial lines. To a great extent, white and black women still speak to one another only in the code of long ago. To a great extent, our children do, too.

Lewis Mumford once stated, "Every culture lives inside its own dream."[1] Throughout my research on this project, this statement comforted me—softening the many and conflicting memories I heard, explaining the ambiguities, rationalizing the unthinking comments. It suggested the universality of dream within cultures, the haziness with which we see our lives and the lives around us.

Yet, even if his comment is universally true, one must still apply it a little differently in studying a culture like the South. In the South there have been two dreams that we have lived inside. Sometimes we have seen both of them; more often we have seen only one or the other. These two dreams, existing side by side in the overall culture, have balanced each other, so that white and black women both have probably operated as best they could in the world given them. But in the process of this balancing, the dreams have also been further obscured and have certainly obscured each other. We have found this obfuscation useful, for reasons that need more consideration, need more acknowledgment.

The dreams have perhaps doubly filtered women's self-images. The culture of women in general, which includes that of both black and white women, has been hidden within our dreams, deemed not worthy of consideration in a male-dominated society, and obscured even to women themselves. Thus, both black and white women generally do not think that domestic work, particularly child-rearing, is a job that should be compensated by more than the minimum wage. It appears then that the dreams of our culture have shaped or allowed others to shape the defini-

1. Lewis Mumford, cited by Richard King, *A Southern Renaissance: The Cultural Awakening of the American South, 1930–1955* (New York, 1980), 26.

tion of work within the domestic sphere. In our acceptance of the dreams, we have helped to continue the hierarchy of customs and responses that exploit all women.

To decipher the dreams, to try to get beyond them or transform them into something good, southern women of both races have had among their clues the memories of their early and infrequent encounters with each other. But it is time now for us to look for other clues of ourselves, to pull our dreams out of the obscured world of the past, to look at how we behave today, and to ask what can be done tomorrow. In looking both backward and forward honestly, we can sort out the ways that class, race, and gender have figured in the history of all people. Doing that could be a beginning for significant, positive change.

The final two narratives touch upon this process of looking backward and forward honestly. Their stories together dramatize ways the South has and has not changed in the last century. They suggest the need for revision and even reconstruction of work within the domestic sphere. Reversing the order maintained throughout the book, a white woman speaks first, and a black woman speaks last.

Regina Manning

Regina Manning (b. 1915), like many of the other white women interviewed, spoke of times gone by. She remembered the plantation South and the help her mother found in the person of a domestic worker named Bette. She took out a large leather photograph album and a large wooden box of loose photographs. She was not questioning the past, but merely showing me "pictures of an era." She described the domestic Bette standing at the foot of her white employer's bed each morning. This was one of the rituals of women's daily lives, of women's place, of women's roles, as known to Manning in childhood and adulthood.

In her tone, however, there was little sense of regret that this era is over. For Manning, as for many others, the passing of this era is absolute and irrevocable. Her tone suggested to me that in some ways, she was glad that it is over. The old ways, at least for some whites, were too much to answer for.

Yet, like many other white southern women, she seemed unwilling to speak of how this past affects us today. The problems created and left by the segregated society are, I think, overwhelming to many southerners today. Some of the white interviewees seemed to hide their concerns about such problems, even from themselves, by speaking of their past understanding of a bond with domestic workers. Thus, many refused to talk about their current relationships with domestics.

In Katherine Anne Porter's "The Old Order," the domestic worker Nannie and her employer Sophia Jane similarly focus on the past: "Who knows why they had loved their past? It had been bitter for them both, they had questioned the burdensome rule they lived by every day of their lives, but without rebellion and without expecting an answer. . . . They wondered perpetually, with only a hint now and then to each other of the uneasiness of their hearts, how so much suffering and confusion could have been built up and maintained on such a foundation."* Regina Manning's memories remind one of "the hint now and then . . . of the uneasiness."

Manning's memories remind one also that the past is a known quantity, unlike the future, unlike even the present. She speculated briefly about the future—for example, about its architecture and its philosophy—before describing so much that was past.

She has a clear, high-pitched voice and a take-charge attitude. She showed me the small courtyard garden where Bette liked to sit in years past. As I left, she called out to me that she had enjoyed our talk more than I will ever know. She had tears in her eyes.

*Katherine Anne Porter, "The Old Order," in Porter, *The Leaning Tower and Other Stories* (New York, 1934), 35–36.

This is a picture of Bette with my oldest granddaughter, Sarah. Sarah was about two and a half, maybe three years old. And it's priceless. Priceless.

That's a picture of an era as well as a relationship between two people. She had no children herself, and she raised us and helped to raise my children and helped then with Sarah, too.

I don't know anyone, *anyone*—I don't care how much they really love their children—[I don't see] how any person can raise children alone. You've got to have some help. I pick up the news articles and read about child abuse and all sorts of abuses, which is nothing new. It's been done ever since the world began. But also, ever since the world began, women have known they had to have help—of some kind.

But now Bette was the one who really I knew the best, who helped my mother and helped me like that. Knew all my life, really—since I was two years old. She was spotted by my mother one day when she was riding with my father through the fields. Bette had a red-and-white-checked square—like a little tablecloth—that she spread down on the ground. And in that pail of hers were her spoons and forks, which were pewter. Now it has become fashionable—pewter. But she opened that red-and-white-checked cloth and put it on the ground and sat down and set her place, and then opened up that pail and had jambalaya or whatever she had that day. And my mother turned to my father and said, "Braxton, I want that girl in the house." And the next day she came in the house.

Mother taught her how to do gourmet things as time went along, but Bette had the instinctive ability to be a good cook, to arrange flowers. I mean, she just *had* it. The things that she learned from my mother and father—white man's schooling, she used to call them—learning how to set a proper table or to serve or which side the glass went on. She learned all this, but she instinctively knew a lot beforehand.

Her mother was half Indian, part white, part black; her father . . . I don't know. But her mother really looked like an Egyptian princess or an Indian princess. And Bette was a fantastic person, and an aristocratic one. It was interesting—Bette in the clothes my mother gave her, which so many people resent as hand-me-downs, but to see Bette with my mother's hats and my mother's clothes and her manner of holding her head high. She was an aristocrat. Somewhere back there, there were aristocratic lines—Indian, blacks, mixture of white.

At that time we lived in the country on a plantation. And Bette and her family had lived there forever. She was only about eighteen or nineteen when my mother first saw her.

I was about two years old when we moved up there. This is a photo of what the quarters looked like, that the colored people, the hands, lived in. My father rebuilt every one—tore them down and rebuilt every house on the place. They were two-family homes.

I've got billions of these pictures if you want to look at pictures. This was farm equipment my father bought. My God, they ran when they first saw it! Here is a road-grading machine. There was not a road on the place. And there's my mother supervising the work on the big house.

This is Rachel's mother. Rachel worked as the housekeeper. She's by the commissary. My father had a commissary put in for everybody to buy from.

As children we thought this life was wonderful—a very happy time. But I can remember that for my parents it was a disaster. I can remember walking with my father through the yard and finding diseased chickens, dead chickens, and the worry of this to my father. Farming was a disaster for him.

And here is the church. My father built them a church. I'll never forget the first time my parents went to this church, the preacher was so thankful for them donating the church. My father that particular Sunday put a ten-dollar bill in the plate as a gift. But the preacher misunderstood. He thought my father wanted some change, so he kept that congregation just singing and singing until he thought my father had enough change for him to take the difference out of the plate.

But, well, we lost everything on that plantation, and we moved back to town in 1924. And Bette, she really had quite a tragedy because she was very much in love with her husband, but some young so-and-so took up with him. They had moved into town when we did, and I really don't remember the details of this, 'cause I was very young, but my mother always stood behind everybody she ever employed, and she and Bette were friends—not just the servant-master thing. But they were friends. And Bette came to Mother and told her that Russell had taken up with someone else. And Bette was never so humiliated in her life! Somehow or other he also went to jail for something.

You have to realize, when we moved into town, every colored person who wanted to come to town—my father got every one of them jobs. Bette's mother and father stayed on the plantation, but all her brothers and sisters came. Russell was a janitor at a building downtown. But anyway the big-city life went to his head. And he subsequently did something and went to jail, and either he got syphilis or gonorrhea and died.

She never remarried and never did have children, and she loved kids, so it was a pity. But there're pros and cons, and it's maybe to our advantage that she didn't.

There was a tremendous amount of responsibility given these women. And then if you hadn't treated them right, they wouldn't have stayed anyway. I remember we lived in South America once, when I was grown and married, and we had a nurse who took care of the children. Nurses there were terribly inexpensive. As a matter of fact, we were in a lot of trouble with a lot of other American people who were living down there for paying the help more.

And when I came home, I told people about the situation. I said that it was different and they got paid a very nominal amount. In fact they just paid the rent. They lived in servants' quarters, and they really had very little free time, and they were like a part of the family.

I said: "Bette, which would you have? Would you prefer the security of living in a house with room, board, and everything else, or would you prefer what you're getting in the way of pay and go home to your own place?" She wanted her place anytime, altogether.

She never owned her house, but she lived in the same house thirty-odd years, just near here. A beautiful high-ceilinged cottage. And she loved to garden, and her garden was exquisite with not only flowers and things but vegetables. She could stick a rose thorn in, and it would grow.

But to her the plantation was always home. You know, I don't care what race you belong to, the expression "I'm going home for Christmas" has meaning. She lived here until she died, but the plantation was home. When we went up for her funeral, my gosh, the countryside turned out. At first, well, long before she died, they told her she couldn't be buried there [in the Catholic cemetery nearest the plantation]. It was on church property, and she was a Catholic. [But] the priest or someone said she couldn't be buried there, and it was most upsetting to her.

We knew something was wrong, but she had someone else straighten it out. Because lots of times she would not tell her sorrows. It used to make you so mad. I said, "Bette, how in God's name do we know what you're thinking, what you're feeling, if you won't tell us what's wrong?" But she was just as stubborn as she could be. She would solve it on her own, which was commendable. But at the same time, it drove you up a wall.

Lydia Malcolm, her niece, straightened it out for her. She was the daughter of Bette's brother, and I'm telling you, she was born too soon, because Lydia, if she was born about one hundred years from now, she'd be president of the United States. In fact, I knew Bette was worried, but we knew Lydia was going to take care of her, 'cause Lydia was the only one who wasn't constantly coming to Bette for money. Bette always had money. My parents left her some money. Lydia was the only member of the family who would come and take Bette around when we weren't taking her.

I mean, before, everywhere my mother went, she took Bette, whether it was to the cemetery or to go shop or to market or whatever. They went riding. And as they were older, it was the blind leading the blind!

Then, when mother died, my sisters and I took her places. And when we couldn't take her, Lydia did. And we knew that Lydia would be the one Bette would live with if it got to the point that she had to live with someone, 'cause she never wanted to live with any of us. She got very sick about two or three years before she died. She was retired by then, because after my parents died, she came to work for me, because you couldn't tell her that she couldn't come.

When she died, I was out of town. My sister found her. But thank God, she just apparently died—no suffering—with prayer beads in her hand. She didn't really become senile. Oh, she became forgetful. She was eighty-six, but she wasn't bedridden, and she would shuffle to church every Sunday morning.

And Peggy, my youngest daughter, would take her to church every Sunday when she was here. As a matter of fact, Peggy had lived for a while in Washington, D.C., and she took Bette there for a visit. Bette stayed with her for two weeks. And Bette met Senator Ervin and got in on these committee hearings, went to the opera, went to the Kennedy Center, and sightseed Washington by night.

When she got home, I put her in this chair, and I invited my sisters and their husbands and their children down here to listen to her. I made a tape of it, and it turns out—well, most of it is not about her memories of Washington, which is not to say she didn't have any. Most of it is about what she remembered of my mother, who she adored probably more than her parents. It is just astounding the things that were recorded on those tapes about my mother.

She was a very wise person, but in other respects she was—I don't know if you wouldn't just say she was too shy and the timing was wrong. She went to the third grade, and she knew her alphabet, and she wrote the grocery list. She'd stand, in the mornings, at the foot of my mother's bed, until my mother told her to sit down, and they talked about what

Bette saw in the paper each day. She'd get the gist of it. But she kept saying, oh, she wished she'd gone to school. After she said this a number of times, I said, "Well, what's wrong with going back to school?"

I found the school for her. And I followed her in the car just to make sure she made the transfers and got there. Well, if I did that once, I did it ten times. She always had trouble doing it alone, though. Those old routines of life . . . She had no problem, but she didn't stick with the class. I'm not quite sure if she didn't become embarrassed or ashamed. As it turned out, one of her relatives was in the class with her. It was too bad, because there are billions of people who learn to read and write as adults.

Maybe it would have been better if I hadn't gone with her at all. Her having the security of knowing I was following her . . . Because she always had my name and telephone number, as well as my sister's name and telephone number. [She knew] that if, in an emergency, she always had that on her person and that whoever found her was to call us. . . . She always had that. And we, for a long time, always had her.

From an interview with Susan Tucker

Linda Barron

Linda Barron (b. 1933) said that the past spoken of by Regina Manning has left many remnants. In the South, one still sees many older, as well as some younger, domestic workers. These new workers are not unlike domestic workers of the past. Underpaid, they still are visible within the community and they still, more often than not, are working parents making do with the little money they do earn. Barron remembers what making do required of her when her children were young. She remembers, too, the evolution of her own understanding of the lives of domestic workers. She remembers the image of one particular domestic worker who walked daily in "crooked over shoes"—shoes so old their sides had been worn down, so old they no longer provided comfort in walking. A younger Linda Barron asked herself why this domestic did not buy new shoes. Now she knows why, and the image of the older domestic has become a memory she uses in describing her own political consciousness.

This memory recalls a passage in Ann Petry's novel *The Street* in which the reader is given a hint of the protagonist's future. Lutie, a young black woman, sees older black women coming home from work, and she remarks upon their slovenly appearance and the society that has made them into "drudges." The narrator comments, "She had no way of knowing that at fifty she [too] wouldn't be misshapen, walking on the sides of her shoes because her feet hurt so badly . . . [going to] church on Sunday and . . . the rest of the week slaving in somebody's kitchen."*

Indeed, working conditions for many domestics have not changed and may not change for the foreseeable future. They are still the lowest paid of all workers. Despite various legislative measures enacted in the 1970s, some still do not receive the minimum wage—though other wage-earners in our society appear to think of the minimum wage only during discussions of teenagers and work. Many domestic workers will not receive Social Security benefits because they cannot afford to have this money withheld from their paychecks. Almost never do they have any insurance paid by their employers. Only a very small percentage belong to the self-help organization called the National Committee on Household Employment.† Thus far, they have been unable to sustain any long-term union. No other large labor group has been so unsuccessful at achieving collective power. The reasons, as Gerda Lerner has noted, center on "the individual nature of the work, the isolation of the workers from one another, their low economic and social status and the intense competition among them."‡ Their working conditions are, in short, still the product of a complicated entanglement of race relations and economics.

*Ann Petry, *The Street* (Boston, 1946), 186.
†Linda Martin and Kerry Segrave, *The Servant Problem: Domestic Workers in North America* (MacFarland, N.C., 1985), 155.
‡Gerda Lerner (ed.), *Black Women in White America: A Documentary History* (New York, 1972), 231.

Domestic work, more than any other kind of work, has been labeled "women's work" and has been hidden within the private world. Linda Barron would like to take it out of the private world and put it into politics.

She offered me a fried fish dinner on her mother's narrow, screened front porch. The porch is about six feet from the street, and as we sat there, I heard the talk of neighbors and the noise of cars. It was a quiet morning, a Saturday, and on weekdays the neighborhood is probably quite different, since the express buses run along the street from Monday through Friday. They shake the house, Barron told me. Her mother washes the walls of the porch once a week to get rid of the dirt caused by the traffic. Her mother fried the fish as we talked, and she served us at noon, bringing fish and white bread and small cans of Colt 45 malt liquor on a flowered tin tray.

I was the oldest of eight children, and all my brothers and sisters finished college but me. My mother, you know, did domestic work. For me, like her, at the particular time there was nothing else to do.

So I've been doing it since I was eighteen years old. I was a sophomore in college when I started full-time. I suppose you wonder why I, who had some college education, would do it, but it's an old story. When you had small kids at that particular time, you had one baby right after another. Nobody told you . . . You didn't know about contraceptives, so actually you had your kids, and to survive, you had to do some type of work.

I was married, but it was a thing where I had five kids. When you came down to the third child, the marriage was mostly trying to fall apart. He'd drink sometimes. He came home, made a whole payday, and there was no money.

I knew my kids had to eat. A lot of times I worked, made three dollars a day. Sometimes I fed them and I didn't eat. But I knew I had to survive.

The people I work for now I've worked for for twenty-four years. I worked there that long because I had to and because domestic work changed over the years. She made the difference. And I made the difference. Some people now still aren't getting W-2 forms, aren't getting paid vacation, aren't getting Social Security. I knew my mother she had to depend on the whites for loans for us and things. I wasn't going to do that. I was going to make a fair wage.

I was college educated. But the part that was hard for me—there were certain type of words that they used that are different. I remember one day she came in and said to dust the prints. I got all upset. I looked up prints in the dictionary. I call them pictures.

Those kinds of things make domestic workers—they don't think high of themselves. At one time I looked upon domestic work as a job that was not skilled, and then I looked at the white people there, and I saw I was not really that less skilled than they were.

A lot of times when the telephone rang, I would not say, "I am the maid." I hate that word. They'd say, "Who is this?" I'd say: "My name is Linda. I work here."

I just hated that word *maid* because way back there [they were] wearing the aprons and the little frilly deals and all that kind of stuff. One time she did buy me an apron like to put over your neck—frilly. I said: "Well, what is this? Who is this for?" She didn't say anything, but she knew that I had too much pride, knowing that my mama before me had did domestic work. That's why they took the Aunt Jemima off the grits box. It was so degrading. You ever thought of that—why Aunt Jemima ain't on the grits box? That apron was not for me, and right now that apron is right there now.

After a while, standing up and saying things like this, I decided that domestic work is not as bad as some people would say it would be. I really would say I'm a domestic engineer because of the fact that if you're an engineer, you've got to put all kinds of stuff together. You're going from the lower part of work to the higher part of work. I think it's a profession.

Course, when you've worked for the same people for twenty-four years, there are people who say you are part of the family. Well, you're *not* part of the family. As long as you work, you have access to the house, the food, the secrets, the stormy life, the fun life. And sometimes you also experience the same things that these people you are working for experience. But so far as you're a part of the family, I can't see that, because you're different than they are.

Like my political differences. They know I'm politically motivated and they're not, and they don't think like I do. They do not try to sway me one way or the other.

Sometimes they tell me they have learned a lot from me. And God knows I have learned a hell of a lot from them. These people they are very very good examples of how people should live. This has brought out a great part of my life, has taught me how to live, has taught me some things about how to care for my family myself. And since I have worked there, I started buying my house. And now I own it. And I think I have accomplished a great bit since I've worked there.

I often think of when I started—not with these people, but when I was eighteen. I made three dollars a day, and the lady who kept my kids, I had to pay her a dollar a day. But I just decided to ask for more money, and now I'm getting it. And in this particular family I get respect, too.

It was that respect, and from the lady and the kids, too. The kids never used . . . There were some people you could work for during the sixties— there were negative words they would call black people, but I never heard them.

It was six kids, and they could come to me and talk to me about things, and there are some things that we have talked about—nobody knows it today. That's the confidence they had in me and the respect.

This particular family, their past life, their family history, black people was always in their life. But I feel they learned from me about blacks. They had a wedding at the Woman's Clubhouse, and we, my family, were invited, and we went to this place and were in the receiving line and all. The lady who was over this clubhouse went to these people that I worked for and told them that blacks were not accepted there. When he came and told me, I said: "You don't have to tell me. You don't have to tell me." We laughed about it, but it hurt them. She cried, and I said: "Don't worry about it. We're used to this kind of stuff." But to let them know that she didn't like it, she got out of this organization.

Now you might notice I have some teeth out. I'm getting them fixed. You'll find most black women who are in the domestic field, you look at their mouths, there are teeth missing. Or they have blood-pressure problems, or they are diabetics or something. Why? I describe it this way: You go to the state hospital, you sit there for hours and hours, you fill out forms, forms, forms. They put you in the back—where the morgue is. This is where they are supposed to tell you about your diet. And there is a white woman, sitting behind the desk—doesn't have very much education, but she has authority. She tells you what you're suppose to eat, sitting next to the morgue. So, I mean, you go back or you don't go back.

Not many white women who hire domestic workers know that feeling. But it is there. At the same time, me, and many others, we've survived. The lady I work for, she knows I know the real world. I know street life, and I know life in general. I know what it means to meet a man and, you know—your kids got to be fed—a one-night affair. When you have a bunch of kids, you must survive.

It's a lot of women knowing that—not only black women, but white women, too. If you go sit in the Piccadilly Cafeteria and look at some of these poor white women working along with some of these poor black women, they have the same old bag. They might not tell it, but they're in the same old bag—just like me, trying to survive.

Some survive and some don't. What makes the difference? Black people call it mother wit. You have an extra sense about yourself. It's an extra sense you got about yourself, something your mother taught you to survive. Your mama tell you to run to the store and hurry up and come back—run, whatever you got to do.

Not everyone has it. I think there should be an organization for domestic workers—to get them what mother wit can't. To get them health care and then to teach them esteem in their work. And there would be seminars—woman to woman, employers to domestic—to make the employer see how to make it a job worth doing.

Like, tell those employers not to write notes. Put in your book after my name: "Hates writing notes." I feel like notes are demeaning. You're going to sit down and write a long note, can't you sit and tell the person what you want them to do? Supposing I can't read?

You learn from experience how to survive and how to help others, and I would really like to help other women like myself. I can remember when I was a young lady, going to school. There was a lady, Mrs. Daniels. I'll never forget that name. That lady would walk . . . I would see that lady walking, and her shoes were turned over. And I used to say, "This lady goes to work every day with shoes turned over, and look like she could buy her some more shoes."

And when I get off that bus today, I have a long ways to go. My shoes begin to turn just like Mrs. Daniels' shoes did. I say to myself: "I see why now this lady wore those type of shoes. She was trying to make it. She had such a long ways to walk."

And often I think of her. Sometimes I go along, and I see a mental picture of her. She used to pass my aunt's house every evening. She had a blue uniform. And those shoes—just crooked over. And she had kids. And I used to wonder why. Now I know why, because I've been in that same situation. That I'm trying to make it.

You get on the city bus. You'll see a lot of people trying to make it. You get on the Goodwood bus. Lot of goodies on the Goodwood bus. Sit there and you listen. Journey along and see what it is. Get the feel of it. See where the women get off the bus. Follow them. They got to walk so far. A long ways to walk.

When you get off that bus, there're a lot of people set their clocks by you. They know you're going to come along. You wave at them. You see them leaving—white people leaving their houses and the blacks coming there to take care of the houses. When they don't see you, they say, "Well, I haven't seen you in a long time." They set their clocks by you, but they don't know what it's like, how to walk back and forth from that bus.

There is a city bus company. Everybody on that board don't ride the bus. They're professional people—never had to stand out in the rain or the sunshine. Why in the hell they don't put some domestic person on there? I would like to be on that board. I been riding the bus when you had to sit in the back, when it was cold and you couldn't close the windows, when the dust blowing in your eyes. I know what needs to go on.

From an interview with Susan Tucker

Photographic Essay

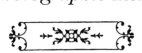

More than any other invention of the past two centuries, photography has changed the way Americans remember their lives—so much so that it is almost impossible to talk to anyone about his or her life without some mention of photographs. By the 1880s, the first decade remembered in this book, the South had photographers in each major city and a number of traveling photographers who ventured out to rural areas. The first marketing of the Kodak cameras in the 1880s, followed by the easily used Brownie in 1900 and by other portable types throughout the century, enabled more and more Americans to preserve photographic memories of themselves and their ways of life.

Thirty-three of the ninety-two women we interviewed showed us photographs, though because they were promised anonymity, none of them are presented here. Many of the photographs whites showed us were of poor quality and had been kept for long years in scrapbooks—sandwiched between bits of bouquets, dance cards, newspaper notices, ball invitations. White women had also saved obituary notices of domestics and, in one case, the church bulletin from the funeral of a domestic. This bulletin listed among the family members of the deceased "a devoted friend"—the domestic's employer. Most of the photos black domestics showed us were school photos and family snapshots. Some had "their" white children's photos in their own family albums, and a few had them in frames on walls or tables. Two black women had large frames with photos of their own children, their grandchildren, neighbor children, and their employers' children all exhibited together. This arrangement showed, in one case, white and black children of the late 1940s and 1950s next to each other in a way they would never have been in the publicly segregated society.

This photograph of a domestic named Sophy was made with an early Kodak camera and is one of many photographs taken between 1885 and 1890 at Evan Hall plantation, the home of the McCall family, near Donaldsonville, Louisiana. Evan Hall was a large sugar plantation, and the photos, probably taken by a family member with his or her first camera, document something of life and work there. "Ol' Sophy," as the inscriptions on the pictures refer to her, appears in three photographs, though her whole name is never given. The word *Old* before the names of favored servants was said by white interviewees to connote respect; black interviewees generally pointed out that they nonetheless felt disrespect in being so addressed.

    This photograph seems to show Sophy in front of her home. The "quarters" on large Louisiana plantations often consisted of many double cabins housing two or more families each. These cabins sat in rows with roads in front of them. The cabins at Evan Hall seem to have been near a railroad track. Fences, such as the one shown here, appear to have separated the roads from the railroad track and divided yards containing small gardens.

The Historic New Orleans Collection, Museum/Research Center, Acc. No. 1978.26.30

Lucy was another worker on the Evan Hall plantation. She is shown here at the back of the big house and its connecting annex. A group portrait in this collection suggests that Evan Hall employed as many as twenty black house servants. Both Lucy and Sophy appear to be among this group. On some plantations, the wearing of the *tignon,* or head handkerchief, and the fabric and color of dress revealed the particular work and therefore the status of different house servants. However, in the Evan Hall photos, the differentiation among dress shows no apparent pattern.

Lucy worked most likely as a cook's assistant, one who spent her time going between the garden, the barn, the kitchen, and the dining room. Here she carries both a milk and a water pail and wears both a head handkerchief and a scarf. The gingham fabric of her dress was thought to be more practical than the white material worn by Sophy and house servants on most other plantations.

The Historic New Orleans Collection, Museum/Research Center, Acc. No. 1978.26.10

This photograph is probably the work of a traveling photographer who visited the prosperous Barrow family's sugar plantation in Terrebonne Parish, Louisiana, in July, 1885. An inscription added later names the subjects as "Mammy or Violet Carter and Mary Delaport, servants; Irene F. Barrow and Robert R. Barrow III."

The photo is the only one that pictures servants among nearly one hundred photos in the Barrow Family Papers. Several of the interviewees recalled traveling photographers and the preparations for sittings with them. The photographer's visit was a big event in the lives of rural people, providing them with not only a picture of themselves but also a gift to be sent to relatives and friends in other areas. The novelty of photography, the fascination with the photographer's equipment and backdrops, and the end product itself all remained vivid memories in the minds of many women. Both the members of the white family and the servants wore their best clothes, and preparation for a sitting required efforts that one woman said were equal to those of getting ready for the biggest party of the year. In this photo the older woman wears the traditional head handkerchief, which was said to reflect her age and maturity.

Barrow Family Papers, Manuscripts Section, Tulane University Library

This woman is probably Mary Howard, who lived and worked on the Belair plantation in Plaquemines Parish in the late nineteenth and early twentieth centuries. Belair was owned during this time by the Dymonds, a prosperous family credited with playing an essential role in the revitalization of the sugar industry in Louisiana between 1880 and 1930. Florence Dymond described Mary Howard as "a generally handy woman, a splendid cook, a natural born nurse, excellent at housework, a good seamstress, [who] could make over mattresses and could turn her hand to anything, even to swinging a side of salt meat against the head of her husband." This photograph was probably taken by Helen Dymond, another daughter in the white family, who seemingly caught Howard ready to smile on the front porch of a small house located in the side yard of the big house. This small house was usually called "Mary Howard's house," for she occupied it, according to Florence Dymond, on a regular basis during spats with her husband. Howard was also remembered for referring to dessert as "the hereafter." At a dessertless meal she would tell guests, "There's no hereafter." This saying was well-known among prominent New Orleanians of the late nineteenth century, many of whom visited the plantation.

Dymond Family Papers, The Historic New Orleans Collection, Museum/Research Center, Acc. No. 1979.145.51

This photograph was taken on Orange Grove plantation, located near Talladega, Alabama, probably in the 1890s. It was found in the scrapbook of a woman who lived between 1896 and 1959. The scrapbook contains other photos that seem to date from just prior to her birth and from her early childhood. Under the picture "Taladia's family" is written in script. Thus, the older woman in the picture may have been named Taladia, and the others may have been her husband and grown children. Whatever the truth, these persons appear to be a family, all of whom worked as house servants. They are dressed well, perhaps for a gathering at the home of the white family who employed them. They are probably descendants of slaves who had labored on the plantation in the pre–Civil War era. These particular workers, however, did not remain there long after this picture was taken. They left around 1900, perhaps to seek work in urban areas, as so many rural southerners did. In later years the plantation employed only two or three house servants.

From a private collection, Mobile, Alabama

This photograph is probably an example of the work of F. B. Moore, a professional photographer who worked in downtown New Orleans in the early twentieth century. The decision of the white family to include the domestic in such portraits as this one obviously attests to their desire to preserve images of their children with caretakers. Many of the white women interviewed felt this desire reflected the centrality of the role of the domestic in the lives of white families and the affection the whites felt for these women. Two black interviewees said that they thought they were included in portraits in part for this reason, but also because whites "liked to dress blacks up" and sought to show that they had "good-looking servants." Such statements and the resulting photos suggest that an attractive, well-dressed black domestic signified the family's membership in "the better class" in the community.

The Historic New Orleans Collection, Museum/Research Center, Acc. No. 1981.309.4

The mulatto woman in this 1907 photograph lived from 1864 to 1944 and was known by the family for whom she worked as Nurse. "Nurse" is written on her gravestone alongside her name. She is remembered as a rural-born woman who at about the age of sixteen went to work for the mother of the baby girl pictured here. Nurse oversaw the upbringing of her young charge and later followed her to the city when she married. Nurse remained with her mistress, raising a second generation of white children.

Nurse typically wore a black or white uniform with a pleated skirt and a white collar. The uniform in this photograph may have been a special one, purchased by her well-to-do employer on one of her trips to England and Scotland. Nurse traveled with the white family throughout the United States and Europe. She is said to have been a tiny woman with an authoritarian air. Throughout her life she was somewhat isolated from other employees in the household, since she frequently looked down on them because of her early attachment to her employer.

From a private collection, Mobile, Alabama

This oil painting by Nell Pomeroy O'Brien (1899–1966) was completed in the 1930s. It shows us the traditional pose found in many photographs of domestics and white children, but here child and nurse—as well as their relationship—are even more idealized. One wonders if the domestic sat for the portrait (and if she wanted to) or if it derives from a photograph. One wonders whether she was ever offered the portrait and whether she would have wanted such a depiction of herself in her working clothes. Historically, very few working-class people have been pictured with their employers, if they have been pictured at all. The black domestic with white child in both portraiture and photography, then, is a highly unusual image of the intersection of races and classes. The artist was a native New Orleanian who must have often seen such domestic workers. Her prolific work, which won her national recognition, almost certainly meant that she herself employed a domestic worker to help her raise her children. Also interesting is the fact that such portraits seem to be rarely kept within either the white family or the family of the domestic worker. One owner of such a portrait had it hidden in the attic. She told me that it felt odd to have a portrait of herself as a child with "a black woman whose name I cannot remember."

Courtesy Tulane University Art Collection. Bequest of Patty O'Brien Strigel

It is likely that this photograph was taken in the late 1920s or early 1930s in uptown New Orleans. Balancing a basket upon her head, this washwoman caught the attention of an unknown photographer, perhaps because she even wears a hat under her basket. But the balancing of baskets of laundry on the heads of washwomen was by no means an uncommon sight. From the post–Civil War period until the advent of commercial laundries and particularly until the increased availability of automobiles, washwomen such as this one could be seen daily. Their pattern of work—going from house to house, doing their work either "on the place" or in their own homes—made them the most visible of all domestic workers. It was said by many interviewees that even the poorest whites employed a black washwoman, and a number of black domestics recalled black families who also had their wash "taken out." In knowing so many more people in the employing class and in not owing allegiance to any particular family, washwomen also played a key role in informing other domestics about prospective employers. It is not surprising, then, that washwomen were frequently remembered quite clearly. When interviewees described the various specialties among domestics, the washwoman was always recalled first, usually with nostalgia.

These three persons are pictured in the kitchen of their white employers' home one Sunday in the 1940s. The man and the woman to his left were husband and wife. He was a butler, chauffeur, and handy man; she was a housekeeper. The woman to the far right was the cook. The white family remembers the man as extremely important in the day-to-day running of the household. He had been born in the country and had first worked for the family on a plantation. He left to attend college, worked in Chicago, and then returned to his employers' new home in the city. His wife, following a pattern common to other black women, did not work during the time their children were small but then followed him into service for the same white family. The cook, who was always called Cookie by the white family, was known by both blacks and whites for her wonderful cooking and her not always cheerful disposition. A good cook's idiosyncrasies were often more readily overlooked than those of other household workers. The cook and the manservant were typically the best paid among all workers in wealthy homes. On Sundays, the three pictured here worked serving the twelve or more guests invited for dinner in the middle of the day.

From a private collection, Mobile, Alabama

This is a type of photograph in which the domestic's presence was often forgotten by the white family. Domestics were usually much in evidence at white gatherings—parties, weddings, Christmas dinners—and yet, most of the white women to whom I spoke told me they did not recall the existence of photographs of domestics at these functions. Many of them nevertheless gave me consent to look through family scrapbooks, and in them, again and again, I found many more pictures of domestics than I had been led to expect. In such photographs the domestics are often obscured and in the background.

The role of the domestic as baby-sitter was thought to be her most important one in the white family. So white mothers often also gave photos such as this one to their black domestics as an expression of gratitude and affection. This was also, then, a type of photograph that I saw in the homes of domestics.

From a private collection, Mobile, Alabama

From the 1950s onward, the wearing of a uniform by a domestic came more and more to signify that she had a permanent position with the white family. On the other hand, the lack of a uniform—even among domestics employed by more well-to-do families—frequently symbolized the stated reluctance of a domestic to dress as her employers wanted her to dress. For example, several of the black interviewees said that they preferred to wear uniforms, but they also emphasized that they did not care to dress in "frilly aprons and lace caps." Other black domestics felt that not having uniforms allowed them to achieve some parity with their employers—at least to control how they chose to look.

The uniform allowed the employers to separate themselves from the domestic and allowed the domestic's presence as a signifier of the family's high social status to be more easily felt. However, some older black women preferred to wear uniforms—not only because these were purchased by their employers but also because wearing the uniforms at work seemed to facilitate their separation of their working lives from their personal lives. Some domestics even kept their uniforms at their employers' homes, changing upon arrival and departure.

From a private collection, Mobile, Alabama

Most domestics, however, arrived and departed in uniform, as the woman shown here did. In this photograph from 1958 she is arriving on Easter morning or Easter Eve. The children often ran to greet her as she walked from the bus stop to their house, and their father, with the leisure of the holiday, recorded this ritual. When I asked the white family for pictures of domestics, this one came immediately to mind. Here the domestic is offering the children a bag that contains chewing gum or candy. She worked for the white family for more than twenty years. Her employer remembers the domestic especially for sitting with her and the young children in doctors' offices and going along with the family to county fairs, puppet shows, and birthday parties—to "all those functions one goes to with young children that one gets so bored and, at the same time, anxious about. My mother had died when most of my children were small, and I always felt that she [the domestic] helped me in the way only an older woman could," said her employer.

From a private collection, Mobile, Alabama

A black domestic holds a white child in a christening gown in 1952. The christening party took place at the baby's grandparents' home, and the domestic came along as extra help. Having the extra domestic allowed the baby to be shown to the guests and then delivered at the proper time to the specially designated domestic who was waiting in the kitchen with the other help. This domestic may have helped the cook as she waited. The "extra" domestic frequently found these situations difficult. To enjoy such an event, one would perhaps need to be particularly adept at giving deference. Parading the baby and then waiting with an older black domestic who felt the kitchen was her own territory required a great deal of tact and diplomacy.

Younger domestics employed by younger branches of white families often commented on the unease they felt in dealing with these older domestics. Jealousy and misunderstanding often existed largely because changing ways resulted in changing expectations on the parts of both employers and workers. One of the black interviewees recalled that her interaction with an older domestic at her employer's mother's home showed her "how domestic work pitted black against black." A high school graduate with college aspirations, the younger domestic called her employer by her first name. The older domestic accused her of disrespect and frequently created situations in which she could make more serious complaints.

From a private collection, Mobile, Alabama

A domestic worker and her daughter finish up the last-minute details before a party in a white home in 1960. Daughters of domestics often were hired to help out in the homes of their mother's employers on special occasions. The black mothers consented because the extra money was needed and because learning how to "serve parties" was considered a valuable lesson. Serving parties was a skill that could help enable them to stay home as young mothers, "working out" only occasionally in the evening. As older women, possibly as older domestics, it could help them supplement their wages. By "carrying the tray just so, fixing those little cakes, knowing just which napkins go where," black domestics worked to help pay for life's emergencies as well as for additions to their homes and college education for their children. The pattern of mother and daughter working for any length of time for the same family, however, was generally something domestics avoided. Most of them wanted better for their daughters. And the daughters wanted better for themselves. Black daughters remembered that, when they helped out in the white homes, they often felt saddened and resentful about their mothers' deferential behavior toward whites. In addition, in these situations white and black teenagers who had played together as children may have met each other again, in new roles that anticipated the adult roles each would later assume.

From a private collection, Mobile, Alabama

This gravestone is located in a corner of the Battle family plot in Magnolia Cemetery, Mobile, Alabama. The Battles were a wealthy entrepreneurial family of the late nineteenth and early twentieth centuries. The small marker pictured above stands across from a twenty-foot monument to the most prominent family member, a leading financier involved in the building of Mobile's largest hotel, which operated from 1852 to the early 1970s. Many black writers have written humorously and derisively of those mammies, like Malinda Battle James, who were buried with "their" white families. Such graves are not an uncommon sight in the South. Most of them date from the late nineteenth and early twentieth centuries. What were they like, these women who were often taken at a young age from their biological families? Did they find comfort in the fact that they would be buried alongside those people known best to them, and thus be equal in death to those people with whom they were denied equality in life? No significant information on Malinda Battle James seems to be available. She was probably a black woman who was born a slave of the Battle family and remained with the family until her death.

Photograph courtesy Jane Tucker